OECD Development Pathways

Production Transformation Policy Review of Chile

REAPING THE BENEFITS OF NEW FRONTIERS

This work is published under the responsibility of the Secretary-General of the OECD. The opinions expressed and arguments employed herein do not necessarily reflect the official views of the member countries of the OECD, its Development Centre or of the United Nations.

This document, as well as any data and any map included herein, are without prejudice to the status of or sovereignty over any territory, to the delimitation of international frontiers and boundaries and to the name of any territory, city or area.

Please cite this publication as:
OECD/UN (2018), *Production Transformation Policy Review of Chile: Reaping the Benefits of New Frontiers*, OECD Development Pathways, OECD Publishing, Paris.
http://dx.doi.org/10.1787/9789264288379-en

ISBN 978-92-64-28833-1 (print)
ISBN 978-92-64-28837-9 (PDF)
ECLAC: LC/PUB.2017/29

Series: OECD Development Pathways
ISSN 2308-734X (print)
ISSN 2308-7358 (online)

The statistical data for Israel are supplied by and under the responsibility of the relevant Israeli authorities. The use of such data by the OECD is without prejudice to the status of the Golan Heights, East Jerusalem and Israeli settlements in the West Bank under the terms of international law.

Photo credits: Cover design by the OECD Development Centre.

Corrigenda to OECD publications may be found on line at: *www.oecd.org/about/publishing/corrigenda.htm*.

Foreword

The current global economic setting is turbulent, complex and fast-changing. Governments, businesses and societies are engaged in better understanding the ongoing technological, digital and industrial reorganisation processes and their profound potential impacts on the economy and the society. At a time in which is clear that growth is a necessary, but not exclusive, condition for development and that incentives are needed to guarantee that growth is inclusive and sustainable, planning and implementing strategies for economic transformation become paramount.

The *Production Transformation Policy Reviews* (PTPRs) are a policy assessment and guidance tool elaborated in response to countries' demand in the framework of the OECD Policy Dialogue Initiative on Global Value Chains, Production Transformation and Development [the Initiative herein forward] to support knowledge sharing and policy dialogue and to increase the evidence on varieties of development trajectories. The PTPR framework is the result of a collective process that started in 2014 with a Working Group on Country Studies set up in the framework of the Initiative and led by Costa Rica, Uruguay and Turkey with contributions from UNIDO and UNCTAD. The PTPRs are a 15-18 month process based on peer-learning and multi-stakeholder dialogue to enable policy makers to better plan and act for the present and the future. The PTPRs assess the economic structure, the upgrading potential and the governance for economic transformation, identify lessons learned and clarify priorities for reform. They rely on peer review mechanisms through the participation of international peers and through a Peer Learning Group that steers each PTPR process. The PTPRs are enriching the OECD Development Pathways Series with their perspective on economic transformation and governance for change.

The PTPR of Chile involved an extensive process of consultation with multiple stakeholders and benefited from peer learning from Sweden, Emilia Romagna (Italy) and Germany. The PTPR of Chile has been a process of dialogue, consensus and trust building and provided an opportunity to identify common grounds for future reforms to enable Chile to reap the benefits of new technological frontiers.

The PTPR of Chile highlights the progress made by the country in maintaining a relatively stable and high growth in the last decades, its effective macroeconomic management and openness to the global economy. The review clarifies the persistent structural weaknesses of the domestic economy, including its low productivity, limited knowledge base and high territorial concentration of economic opportunities. It clarifies how the ongoing geopolitical and technological changes could open a window of opportunity for Chile to transform its economy and overcome its structural weaknesses. To this end it reviews the current strategy for economic transformation, including the strategic programmes Chile has put in place to reap the benefit of new technologies and global trends in solar energy, green mining and functional agro-food and identifies game changers for future reforms.

Acknowledgements

The PTPRs are the policy assessment and guidance tool of the OECD Initiative for Policy Dialogue on GVCs, Production Transformation and Development (The Initiative herein after). This report is the result of a 18-month in-depth policy review consensus building process in Chile.

The report has been produced by the OECD Development Centre in cooperation with the Economic Commission for Latin America and the Caribbean (ECLAC) of the United Nations and the United Nations Conference on Trade and Development (UNCTAD), under the leadership of Mario Pezzini, Director of the OECD Development Centre, Mario Cimoli, Deputy Executive Secretary, ECLAC and Richard Kozul-Wright, Director, Division on Globalization and Development Strategies, UNCTAD. Annalisa Primi, Head of Structural Policies and Innovation and of the OECD Initiative for Policy Dialogue on GVCs, Production Transformation and Development at the Development Centre led the PTPR process and report elaboration. Manuel Toselli, junior economist at the OECD Development Centre acted as project coordinator and main analyst. The report has been drafted by the OECD Development Centre with key inputs from Nadim Ahmad, Head Trade and Competitiveness Division of the Statistic Directorate of the OECD, Fabienne Fortanier and Guannan Miao OECD, Piergiuseppe Fortunato UNCTAD, Mario Castillo, Felipe Correa, Marco Dini, Nicolo Gligo and Catalina Achermann ECLAC. The report benefited from valuable comments from Naoko Ueda, Deputy Director of the OECD Development Centre. Chloé Desjonquères, Jing Zhao and Vasiliki Mavroeidi from the OECD Development Centre provided valuable contributions to the report and Lucia Perez Villar contributed to the drafting during the initial phase of the project. Kim Millin provided essential assistance during the whole project. Duncan Cass-Beggs, Counsellor, Strategic Foresight, General Secretariat, OECD, Joaquim Oliveira Martins, Acting Special Advisor to the Director, Centre for Entrepreneurship, OECD, Antoine Goujard, Senior Economist at the OECD Economic Department, José Enrique Garcilazo, Head of Regional and Rural Policy at the OECD Centre for Entrepreneurship, Michele Clara and Manuel Albaladejo from the United Nations Industrial Development Organisation (UNIDO), Paolo Frank and Cedrick Philbert from the International Energy Agency (IEA), Rainer Quitzow, Senior Research Associate at IASS Potsdam, Germany, Professor Stephany Griffith-Jones, Initiative for Policy Dialogue, Columbia University and Professor John Mathews, Macquarie University of Sydney provided highly valuable comments to the report. Anne-Lise Prigent provided her usual high quality editorial advice. Delphine Grandrieux coordinated the publication process with key graphic inputs from Aida Buendía, Elisabeth Nash and Irit Perry. The report benefited from editing by Fiona Hinchcliffe and editorial advice by Linda Herda Smiroldo.

The PTPR of Chile has been requested by the Chilean Economic Development Agency (CORFO) and the General Directorate for International Economic Affairs of the Ministry of Foreign Affairs of Chile with the objective to identify future priorities for the national development agenda of Chile and to share lessons learned with other OECD, emerging and developing economies in the framework of the OECD Initiative for Policy Dialogue on GVCs, Production Transformation and Development (the Initiative herein after). The PTPR of Chile is the result of a longstanding cooperation between Chile and the OECD Development Centre. It also highlights the commitment of Chile to the Initiative, as DIRECON is a member of the Bureau of the Initiative since its inception. The PTPR has benefited immensely from the commitment and dedication of CORFO and DIRECON during all project implementation. Eduardo Bitran, Vice President of CORFO shared information, visions and ideas with generosity throughout the whole process and ensured a high quality mobilisation of executives in CORFO to access information. The authors are particularly grateful to Claudio Maggi, Pedro Sierra and Juan Rada for sharing their knowledge with the review team and for facilitating access to key contacts. Carlos Ladrix, Marcela Angulo, Rodrigo Mancilla, Mauro Valdés and Pablo Tello and Cristian González Urrutia. also provided valuable information. Paulina Nazal, Director General for International Economic Relations provided strong support to the project. Viviana Araneda led DIRECON's participation. Felipe Lopeandía has been essential in ensuring smooth project implementation. Claudia Marró and Maximiliano Carbonetti provided valuable comments provided excellent organisational support and project coordination. Claudia Serrano, Ambassador of Chile to the OECD provided strategic guidance to the project and Rodrigo Monardes has been essential in ensuring effective project implementation, smooth contact with local counterparts and provided highly relevant comments to the report. The OECD Development Centre is also thankful to Christian Rehren Ambassador of Chile to Thailand for its support to the PTPR process and its participation to the 9th Plenary Meeting of the Initiative, hosted by ESCAP in Bangkok in November 2017.

Peer learning and knowledge sharing lie at the heart of the PTPR process. This report has been shaped and enriched by the contributions of the peers, the Peer Learning Group (PLG) set up to steer the review process and the debates in the Plenary Meeting of the Initiative. The PTPR of Chile benefited from the participation of three peers: Jonas Borglin, CEO, International Council of Swedish Industry (NIR Sweden); Patrizio Bianchi, Assessor for School, Universities, Research and Labour Policies, Government of Emilia Romagna Region, Italy; and Christoph Richter, Project Manager at DLR Solar Research, Germany; provided valuable and outstanding intellectual guidance and shared concrete insights on managing policies for economic transformation. The Government of Emilia Romagna also contributed with two additional experts: Sofia Miceli EU project manager at ASTER, and Annaflavia Bianchi University of Ferrara. The OECD Development Centre is also thankful to Jakob Kiefer, Ambassador of Sweden in Chile and Marco Ricci, Ambassador of Italy in Chile, and Simone Balzani, Director of Economic and Trade section, Italian embassy in Chile. Valuable inputs originated from the PTPR Peer Learning Group, hosted by the OECD in May 2017. In particular we are thankful to Taoufik Oukessou, Head of Division, Evaluation of Sectoral Policies of the Moroccan Ministry of Economy and Finance for contributing to the PTPR drafting and to those who made the kick off interventions to steer the dialogue, including, Keiji Katai, Senior Deputy Director, Private Sector Development, Japan International Cooperation Agency (JICA), Japan; Santiago Matallana, Director of Enterprise Development, National Planning Department (DNP), Colombia; Peter Padbury, Chief Futurist, Policy Horizons Canada; Peter Wostner, Secretary, Government Office for Development and European Cohesion Policy and Head of Smart Specialisation Unit; and Nimrod Zalk, Industrial Development Policy and Strategy Advisor, Department of Trade and Industry, South Africa, in addition to OECD colleagues from the General Secretariat, Centre for Entrepreneurship, Economics Department and Development Centre.

The PTPR is the result of an extensive and open consultation process with diverse stakeholders in Chile. The PTPR benefited from:

- Five meetings of the Task Force on Production Transformation. The Task Force has been set up to steer the PTPR process. It was chaired by CORFO and DIRECON and composed by high level representatives from nine key government agencies, including the Ministry of Economy, Agriculture, Energy and Finance, the agency for FDI promotion (InvestChile), the National Council for Innovation and Development (CNDI) and the National Productivity Commission (CNP). The Task Force provided strategic advice since project's inception and valuable comments to the report. Carlos Alvarez, Javier Bustos, Cristobal Marshall, Joseph Ramos, Gonzalo Rivas, Claudio Soto, provided valuable inputs and comments;

- Presentation and debate at the Budget Commission in the Senate held in January 10th 2017. The authors are grateful to Senator Carlos Montes Cisternas, chair of the Budget Commission and to all the members of the Commission for their insightful comments.
- Four Government-Business Roundtables hosted by CORFO on future trends with a focus on solar energy, agro-food, smart mining and industry 4.0. The four roundtables gathered in total more than 100 high level participants. Leading companies have been key in sharing their views about the future and shaping the content of this report, in particular we thank, ACTI BNamericas, Amazon web services, AMSA,BhP, CISCO Chile, Codelco, Cerro Dominador, EDF, Enel,Engie, Granotec, Minnovex A.G, Oracle, Telefonica. Their contributions have been key to inform the PTPR process.
- One high level, closed-door event on "Trust, growth and sustainable development" co-organised by CORFO, Trade and Production Confederation of Chile (CPC), the OECD Development Centre and the Consensus Building Institute. The event was hosted by CPC in June 2017 and gathered 100 high level representatives from business and government and key opinion shapers in the country including ministers, former ministers and CEO of major companies. David Plumb managed the event and ensured that the debate delivered key inputs to the PTPR process.
- Semi-structured interviews with more than 50 experts from business, government and academia in Chile. All interviews have contributed to the process and have been extremely relevant to shape the report. In addition to the people mentioned above, in particular we acknowledge the time and contributions of (in alphabetical order): Kathleen Barclay, President, AmCham Chile; Raphael Bergoeing, Centre for Public Studies (CEP); Gonzalo Blumel, Director, Fundación Avanza Chile; Gonzalo Braham, Director, Association of Latin America Entrepreneurs (ASELA); Hernán Cheyre, Director, Universidad del Desarrollo; Juan Esteban Musalem, President, Chile-China Chamber of Commerce; Carlos Finat, Director, Chilean Association for Renewable Energies ACERA; Marcos Kulka , Director, Fundación Chile; Mario Marcel, President, Central Bank of Chile; Alfredo Moreno, President, CPC; Rodrigo Palma, Director, Solar Energy Research Center SERC; Fernando Prieto, CEO and Founder, Gal&Leo; Christian Santana, Director, Renewable Energy Divison, Ministry of Energy; Klaus Schmidt-Hebbel, Professor, Catholic University of Chile, Cristóbal Undurraga, Chairman, Ekonometrika., Felipe Morandé, NSG Chile, Ignacio Briones, Dean of the School of Government at University Adolfo Ibanez (UAI), Patricio Caceres, director of regulation, Telefonica Chile, Osvaldo Urzua, Head of Public Relations BHP Billiton, Jaime Rivera, Director of Business and Innovation, CODELCO, Juan Andrés Fontaine, economist and management consultant . The review also benefited from in-depth discussions with key stakeholders in the region of Concepción in January 2017. Roberta Lama, Desarolla Bio-bio, organised the government, businesses and academia consultations in the region. Carlos Claro CORFO organised the visit to Antofagasta in April 2017. For this occasion we would like to thank Cristian Varas Medalla, Director of Communication of CODELCO- Chuquicamata and Jorge Medina Sandoval, Cummins Antofagasta.

The PTPR of Chile has benefited from a targeted financial contribution from the Chilean Economic Development Agency (CORFO) and the General Directorate for International Economic Affairs of the Ministry of Foreign Affairs of Chile.

Table of contents

Figures

Acronyms and abbreviations

CLN	Chilean pesos
CNID	National Council for Innovation and Development
CNP	National Productivity Commission
CONICYT	National Council for Science and Technology
CORFO	Chilean Economic Development Agency
CSP	Concentrated Solar Power
DIRECON	General Directorate for International Economic Affairs
DLR	German Aerospace Center
ECLAC	Economic Commission for Latin America and the Caribbean
EU	European Union
EUR	Euro
FDI	Foreign Direct Investment
FIA	Agriculture Innovation Foundation
FIC	Fund for Innovation and Competitiveness
FIE	Strategic Investments Fund
GDP	Gross domestic product
GVCs	Global Value Chains
ICT	Information and communication technology
IEA	International Energy Agency
JICA	Japanese International Cooperation Agency
NCREs	Non-conventional renewable energies
NIR	International Council of Swedish Industry
OECD	Organisation for Economic Co-operation and Development
PLG	Peer Learning Group
PROCHILE	Chilean Agency for Exports Promotion
PTPR	Production Transformation Policy Review
PV	Photovoltaic
R&D	Research and development
RMS	Metropolitan Region of Santiago
SENCE	National Service for Training and Employment
SERCOTEC	National Service for Technical Cooperation
SMEs	Small and medium-sized enterprises
TFP	Total factor productivity
TiVA	Trade in Value Added
UNCTAD	United Nations Conference on Trade and Development
USD	United States Dollars
WTO	World Trade Organization

Editorial

No unique pathway to development exists. Each country's experience enriches our understanding of how development occurs in different contexts and of the role that institutions and polices play in shaping development outcomes.

In an uncertain, complex and fast-changing global landscape, governments constantly need to anticipate and adapt to new scenarios to sustain growth and deliver benefits to societies. The Production Transformation Policy Reviews (PTPRs) respond to this challenge by providing a novel and timely assessment that relies on peer learning and consensus building. The PTPRs are implemented in the framework of the OECD Initiative for Policy Dialogue on GVCs, Production Transformation and Development and provide an opportunity for our Organisations to cooperate to respond to countries' demand.

Each country, region or city is unique and, as such, no "one size fits all" approach applies to development strategies. Still, some cross-cutting principles that enhance the quality and effectiveness of policies are possible. Thus, policies need to anticipate change, adapt to changing circumstances, promote learning, facilitate interactions and build resilient linkages. The policies of tomorrow need to increasingly be able to bring together all relevant stakeholders. This not only enhances ownership and accountability of the policy process, but also represents a key requisite for implementing effective policies and enabling an inclusive and sustainable economic transformation.

Chile is a successful natural-resource-based economy, which is now looking at how to mobilise drivers of change to transform its economy to respond to the multiple aspirations of its society and achieve inclusive and sustainable growth. Building on solid macroeconomic management, Chile is mobilising partnerships and investments for innovation and technological development to reduce its dependency on natural resources and to enlarge its production and export base by leveraging some of its unique assets. The Atacama Desert in the north, for example, has unique characteristics that could enable transformative changes linked to solar energy. Emerging and developing economies need to increase their awareness of advanced manufacturing and of the Internet of Things and their potential impact on the economy and society to mitigate risks or enable leapfrogging. In keeping with international trends, CORFO (the Chilean Economic Development Agency) is engaging with lead research and business partners to scout out potential long-term scenarios to better orient incentives and regulations and define adequate road-maps. Chile has also developed a strategy to increase participation in regional and global markets by investing in innovation, promoting development in strategic industries and gradually shifting towards a place-based approach to policy. Achieving results will depend on implementation and on the private sector's commitment to change.

With a per-capita income of around USD 14 000, Chile is no longer an eligible recipient of Official Development Assistance. The country, however, still needs to make further progress to achieve shared prosperity. The OECD Development Centre, ECLAC and UNCTAD are ready to support Chile's development through knowledge sharing and peer learning through the OECD Initiative for Policy Dialogue on GVCs, Production Transformation and Development. This Production Transformation Policy Review is one concrete way to support Chile in scanning potential futures and in identifying key priorities for seizing the opportunities of the current global landscape and enabling an economic transformation that creates better jobs and lives for all Chileans.

Mario Pezzini
Director, OECD Development Centre and Special Advisor to the OECD Secretary-General on Development

Richard Kouzul Wright
Director, Globalisation and Sustainable Development UNCTAD

Alicia Bárcena
Executive Secretary ECLAC

Executive summary

Chile is a relatively stable and open economy. Sound macroeconomic management, coupled with effective penetration in global markets (trade equals 60% of GDP, a figure that is 20 percentage points higher than in Australia and 40 percentage points higher than in Argentina) and Chinese appetite for raw materials, enabled the country to enjoy sustained and relatively stable growth since the early 1990s. This reality also insulated Chile from the more volatile growth patterns of other economies in Latin America (Chile has been growing on average 4% since 2000 whereas Latin America at 2.8%). As a consequence, Chileans today are better off than in the past. They have higher incomes. They are progressively closing the gap with more advanced countries: the per-capita income of Chile was only 26% of the one in the United States in the 1990s, while nowadays the average income of a Chilean equals 40% of the one of a US citizen. And they have access to better services and improved infrastructure; 16 out of 100 Chileans have a fixed broadband connection; a figure that doubles the one of ten years ago and that is well above the current average of 10 out of 100 in Latin America.

Low productivity holds back Chile's growth. Most workers in Chile are employed in low productivity activities that contribute little to value addition. Total factor productivity (TFP) has remained stagnant since the beginning of the 1990s, mostly because of the dynamics in the mining industry (TFP in mining has been declining at an yearly average of 4.7% between 1993 and 2015). The deterioration in copper ore grades has demanded a shift to underground mining and an increase in energy intensity resulting in lower productivity. In addition, the number of workers per unit of output in mining is three times higher in Chile than in Sweden. Improving skills will be important to increase productivity. According to PISA estimates, the proficiency in literacy, mathematics and science of 15-year-olds in Chile is among the lowest in OECD countries; 28% of students lack the elementary skills required to read and understand simple texts or to master basic mathematical and scientific concepts and procedures. Graduate, post-graduate and vocational training are poorly connected to the needs of the private sector. Continuous updating of vocational programmes, as well as of university curricula, will be essential to close the gap between supply and demand in the labour market.

The limited diversification of the economy, both in terms of activities and markets, leaves Chile vulnerable to external shocks. Domestic economic growth still highly relies on natural resources. Mining accounts for more than half of Chilean exports. Three countries – China, the United States and Japan – are the recipients of more than half of total exports. A contraction in demand by any of these countries can therefore affect the entire economy. Fluctuations in cooper prices also have major effects, despite the effort to maintain macroeconomic stability through the stabilisation fund. Such swings affect business and citizen perceptions, limiting pro-innovation, risky and long-term investments. Indeed, the boom in copper prices in the mid-2000s significantly increased the profitability of mining, sustaining economic growth but limiting the incentives to invest in other activities. Chile accounts for over one-third of the world's total copper reserves, and is among the top three producers of lithium. Mining will therefore continue to be a key driver of growth in the future; however, the sector faces limits in terms of labour absorption given the characteristics of the production process and the move towards automated mining. Diversifying the economy by generating business opportunities for suppliers in related economic activities, and by enabling business development in new areas, is critically important to sustaining growth and creating jobs. In summary, achieving successful diversification in Chile does not mean dismissing mining but rather transforming it, making it more productive, and exploiting its synergies with emerging industries and technologies, including digital technologies and solar energy. Furthermore,

Chile has the potential to benefit more from its openness and improve its participation in global value chains (GVCs) by seeking opportunities beyond mining, including in services. In 2014, the services value-added content of Chile's total exports was 38.4%, below the OECD average of 55.5%.

A high concentration of economic opportunities in few activities, firms and regions hampers future progress and limits innovation. Large firms play a dominant role in the economy, but they innovate less than their peers in advanced countries. In Chile, large firms explain 73% of the domestic business turnover and 57% of total business research and development (R&D) expenditures, while in Germany such firms account for 53% and for 85% of total business R&D expenditures. Chile has one of the lowest R&D intensity of all OECD countries (0.39% of GDP), and its private sector's contribution – only 33% of total R&D expenditure – is significantly below the OECD average of around 68%. The difference between the top and the bottom regions in per-capita income is the second highest of all OECD countries, after Mexico. Foreign direct investment is concentrated in Santiago, Antofagasta and Atacama, and 80% of start-ups are created in the capital region. In Colombia, by comparison, the capital region accounts for less than half of total national start-ups.

The Chilean model requires an "update" to continue succeeding. Society's aspirations change with progress, and the Chilean society – with its growing middle class – is no exception. Chileans are demanding more opportunities for their youth and access to new services. The traditional, highly concentrated export-led model will struggle to deliver these opportunities. Matching the aspirations of an inclusive society requires therefore adjusting the model and finding new sources of growth to broaden society's participation in the economy and achieve shared prosperity.

The global march towards inclusive and sustainable development, captured in the Sustainable Development Goals and coupled with ongoing major technological changes, opens up new opportunities for Chile. The call for "green" products and services could transform the Chilean economy, offering opportunities for domestic entrepreneurs and research centres to generate new businesses along the whole value chain. This holds true in traditional activities such as mining and agro-food and in new areas including solar energy and big data. Most countries in the world, including Germany, Sweden and Italy, are growing in their awareness of the potential disruptive impacts of ongoing technological change and, in fact, are taking steps to shape their futures by defining long-term visions, scanning potential options and investing for the long term.

Chile, in line with international practices, has embarked upon reforming institutions to increase impact and deliver more effective results. It created, for example, the National Productivity Commission to better prioritise policy actions and Invest Chile to attract foreign direct investments in strategic areas. The government, through CORFO, also led an effort to enable public-private partnerships to identify future road-maps and enable change in key industrial ecosystems. And this Production Transformation Policy Review (PTPR) of Chile, based on peer learning, identifies three game changers for future reforms: 1) updating institutions and governance to cope with the broader and more sophisticated roles that the government is called on to play now and in the future; 2) strengthening and institutionalising the anticipation capacity and the foresight process at the highest strategic level to increase long-term planning capabilities, and 3) shifting to a place-based approach to policy making. The PTPR provides an in-depth analysis of the strategic programmes that Chile has put in place to benefit from new technologies and global trends, focusing on solar energy, green mining and functional agro-food.

A new pact between the government, business community, academia and society is needed to allow Chile to embark on its path to prosperity. Being a stable and open economy will not be enough to sustain business development or respond to society's demands. The world is moving fast, and for Chile to be part of the global wave of change, a renewed approach to policy making and to the government-business-society relationship is needed. Going beyond ideological divides and finding common ground to mobilise private and public actors is of critical importance for Chile to avoid marginalisation in the changing global context. It will help identify national development challenges – such as greening the economy – that can align interests and enable change in the economy and society alike.

Assessment and recommendations

The Production Transformation Policy Review (PTPR) of Chile reviews the national agenda for growth and economic transformation and identifies game changers for future reforms. This overview summarises the PTPR's main results and recommendations. The PTPR highlights the progress made by the country in maintaining relatively stable and high growth during the last decades, its effective macroeconomic management and its openness to the global economy. It identifies the country's persistent structural weaknesses, including low productivity, limited knowledge base and persistent concentration of economic opportunities. It clarifies how the ongoing geopolitical and technological changes could open a window of opportunity for Chile to transform its economy and overcome its structural weaknesses. It assesses the current governance, policies and tools for economic transformation, including the strategic programmes that the country has put in place to reap the benefit of new technologies and global trends in solar energy, green mining and functional agro-food. The PTPR of Chile calls for an "update" of the Chilean model to continue succeeding. The PTPR process involved extensive consultations with multiple stakeholders. It benefited from peer review mechanisms through the participation of peers from Sweden, Emilia Romagna (Italy) and Germany and through a Peer Learning Group that steered the PTPR process in the framework of the OECD Initiative for Policy Dialogue on GVCs, Production Transformation and Development.

Chile is a relatively stable, high growth and open economy.

The Chilean economy has been growing on average 4% annually since 2000 (the annual average GDP growth for Latin America in the same period has been 2.8%), (Figure 0.1). Sound macroeconomic management, coupled with effective penetration in global markets (trade equals 60% of GDP in Chile, while in Australia the same figure equals 40%) and Chinese appetite for raw materials explain this positive performance. Targeted policies to foster trade and investment have also been central: Chile has 21 free trade agreements in force, including with the European Union (2003), the United States (2004), the People's Republic of China (2006) and Japan (2007). Additionally, since the 1990s, the country has received a fair amount of FDI, especially in capital-intensive activities such as mining. In 2015, Chile's inward stock of FDI was among the highest in the OECD (around 80% of GDP, double the OECD average of 40%). Over the last decade, Chile has also seen some of its large companies grow and become regional leaders in forestry, retail and the airline business.

As a consequence, Chileans today are better off than in the past. They have higher incomes and they are progressively closing the gap with more advanced countries: the per-capita income of Chile was only 26% of the United States in the 1990s, while nowadays the average income of a Chilean equals 40% that of a US citizen.

Figure 0.1 **Chile's GDP growth and GDP per capita**

Annual GDP growth rate (HP filter, left axis) and GDP per capita (right axis), 1950-2016

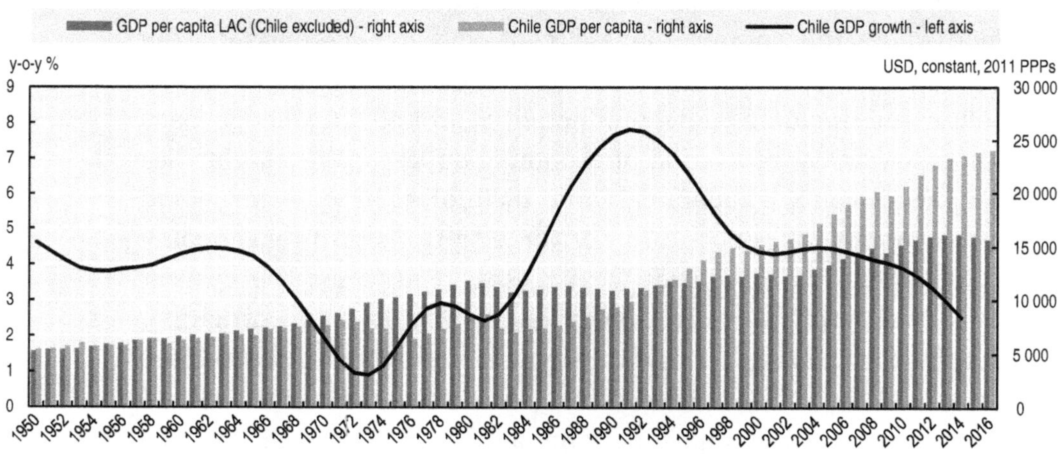

Note: GDP: gross domestic product; LAC: Latin American countries; y-o-y: year on year; PPP: purchasing power parity; HP: Hodrick Prescott Filter. The Lambda in the Hodrick Prescott filter has been chosen according to OECD (2016a), OECD Compendium of Productivity Indicators 2016, http://dx.doi.org/10.1787/pdtvy-2016-en.

Source: Authors' analysis based on the Conference Board (2017), Total Economy Database™ (Adjusted version), https://www.conference-board.org/data/economydatabase/index.cfm?id=27762.

Low productivity holds back Chile's future growth.

Despite the positive growth performance, weak productivity is holding back Chile's future growth potential. Total factor productivity (TFP) has remained stagnant since the beginning of the 1990s, mostly because of mining (TFP in mining has been declining at a yearly average of 4.7% since the early 1990s, Figure 0.2). The deterioration in copper ore grades has demanded a shift to underground mining and an increase in energy intensity resulting in lower productivity (Figure 0.3). In addition, most workers in Chile are employed in low productivity activities. Moreover, the number of workers per unit of output in mining is three times higher in Chile than in Sweden.

Figure 0.2 **Total factor productivity growth in Chile, 1993-2015**

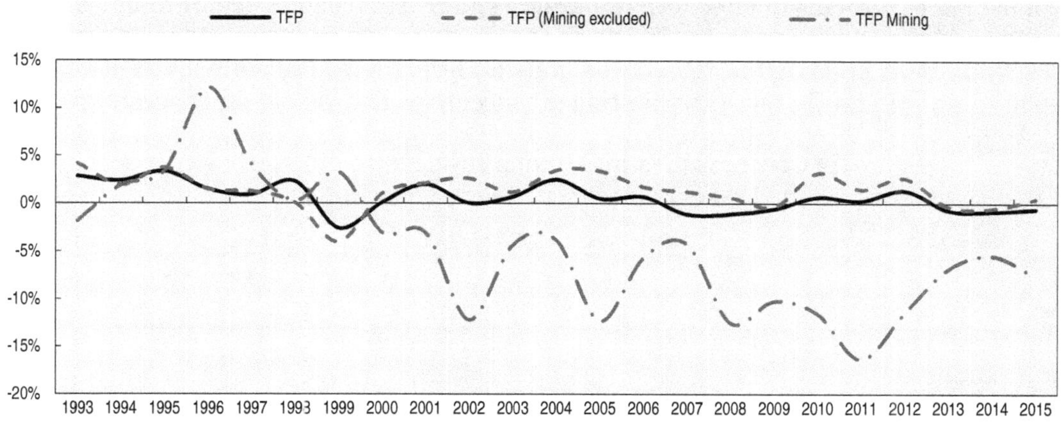

Source: Authors' analysis based on data from UAI/CORFO (2017), "Boletín trimestral Evolución de la PTF en Chile" (Quarterly Evolution of the TFP in Chile).

Figure 0.3 **Chilean ore grades are falling while energy consumption is rising, 2001-15**

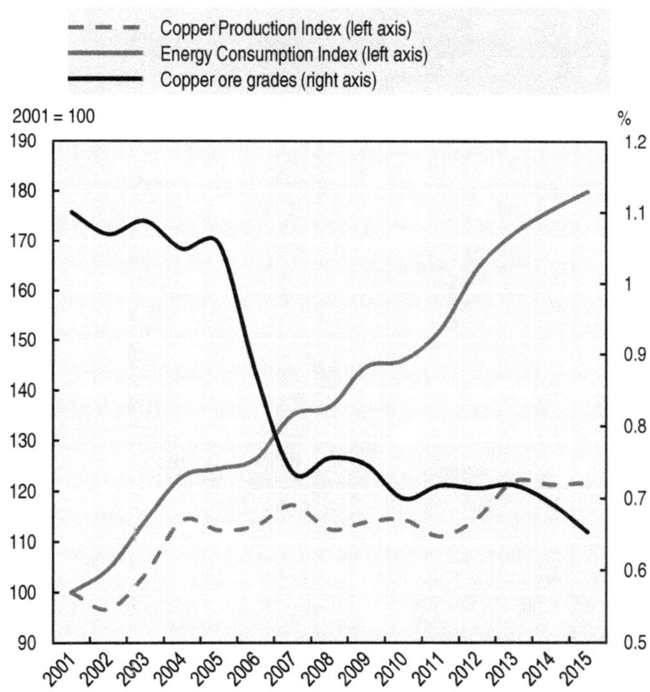

Note: Index is constructed for copper production by referring to thousands of tons extracted, and for energy consumption to terajoules necessary for extraction.

Source: Authors' analysis based on US Geological Survey and COCHILCO (2017), database, https://www.cochilco.cl.

The limited diversification of the economy, both in terms of activities and markets, leaves Chile vulnerable to external shocks.

Domestic economic growth is still highly reliant on natural resources. The Chilean economy remains only modestly diversified (Figure 0.4). Its exports are mostly concentrated in natural resource-based and primary products, characterised by relatively low levels of sophistication and poor linkages with the rest of the economy. Despite the effectiveness of the stabilisation fund which guarantees macroeconomic stability, fluctuations in copper prices have major effects on businesses and citizens' perceptions. Pro-innovation, risky and long-term investments are limited when prices are on the upturn. Indeed, the boom in copper prices in the mid-2000s significantly increased the profitability of mining, sustaining economic growth but limiting the incentives to invest in other activities.

Figure 0.4 **Commodities make up a high share of Chile's exports**

Share of gross exports by technology content towards selected regions, Chile and selected countries, 2016

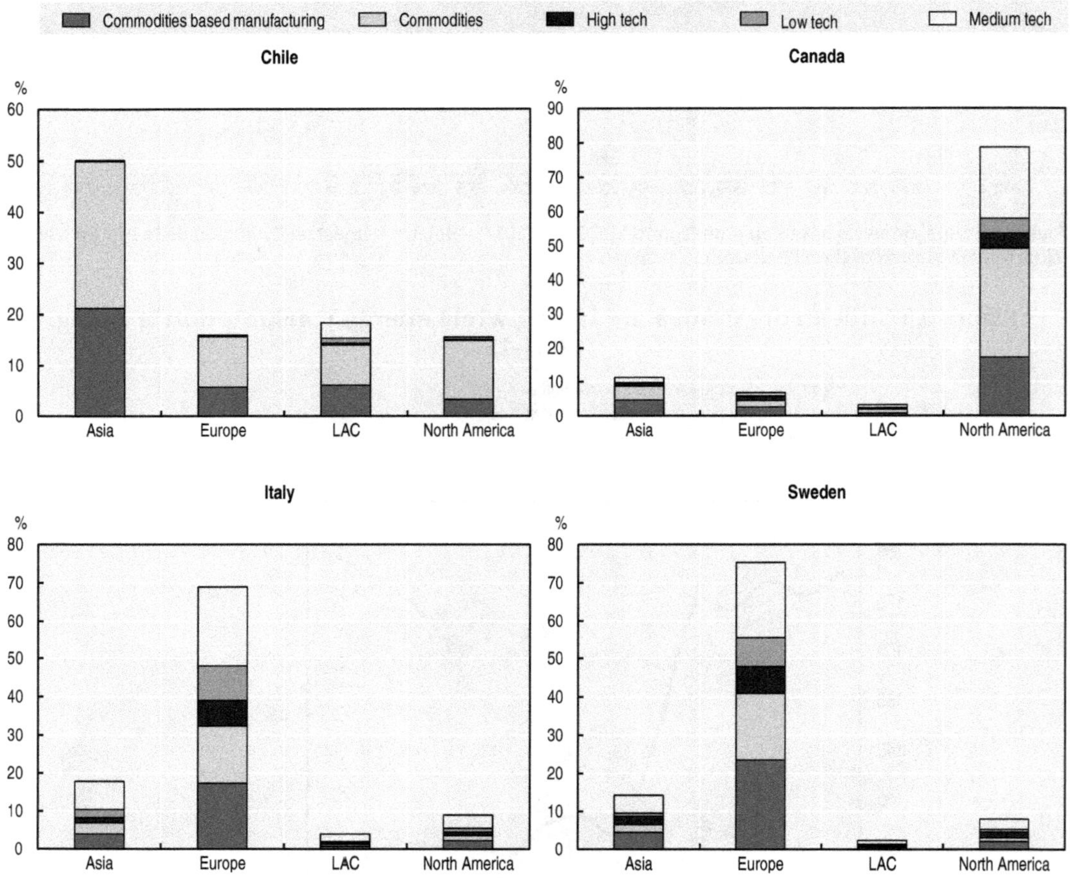

Notes: LAC: All Latin American and Caribbean countries.

The technological classification follows Lall, S. (2000) and Aboal et al (2015).

Source: Authors' analysis based on UN (2017), Comtrade Database, https://comtrade.un.org.

The country is the biggest producer of copper in the world, accounting for over one-third of global total reserves. It is also the world's leading producer of iodine, rhenium and lithium (Chile accounts for 63.2%, 50% and 39% of world production, respectively). Mining is the backbone of the Chilean economy. It employs around 220 000 workers and in the last decade, it accounted on average for 13% of GDP and for more than 55% of Chilean exports (50% of which are explained by copper alone).

Mining will continue to be a key driver of growth in the future, but it needs to shift up a gear. Mining in Chile is mostly linked to extraction and benefits less from foreign inputs than in other countries. Chile has, for example, a lower foreign value added content in gross exports (20%) than Sweden (25%). Chilean mining exports also embed fewer inputs from other sectors than Swedish ones. In Sweden, business services and manufacturing contribute, respectively to 30% and 10% of the value added of mining exports, while in Chile these shares are down to 21% and 7%, respectively (Figures 0.5 and 0.6). In addition, the sector faces limits in terms of its future capacity to generate jobs given the move towards automated mining. Mining will also need to address its growing energy intensity: it accounted for 20% of total domestic energy consumption in Chile in 2015, 7 percentage points higher than in 2000.

Figure 0.5 **Decomposition of Chilean gross exports by origin and destination, mining, 2014**

Value added of gross exports by origin and destination (%)

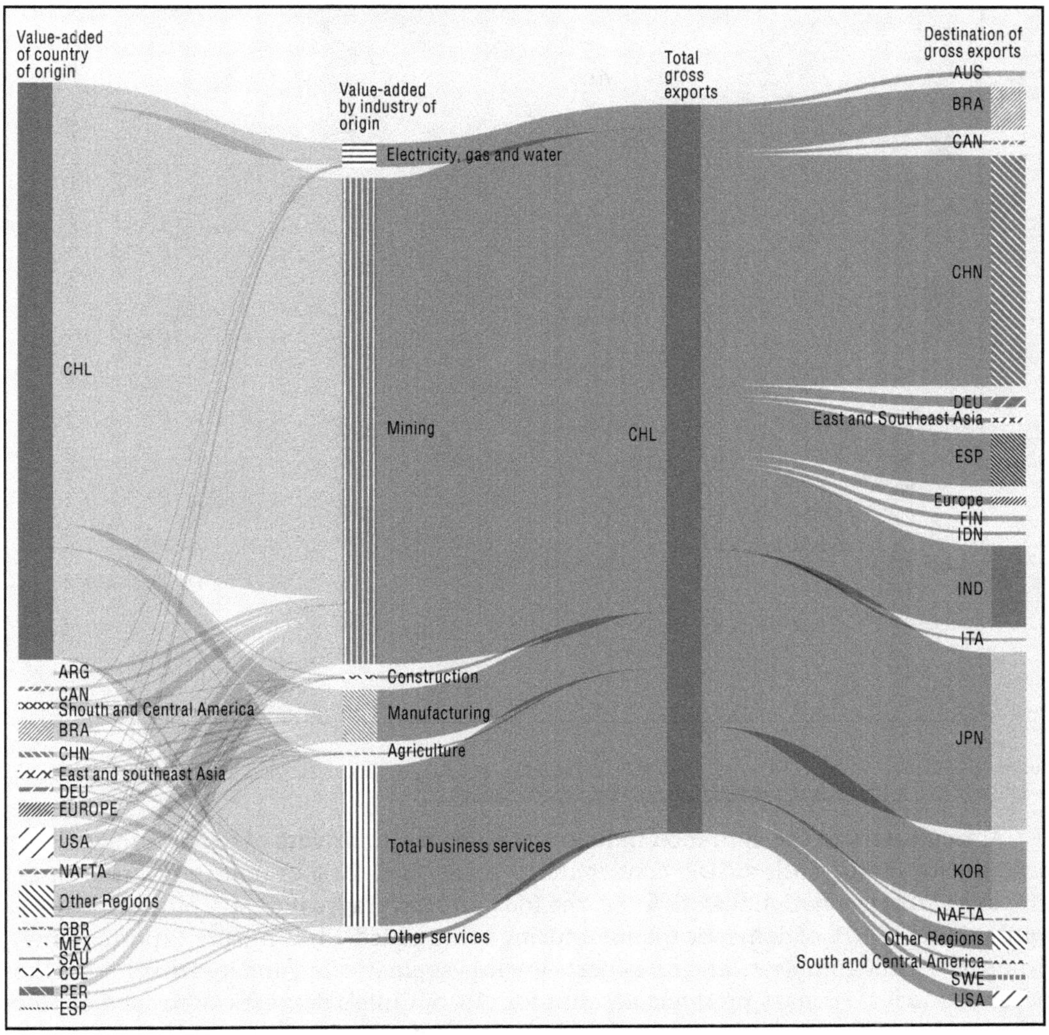

Note: Regional aggregates exclude member countries reported in the graph.

Source: OECD (2017b), TiVA Nowcast Database, http://stats.oecd.org/Index.aspx?DataSetCode=TIVA_NOWCAST; see also www.oecd.org/std/its/tiva-nowcast-methodology.pdf

Figure 0.6 **Decomposition of Swedish gross exports by origin and destination, mining, 2014**

Value added of exports by origin and destination (%)

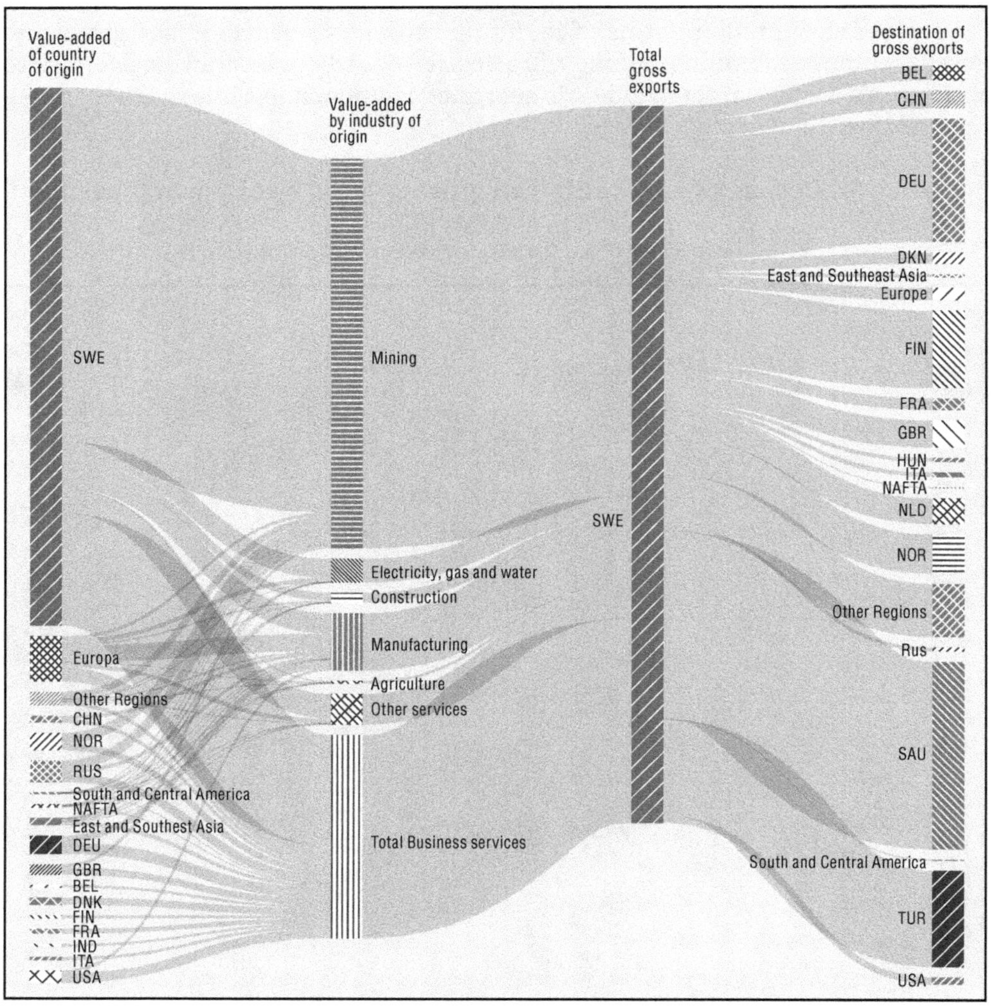

Source: OECD (2017b), TiVA Nowcast Database, http://stats.oecd.org/Index.aspx?DataSetCode=TIVA_NOWCAST; see also http://www.oecd.org/std/its/tiva-nowcast-methodology.pdf

Agriculture and the agro-food industry are also major drivers of export growth. They account for 8% of Chile's GDP, contribute to more than 20% of domestic exports, and employ 17% of the national work force; the food and beverages industry only accounts for approximately 40% of domestic manufacturing value added. Chile mostly exports primary products for consumption, and its exports are less sophisticated and less diversified than other countries. Primary products account for 41% of Chile's domestic agro-food exports, compared to 15% and 11% in Italy and France respectively. In 2016, 49 products accounted for 90% of Chilean agro-food exports, while 112 products explain 90% of Italy's exports. Chile's top 10 destination markets (of which the US is by far the most important) account for 75% of total domestic agricultural exports and 70% of agro-food industry exports.

Achieving successful diversification in Chile does not mean dismissing mining and traditional activities such agriculture and agro-food. But rather transforming them, making it more productive, and exploiting the synergies with emerging industries and technologies, including digital technologies and solar energy. Generating business opportunities in new areas will be essential to sustaining growth and creating jobs.

Chile has the potential to benefit more from its openness and improve its participation in global value chains (GVCs). Its businesses are integrated in GVCs, but mostly as commodity producers. In fact, most of the country's participation to GVCs is explained by the provision of un-refined copper to China, (Figure 0.7). Chile could improve its participation in GVCs by seeking opportunities beyond mining, including in services. In 2014, the services value-added content of Chile's total exports was 38.4%, below the OECD average of 55.5% (Figure 0.8). This could also contribute to increase SMEs' participation to GVCs, as in Chile only 10% of SMEs are involved in export activities, one of the lowest shares in OECD countries.

Figure 0.7 **GVC participation by partner country, Chile, 2014**

Billion USD

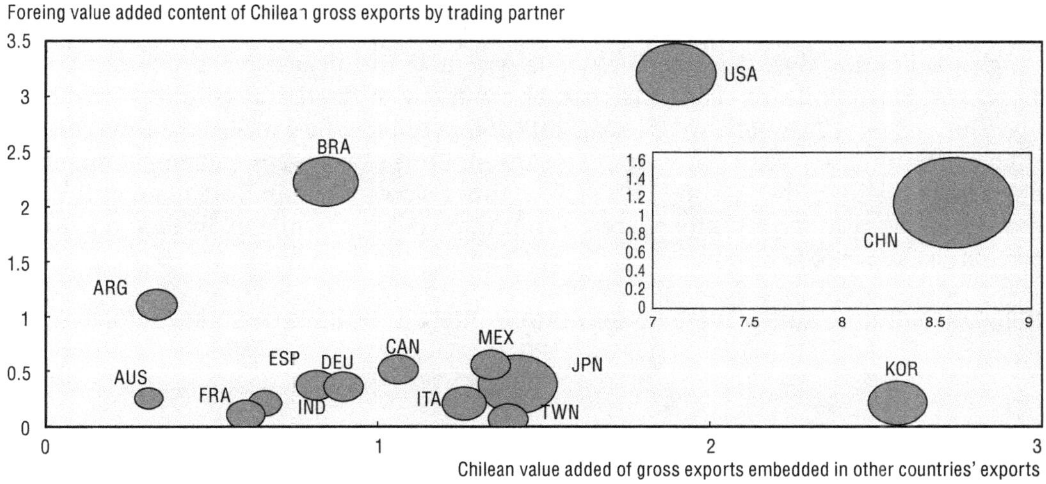

Note: Bubble size represents the share of Chilean exports to that country. Only countries that account for at least 2% of Chile's exports are displayed.

Source: Authors' analysis based on OECD-WTO (2017), Trade in Value Added database, http://stats.oecd.org.

Figure 0.8 **Chile's services content of gross exports, by industry and service category, 2014**

Share of industry gross exports

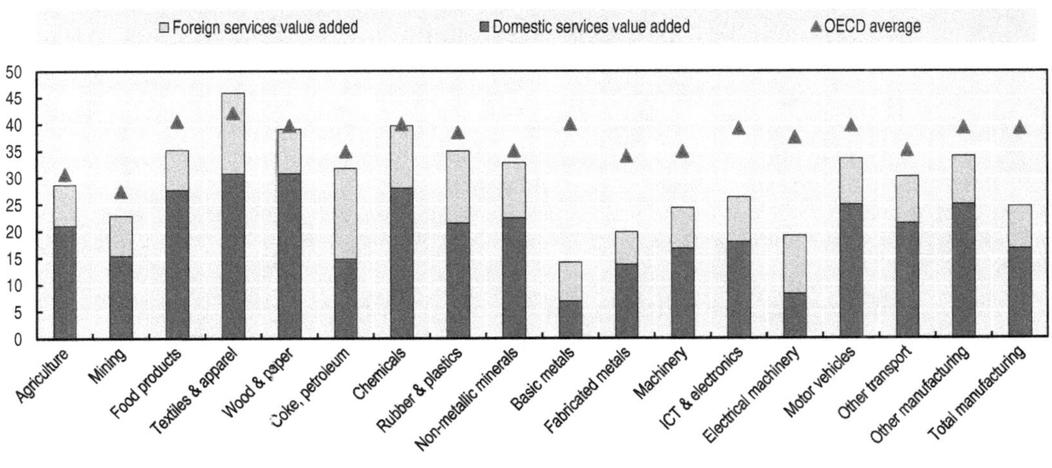

Source: Authors' analysis on OECD (2017d), TiVA Nowcast Database, http://stats.oecd.org/Index.aspx?DataSetCode=TIVA_NOWCAST.

The persistent specialisation in low value added activities and the high concentration of economic opportunities in few activities, firms and regions hamper future progress and limit innovation.

Despite the progress of the last decade, Chile still has a limited knowledge base. A growing number of Chileans pursue graduate degrees, but few do so in relevant areas for future competitiveness: 3% of graduates are in information and communication technology (ICT), and only 1% in natural sciences, mathematics and statistics (the lowest share of all OECD countries). This skills gap hampers the capacity to be connected to global production systems, which will be increasingly dominated by digitalisation and new technologies and to innovate in strategic areas for the country, such as earth science and natural resources.

Chile has advanced in digital connectivity, but much progress still needs to be made. A high performing digital infrastructure is essential to fully reap the benefits of the digital era. More Chileans using internet, the number of fixed and wireless broadband subscriptions per 100 inhabitants is 16 in 2017 compared to only 9 in 2008, but the country still lags behind the frontier in connection speed. Chile's average broadband connection speed is 5 megabytes per second (Mb/s), four times slower than in Korea and only 2% of broadband connections in Chile operate faster than 15 Mb/s, while in Sweden and Korea the share is above 35%.

Figure 0.9 **Public and private investment in R&D in Chile remain below average, 2015**

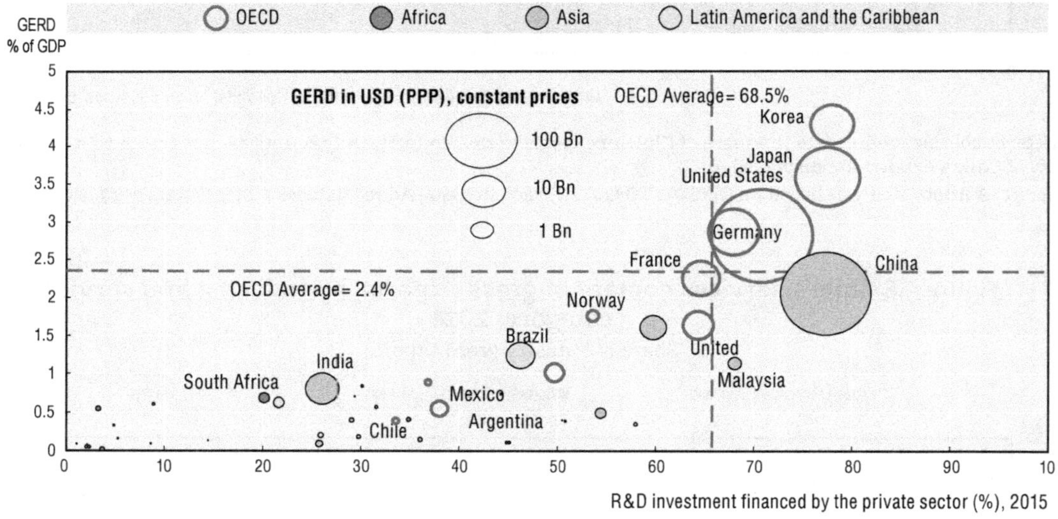

Note: GERD: Gross domestic expenditure on research and development.

Source: OECD (2016e), "Main science and technology indicators", http://oe.cd/msti; RICYT (2015), *Red de Indicadores de Ciencia y Tecnologia* (database), www.ricyt.org; UNESCO (2016), *Institute for Statistics Database*, http://data.uis.unesco.org.

Chilean businesses invest little in innovation. With roughly USD 1.2 billion of gross domestic expenditure on research and development (GERD) (0.39% of GDP), Chile has one of the lowest R&D intensities of all OECD countries (Figure 0.9). Moreover, the private sector's contribution -at 33% of total R&D expenditure- is significantly below the OECD average of around 68%. In mining, the increasing specialisation in extractive activities and the high returns of the super cycle of commodity prices during the 2000s reduced the incentives to invest in innovation. Total business expenditures in R&D over total gross value added is 0.15% in Chile, versus 2% in Australia and 1% in Sweden (Figure 0.10). And, while in Australia 21.4 out of 1 000 employees and in Sweden 13.3 are dedicated to R&D, the figure in Chile is 1.2. The lag in business investment in innovation is also large in manufacturing: Chilean firms invest only 0.4% of their gross value added in R&D, which compares poorly to the 5% invested by Australian manufacturing firms (Figure 0.11). In the food processing industry, the private sector commitment to innovation is also below that of international leaders. Fewer firms innovate and, among the innovators, Chilean firms tend to be less radical than the ones in other countries and they tend to focus on process, rather than on product innovations. In Chile, 40% of food processing companies declare being active in innovation, compared to 70% in Belgium and around 60% in France and Italy (Figure 0.12).

Figure 0.10 **Chile lags behind world leading mining countries in innovation**

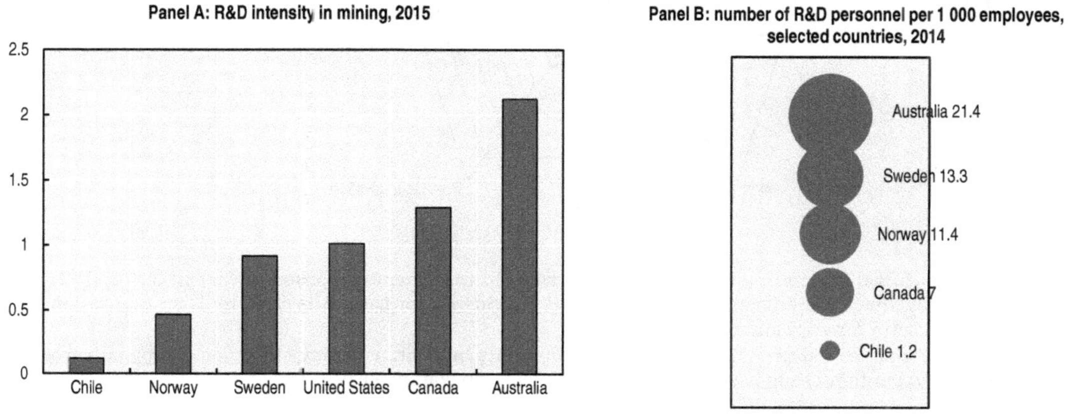

Note: Panel a: R&D intensity in mining is the ratio of total business enterprises' expenditure on R&D over total gross value added in the mining sector (ISIC rev 3.1); Panel b figures refer to private sector employment, 2015: Chile, 2014: Norway, 2013, Australia and Canada, 2010: Sweden.

Source: Authors' analysis based on OECD STAND stats.oecd.org; ILO Statistics, www.ilo.org/ilostat; and Australian Department of Employment, https://www.employment.gov.au (databases), 2017.

Figure 0.11 **Chile's manufacturing sector invests little in R&D**

R&D investment as share of manufacturing value added, 2015

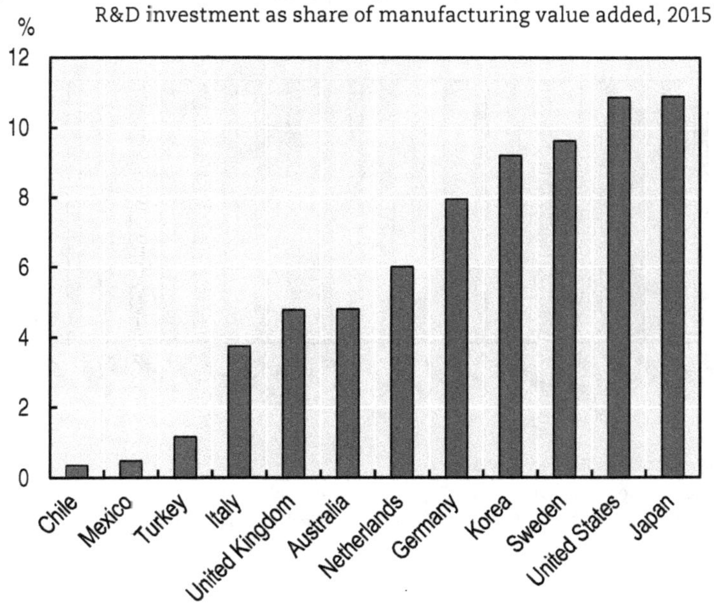

Source: Based on OECD (2017e), National Accounts Data, http://stats.oecd.org/; and OECD (2017i), Structural Analysis Statistics (TAN) Database, http://stats.oecd.org.

Figure 0.12 **Share of food processing firms engaged in innovation activities by type of innovation, 2014**

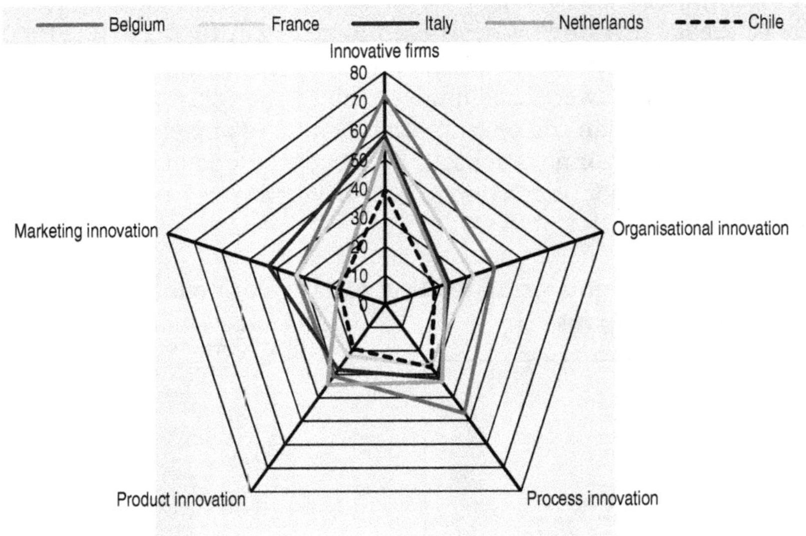

Note: For comparing different innovation surveys we adopted the scheme proposed by Crespi, G., Tacsir, E. and F. Vargas (2016), "Innovation dynamics and productivity: Evidence for Latin America", in: Firm Innovation and Productivity in Latin America and the Caribbean.

Source: Authors' analysis based on Eurostat (2014), "Community Innovation Survey", http://ec.europa.eu/eurostat/web/microdata/community-innovation-survey; and Chilean Innovation Survey 2013-14, 2017.

Large firms play a dominant role in the economy, but they innovate less than their peers in advanced countries. Large firms in Chile are responsible for 73% of business turnover and 57% of total business R&D, while in Germany such firms account for 53% of turnover and for 85% of R&D (Figures 0.13 and 0.14).

Figure 0.13 **Large firms play a dominant role in Chile's economy**

Share of total turnover in business activities by firm size, selected countries, 2015

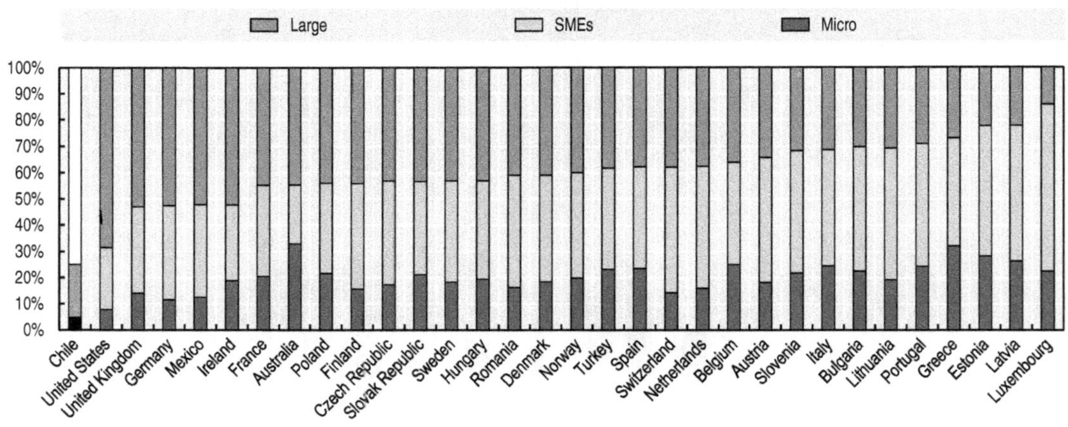

Note: Business activities comprises ISIC 4.0 Div 5-90.

Source: Authors' analysis based on OECD (2017g), *Structural and Demographic Business Statistics database*, http://stats.oecd.org; and SII (2017), "SII statistics and studies", www.sii.cl/estadisticas.

Figure 0.14 **Business enterprise R&D expenditure by firm size, 2015**

Share of total business R&D expenditure by firm size, 2015

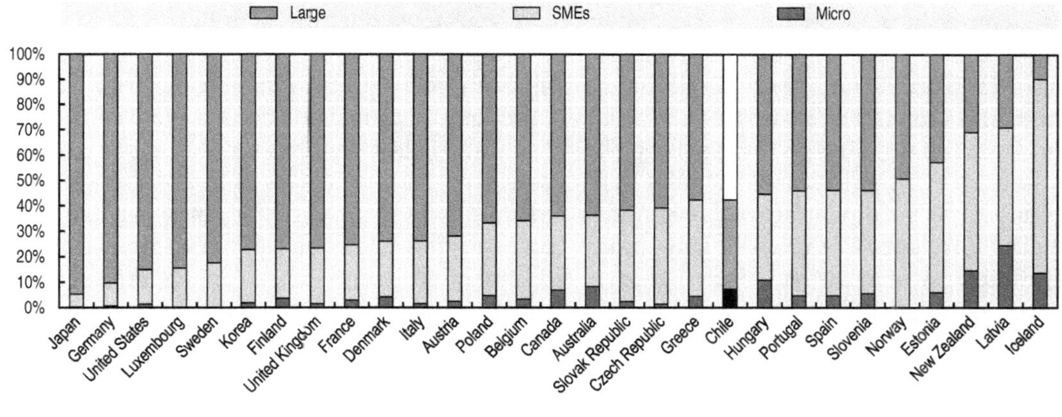

Source: Authors' analysis based on OECD (2017h), *OECD Science, Technology and Patents Database*, http://stats.oecd.org.

In addition, economic opportunities are unequally distributed across the country. Chile is the most territorially unequal country in the OECD. Population, GDP growth and productivity are concentrated in the capital city. According to the latest census, 40% of Chileans live in the Santiago Metropolitan Region (RMS) and generate 48% of national GDP, higher than other countries in which the capital city plays an important role (Paris, for example, accounts for 18% of France's population and for 30% of national GDP). Chile's regional disparities in GDP per capita are the second highest of all OECD countries. Foreign direct investment concentrates in Santiago and the mining regions of Antofagasta and Atacama, while the creation of new firms is concentrated in Santiago. These trends hamper the possibilities to identify new sources of growth and to connect local ecosystems with emerging business opportunities.

New technologies and the global call for inclusive and sustainable development open a window of opportunities to overcome the country's structural weaknesses.

Major scientific, technological and production changes are revolutionising the economy and society at an unprecedented speed. A high level of uncertainty characterises the global landscape at multiple levels – from the kind of technology that will dominate in a given domain, to the forms of social contracts that will be needed to regulate work in a platform-based economy, and the global race for leadership in the standards that will define competitive advantages in the future. These changes are coupled with stronger demands for shared prosperity and more sustainable and inclusive development, calling all countries – at different levels of development and wealth – to revise their strategies and to define new policy approaches.

New technologies are transforming businesses. Most countries in the world, including Germany, Sweden and Italy, are increasingly aware of the potential disruptive impacts of ongoing technological changes and, in fact, are taking steps to shape their futures by defining long-term visions, scanning potential options and investing for the long term. For example, automation and artificial intelligence are driving productivity growth in mining, and are enhancing safety in the work place. In 2014, Sweden invested almost half a USD billion to set up the world's most automated mine which enabled a doubling in the extracted output and energy savings of 25%. In addition, the agro-food value chain is increasingly sophisticated and a growing number of scientific and technological areas will drive competitiveness in the future, including biotechnology, nanotechnology, pharmaceuticals, and smart packaging. Data science will also benefit the sector through enhanced traceability and greater food safety.

The call for "green" products and services and new consumers' preferences are also transforming the way to do business. This holds true in all activities, from mining to agro-food and solar energy. Greening mining is already a global business priority, due to high and growing energy costs and to a demand for greening value chains. New consumer preferences are also changing the global agriculture, food and beverage markets. While a decade ago the demand for sustainable, safe and healthy food was limited to a niche, today it has become more diffused and is expected to keep growing. Demand is shifting to "local" products (0-Km products), and to "authentic" and unique products, often coming from distant markets but with a recognised impact on health. These trends require new forms of traceability and standards and open new opportunities for business development.

Solar energy is becoming globally competitive thanks to falling prices. Chile's natural endowments (the Atacama Desert has the highest solar incidence in the world and UV-B radiation 65% above the European average) together with falling renewable energy prices and ongoing technological changes are opening a window of opportunities. Chile is already the biggest solar energy producer in Latin America, accounting for almost half of total installed capacity in the region (Figure 0.15). Since 2015, Chile also has a national vision with a roadmap for energy towards 2050. All scenarios estimate that solar will be the leading energy source in Chile by 2045. Solar energy can help not only to green the energy matrix, but also to transform the economy and its growth model. Unlike fossil-fuel based energies, solar is not extracted through drilling or mining. It involves a manufacturing value chain and can be produced and used locally, opening new business opportunities in Chile.

Figure 0.15 **Chile is Latin America's biggest solar energy producer**

Installed capacity in solar energy, 2016

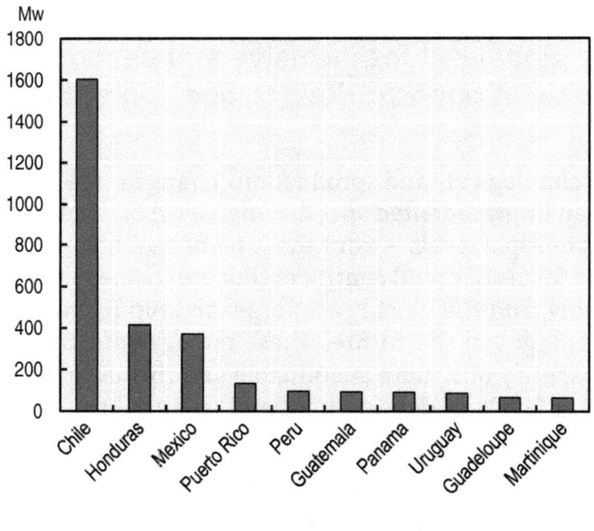

Source: Authors' analysis based on IRENA (2017), IRENA Dashboard, http://resourceirena.irena.org/gateway/dashboard/

Chile has taken steps to transform the economy and reap the benefits of new demands and technologies.

The Chilean approach to economic development shows relative continuity over time. Since 2014, the government has embarked on an ambitious programme that included an educational reform to respond to the demand for better and more inclusive education, targeted efforts to promote environmental sustainability, reforms to increase decentralisation and autonomy in the regions, and reforms for enhancing productivity, innovation and growth. The pro-growth reforms had a budget of approximately 1 USD billion in 2017 (0.4% of GDP) of which 45% went to skills development. This budget has been increasing in the last decade, but it is still considerably below international trends. The growth agenda since 2014 can be summarised in four main areas:

1. **Modernising the state for greater impact**. The government has been active in reforming institutions to increase impact and deliver more effective results. The main actions have included: i) The creation of the National Productivity Commission (CNP), by decree in 2015, as a public-private consultative body to facilitate co-ordination and to better prioritise action; ii) The creation in 2016 of InvestChile as the national agency in charge of FDI attraction; iii) A proposal for creating a Ministry for Science and Technology, responsible for financing the training of advanced human capital and research, to which CONICYT would respond to as an implementing agency, and; iv) a renewed impetus to the decentralisation agenda. Recent reforms increased the decision-making and financial autonomy of regions. CORFO has also started pilot programmes in regions with the aim to decentralise 40% of its budget by 2021.
2. **Facilitating business development**. Chile has updated its policies for business development by reducing red tape and fostering start-up creation and expansion. The country has reformed the policy mix based on the results of its monitoring and evaluation, and now prioritises retaining more talent and businesses in the country and the creation of start-ups in the regions outside the capital city, Santiago. As a result the concentration of start-up creation in Santiago has decreased from 75% (during the first assessment of Start-up Chile) to around 50% in 2017. The government has modernised services to entrepreneurs through more flexible mechanisms tailored to the needs of start-ups, such as collaborative workspaces and mentoring networks; and it has simplified the regulations for starting and winding down a business. Private investment at the expansion stage and angel investors remain weak links in Chile's financing chain.
3. **Fostering human capital and innovation**. The government has continued to support human capital and innovation through several tools managed by CONICYT and CORFO. BecasChile has financed more than 2 300 PhDs in the last five years; however, the programme is not sufficiently articulated with emerging skills demand as more than 40% of the beneficiaries were trained in social sciences. CORFO manages multiple lines of financing to foster innovation in firms from precompetitive research to piloting and scale up. Some instruments specifically target SMEs. Since 2008, Chile has also put in place fiscal incentives for innovation; they have been reformed in 2011 to broaden the scope of the tax credit for R&D to include internal expenditures, increase the annual tax ceiling, simplify administrative requirements and encourage co-operation in R&D with domestic and international science and business partners. Between 2012 and 2016, CORFO certified more than USD 60 million in tax credits (50% of which went to mining, 35% to agriculture and forestry and 18% to agro-processing).
4. **Enabling public-private partnerships to address strategic challenges**. Starting from increasing awareness about the major technological changes that are transforming businesses and societies worldwide, and in line with global trends, the government has embarked in a new effort to facilitate public-private dialogue to identify future challenges and opportunities in its different industrial ecosystems. The Strategic Investments Fund (FIE) managed by the Ministry of Economy was set up in 2015 to finance high-impact strategic projects jointly selected by the government and the private sector. CORFO has introduced the strategic programmes. These represent a novelty in the Chilean policy approach: they build on previous

successful experiences of public-private dialogue, especially in mining, and scale it up to add a forward-looking dimension. Through a process of multi-stakeholder dialogue, CORFO acted as a coordination facilitator between businesses, academia, civil society and government to identify gaps and road-maps with a 10/15-year timeframe. This process has been conducive to identify future priorities, including the need to ensure resilient, reliable and safe Internet connection; to define standards for interoperability and digital trade and to modernise training at all levels – from vocational to post-graduate – to endow the next generation of workers and managers with the skills needed for the future. It has also contributed to identify competitiveness gaps that need public-private action, including for example: knowledge, technology, skills and infrastructure gaps.

Table 0.1 **Progress overview of Chile's strategic programmes, 2017**

Governance dimensions		
Anticipation capacity	√	Having road-maps with a long-term horizon (to 2025-30) takes Chile a step forward in line with international good practices. Aligning financing with the time-line of the road map will be an additional step forward.
Adaptation capacity	≈	In the fast changing technological environment the time for design and validating road-maps could be shortened from the current 13 months, while adaptability could be increased by introducing periodical revision of road-maps.
Learning and upgrading potential	√	The public-private consultations led to an effective identification of gaps in skills needed to compete in the future and of priority actions to bridge them. Growing cooperation between businesses, training centres and academia is a positive step. Overcoming barriers, including aligning educational accreditation processes with emerging needs, will be important to getting the right skills for tomorrow.
	≈	Setting up mechanisms to generate synergies between the different programmes and to enable learning and cross-fertilisation could align multiple-stakeholders to take actions and provide public goods which would act as competitiveness enhancers across all industries and firms, including digital infrastructure and skills. The creation of the Solar Research Institute, if endowed with a broader science base and mission could contribute to enhance learning opportunities in the whole economy.
Interconnectedness propensity	√	**Within government**. The programme benefits from multi-agency co-ordination.
	≈	**Private sector**. Businesses participated in the road-map process, but enhanced. participation of start-ups and SMEs would be needed as well as increased commitment by lead firms and investors would be needed in going forward.
	√	**Academia**. The programme benefits from commitment and co-operation mechanisms with academia and international research centres.
	√	**Civil society**. There is room to increase the participation of civil society in the process, and to identify new mechanisms to strengthen business-community relationship.
	x	**Regional.** Strengthening regional ties could help to scale up investments and reach the critical mass needed to compete effectively at the global level.
	√	**International**. Scaling up on international cooperation could help closing knowledge and technology gaps.
Embeddedness potential	≈	There is a need to clarify procedures and standards to ensure environmental and social sustainability.
	×	There is a need to increase the role of regions & territories in planning, implementation and monitoring.
	≈	Open government and effective monitoring and evaluation are needed to track progress and performance and identify areas for reform.
Future challenges		
Ensuring the long-term commitment of the private sector. Mechanisms to avoid rent seeking and capture need to be in place to ensure that publicly-financed actions benefit all stakeholders and deliver public and club goods not available otherwise		
Aligning the budget with the strategy's objectives. Chile has an initial budget of USD160 million for three years (0.1% of 2016 GDP). In comparison, the Emilia Romagna region (Italy) has a USD 700 million budget for the period 2014-2020 in the context of the European Union Smart Specialisation Strategy		
Avoiding the overlap of programmes and actions and foster synergies among the different sectoral programmes. It is important to convey resources towards economic activities that have the greatest spill-over effects for the economy and society		
Ensuring high-level political ownership. The programmes are designed, implemented and revised within the Ministry of Economy through CORFO and with the financial support of FIE and FIC. In order to scale-up and foster production transformation it will be important seek higher political commitment		

Note: √: positive progress; ≈: margin for improvement; x: reform needed.

Through the strategic programmes, Chile seems to have found an effective policy approach by identifying enabling areas that are relevant for all industries (i.e logistics, solar energy, smart industries and advanced manufacturing) and by creating opportunities for the actors operating in different industries to share visions and challenges and define future specific needs in terms of skills, infrastructure, supply chain development, R&D and standards. This process is a step forward in consensus building and in fostering public private co-operation for economic development (Table 0.1). Examples of actions to close competitiveness gaps derived from the road-mapping process include: i) the proposal of the creation of the International Institute of Solar and Mining (IISM) to foster applied research in solar energy, mining and production of clean hydrogen and other energy-storage components that aims to fill the knowledge gap that hampers Chile to participate to natural resource-based value chains in a more sophisticated way; ii) the open platform, launched in 2017 and managed by Fundación Chile, to match demand and supply for developing innovative solutions to foster supply chain development in mining; and iii) the clarification of the need to develop standards for enabling the development of new food categories and high-value ingredients to enable upgrading in agro-food.

To consolidate the progress made Chile will need to:

- **Mobilise public resources and scale up public investments to amounts that reflect global challenges.** Ensuring a high speed, resilient and reliable internet connection across the whole territory will require high investment. In addition, the competitiveness challenges posed by the ongoing technological and demand revolutions require high mobilisation of resources. For example, the Emilia Romagna region, with less than 5 million inhabitants, is mobilising USD 800 million between 2015 and 2020 for investments to improve the competitiveness of its agro-food system. Chile, according to current plans, is aiming to mobilise one-eighth of this amount (USD 100 million from 2014 to 2025). Considering Chile's future priorities to reduce public debt, actions involving regional and global partnerships could help the country overcome the funding gap.
- **Strengthen opportunities for learning and innovation.**
  - **Bridging the skills gap** to enable operating in global production systems, which will be increasingly dominated by digitalisation and new technologies and to innovate in strategic areas for the country, such as earth sciences and natural resources. Chile would benefit from consolidating and expanding current initiatives of greater involvement of private sector in technical, graduate and post-graduate levels, modernising vocational training, updating curricula at all levels to endow the next generation of workers and managers with the skills needed for the future and aligning educational accreditation processes with emerging needs. Increasing quality and access of the overall educational system is a precondition.
  - **Leverage on mining as a driver of change.** Chile could further leverage on the transition of mining towards industry 4.0 to address the competitiveness gaps that limit the country's potential to benefit from new technologies, including by improving internet connectivity and by creating opportunities for domestic universities, firms and research institutes to develop solutions for digital industrial systems.
  - **Enable partnerships and explore the potential of technological convergence.** The new industrial landscape will be characterized by growing interrelation between knowledge and technology fields; innovating will require cross-fertilization from different areas and disciplines. For example, it would be appropriate to enlarge the mission of the solar institute in Chile beyond

mining applications and to explore synergies with other renewable energies. World leading research centers in solar, including the German Aerospace Center (DLR), benefit from a wide science base and with networks with multiple technological and industrial fields. Europe, in its plan for renewable energies has also shifted from a technology-specific to an integrated approach that fosters complementarities between renewables and with other enabling technologies, such as ICT, advanced manufacturing, new materials, industrial biotechnology, nanotechnology, photonics and nano-electronics, among others.

- **Strengthen national, regional and international co-operation in research and supply-chain development.** Building capabilities in a rapidly changing technological environment takes time and requires benefiting from local and global research and production networks. Chile needs to increase private sector commitment to innovate and needs greater co-operation between science and businesses.Chile is on a good track as it is exploring opportunities to strengthen its learning and knowledge base through global partnership; the country could further build on its reputation as a reliable partner and scale up its efforts to co-operate within the region and globally. Pooling resources for research and exploiting synergies in Latin America could also help to scale up investments and reach the critical mass needed to compete effectively at the global level. International co-operation is also relevant. An interesting step in this direction is the South-South co-operation programme that Chile signed in 2017 with Morocco to foster learning and co-operation to strengthen capabilities in the solar value chain.

- **Getting the right stakeholders at the table**. Setting up effective public-private consultations is an important step in defining better policies. The effectiveness of these consultations depends, however, on the representativeness and inclusiveness of the participants. Over the last decade, Chile has strengthened the public-private dialogue with lead firms, especially in mining. Going forward it would be important to strengthen the participation of civil society, entrepreneurs along the entire value chain and local governments and communities. For example, the social acceptability of solar energy should not be taken for granted. The social license from which these energies currently benefit from will only be sustained in the long run if new agreements, negotiations and benefit sharing with the local communities are developed. New forms of dialogue and partnership with local communities will therefore be needed.
- **Being actively involved in international discussions on future standards and norms**. Especially in the ones that will be increasingly relevant in the value chains that matter to the country, such as mining, renewable energies and agro-food.
- **Monitor implementation and assess impact**. New technologies offer new opportunities to guarantee easier and real-time access to information linked to the implementation of public action. CORFO has good experience in project monitoring and evaluation. Going forward, it would be desirable to benefit from new technologies and set up a simple, easy-to-access mechanism for tracking implementation to increase accountability and enable adjusting actions when expected results are not achieved.

The Chilean model requires an "update" to continue succeeding: a renewed pact between government, businesses, academia and society is needed to allow Chile to advance on its path to prosperity.

Society's aspirations change with progress, and the Chilean society – with its growing middle class – is no exception. Chileans are demanding more opportunities for their youth and access to new services. Matching the aspirations of an inclusive society requires an 'update" of the growth model to unleash new sources of growth and to broaden society's participation to the economy to achieve shared prosperity.

Chile's has the potential to be part of the next production revolution. The country, in addition to its natural endowments, has a sound reputation as a business partner and as a stable economy, and it counts on an extensive network of investors and trade partners. However, being a stable and open economy will not be enough to reap the benefits of new frontiers. Chile could build on its effective partnerships with lead firms in the value chain to participate in this transformation at an early stage. This will require a pro-innovation attitude from the business community, and targeted policies to foster learning and innovation. The speed of global change and the competition for lead positions mean that this window of opportunity will not remain open forever. Development is a moving target – successful countries are those that are able to seize opportunities at an early stage. Taking full advantage of global opportunities will require Chile to address its structural weaknesses, from ICT infrastructure and skills to strengthening the national production and innovation system. This can be achieved only through investment and renewed and effective partnerships among government at all levels, businesses, academia and society. To make Chile advance on its path towards prosperity and build the trust that is needed, three game changers are of particular importance in the near future:

1. **Advancing in modernizing the state to cope with a fast-changing, uncertain and complex landscape.** Chile's governance needs an "update" to continue succeeding. Over the years, several institutional reforms have been implemented within and across organisations. In some cases the reforms have improved governance, in others successive changes created several institutional layers and a high level of complexity in the bureaucracy. In the future it would be important to preserve the state's modernisation agenda and make it more agile, effective and capable of responding to future needs. Ensuring high-level leadership for the transformation agenda would help to achieve consensus and mobilise actions across ministries. Co-ordination at the ministerial level on innovation and economic transformation needs to be strengthened. The current negotiation process for annual budgeting between finance and each line ministry, coupled with weak co-ordination at the strategic level, weakens the capacity to prioritise actions in a more effective way. In going forward, it would also be desirable to reduce the multiplicity of co-ordination and advisory bodies and aim for a unique, but empowered and strengthened, body directly answering to the President. Enabling long-term financing for strategic investment is also important. The creation of the Strategic Investments Fund (FIE) is a positive step forward, even though its nature as a treasury fund limits the long-term orientation. To consolidate the fund and to simplify procedures it could be shifted to the responsibility of the implementation agency (CORFO), rather than being directly managed at the ministerial level. As the challenges of global, digital, inclusive and environmentally sustainable economies are multidimensional and complex, renewed co-ordination among the production, investment, trade and education agendas would also be desirable. The government has consolidated the dialogue with leading domestic and international firms. The next step would be to enlarge the consultation base and increase the capacity for dialogue with entrepreneurs, small businesses and civil society. In the new technological

paradigms, disruptive innovations could also come from start-ups and small firms – having a governance structure capable of interacting with them will increase the capacity to design better policies.

2. **Strengthening and institutionalising anticipation capacity at the highest strategic level.** The pace of change at the global level is so rapid and uncertain that it is almost impossible to do responsible policy making without preparing for a range of alternative possible futures. Since the Ministry of Planning has been transformed into the ministry in charge of social development, Chile lacks a formal process, or an institutionalised space for planning and scenarios building. There are some initiatives, including the 2050 energy policy and the strategic programmes for economic transformation with their road-maps to 2030, but there is no high level strategic function dedicated to scanning potential futures to inform the policy process. In going forward, stronger anticipatory capacities could increase the ability to identify needs, prioritise actions and generate consensus on what is needed in the short, medium and long term. A future-oriented space for strategy setting is essential to contribute to aligning different stakeholders on a modernisation path and avoid the risks of being captured by current established interests. It would be important to set up a mechanism to ensure that the results of the strategic foresight processes are embedded into the national strategy and that they trickle down to each policy area.
3. **Advancing towards a place-based approach to policy making.** At the global level, regions and cities are becoming key units for planning and implementing economic transformation strategies. Chile would benefit from continuing advancing in its regional agenda to identify new sources of growth and make it more inclusive. In this process, it is also important to identify mechanisms for cross-regional cooperation to take into account not only administrative regions, but also functional ones. Regional governments in Chile suffer from capability gaps with respect to the national administration, it is important to complement the decentralisation agenda with efforts to increase capabilities in regional and local governments as well as implementing effective mechanisms for resource transfers between the national and regional governments.

The world is moving fast, and for Chile to be part of the global wave of change, a renewed approach to policy making and government-business-society relationships is needed. The current strategy has marked some positive steps towards building consensus for change. From now on, going beyond ideological divides and finding a common ground to mobilise private and public actors is of critical importance to reap the benefits of international trends and avoid marginalisation in the evolving global context.

Chapter 1

What's next on Chile's growth and development agenda?

Chile has been growing in a sustained and relatively stable manner since the 1990s, thanks to effective macroeconomic management and its open economy. Today the Chilean model requires an "update" if it is to capture the gains offered by global technological and geopolitical changes and to meet the aspirations of its growing middle classes. Finding new sources of growth and broadening its economic base will be crucial for achieving shared prosperity. This chapter reviews Chile's economic transformation and identifies four structural weaknesses that will need to be overcome to benefit from the window of opportunity opened in today's global context.

Chile is a relatively stable, open and highly connected economy

Chile's economic growth has been sustained and relatively stable since the 1990s. Effective macroeconomic management has insulated Chile from the more volatile growth patterns of other Latin American countries. It has outperformed other economies in the region, overturning the persistent income per capita gaps of the 1980s. For example, its average gross domestic product (GDP) per capita is 40% higher than the Latin American average (Figure 1.1). Chile's performance has also allowed it to converge with more advanced economies in terms of income per capita: while Chile's average GDP per capita was only 26% of that of the United States in 1990, it reached 40% in 2016 (in 2016, Chile had an average GDP per capita of USD 24 000 in purchasing power parity in 2011 constant prices; Figure 1.1).

Figure 1.1. **Chile's GDP growth and GDP per capita**

Annual GDP growth rate (HP filter, left axis) and GDP per capita (right axis), 1950-2016

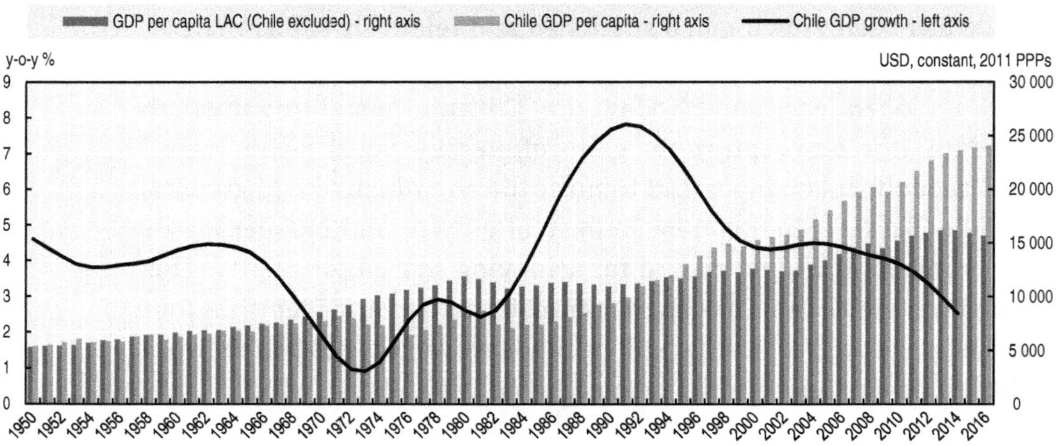

Note: GDP: gross domestic product; LAC: Latin American countries; y-o-y: year on year; PPP: purchasing power parity; HP: Hodrick Prescott Filter. The Lambda in the Hodrick Prescott filter has been chosen according to OECD (2016a), OECD Compendium of Productivity Indicators 2016, http://dx.doi.org/10.1787/pdtvy-2016-en.

Source: Authors' analysis based on the Conference Board (2017), Total Economy Database™ (Adjusted version), https://www.conference-board.org/data/economydatabase/index.cfm?id=27762.

Chile is an open economy. In 2016, total trade amounted to 60% of GDP. This figure is higher than for other countries in Latin America, such as Argentina (where trade as a share of GDP is 24%), and other natural resource-rich countries such as Australia (where trade amounts to 41% of GDP). Yet Chile's performance lags behind economies such as Sweden and Germany, where overall trade amounts to 86% and 84% of GDP (Figure 1.2). Central to Chile's positive growth performance has been the implementation of open trade and investment policies, co-ordinated by the General Directorate for International Economic Affairs (DIRECON). Chile has been a World Trade Organization (WTO) member since 1995, and has 21 free trade agreements in force, including with the European Union (2003), the United States (2004), the People's Republic of China (2006) and Japan (2007). The country also has five preferential trade agreements with Bolivia, Ecuador, India, Venezuela and the Mercosur custom union. The extensive trade network has led to an applied tariff of 0.93%. In 2000 Chile abandoned the floating exchange rate regime and introduced inflation targeting as its main monetary policy objective. Increasing liberalisation in the services sector has also played a role in sustaining growth by facilitating access to foreign upstream service providers and, in turn, improving the competitiveness of Chile's exports. Nowadays, Chile has a lower score than the OECD average in 18 out of 22 sectors in the OECD Services Trade Restrictiveness Index, signalling its above-average openness with respect to other OECD countries (OECD, 2017a; UNTAC, 2016).

Figure 1.2. **Chile is a very open economy**

Trade as % of GDP, selected economies, 1990-2015

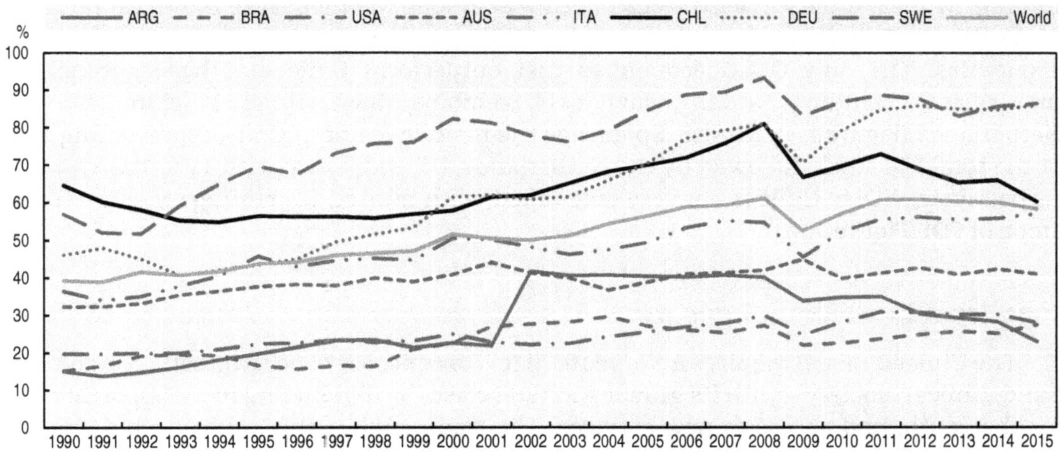

Source: Authors' analysis based on World Bank (2017), National Accounts Data, https://data.worldbank.org/indicator/NY.GDP.MKTP.CD; and OECD (2017e), National Accounts Data, http://stats.oecd.org.

Figure 1.3. **Chile is among the top economies for its share of FDI stock**

FDI as % of GDP by economic activity, top three and selected economies, 2015

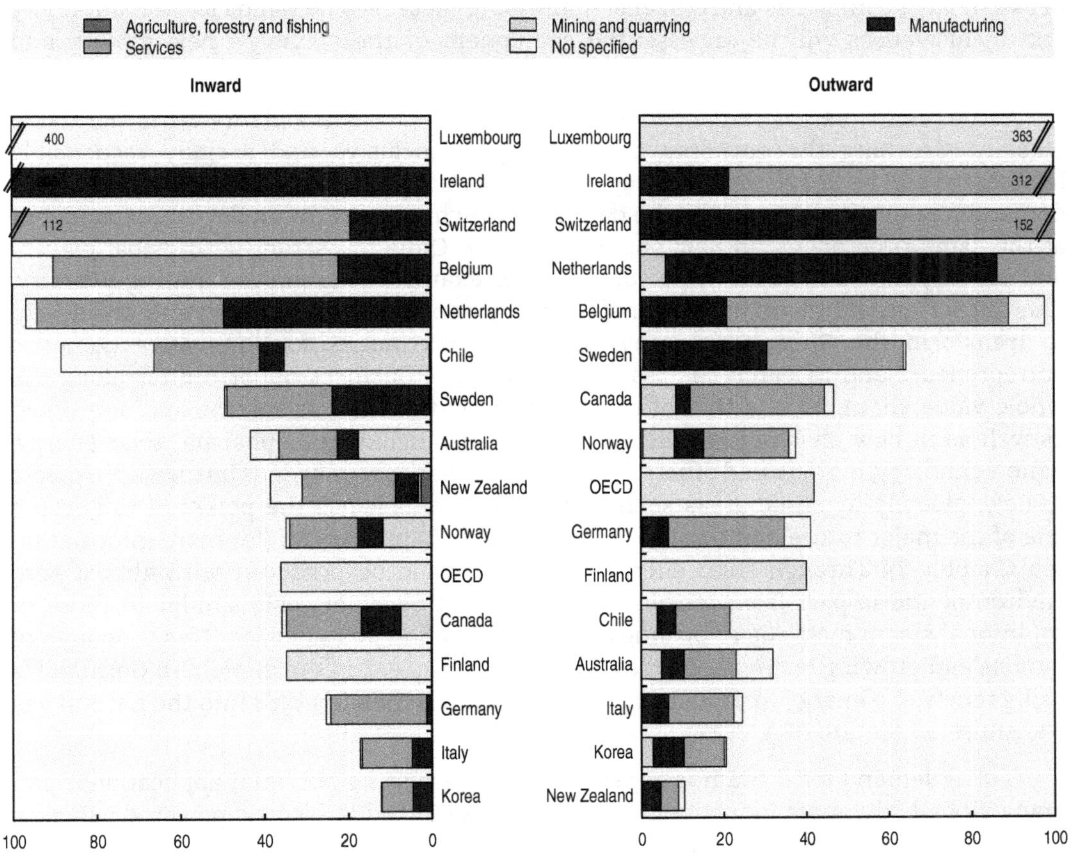

Note: Data refer to 2015, or latest available year. Foreign direct investment (FDI) data exclude resident Special Purpose Entities (SPEs) with the exception of Australia, Canada, Chile and Ireland. Inward and outward FDI positions as a share of GDP are calculated using GDP at current prices and current exchange rates. Not Specified: For Luxembourg, Finland and aggregate OECD breakdown by sectors is not available.

Source: Authors' analysis based on OECD (2017f), International Direct Investment statistics, http://stats.oecd.org; and OECD (2017e), National Accounts Data, http://stats.oecd.org.

The opening up of the economy since the 1990s has encouraged foreign direct investment (FDI) into the country, especially in capital-intensive activities such as mining. In 2015, Chile's inward stock of FDI was among the highest in the OECD (around 80% of GDP). This figure is well above the OECD average of 40% and of similarly sized economies. The only OECD economies that outperform Chile are those specialised in services, including banking, such as Luxemburg, Switzerland, Belgium and the Netherlands (Figure 1.3). In 2015, Spain was the main investor in Chile, representing 12% of the total FDI stock, followed by the Netherlands, US and Japan (with 11%, 11% and 6%, respectively). FDI to Chile is not very diversified, with mining accounting for 40% of total stock of FDI (Figure 1.3).

New global and local challenges present a window of opportunities to Chile

The Chilean model requires an "update" if it is to continue to be successful. On the one hand, Chilean society – with its growing middle class – is demanding more opportunities for the youth, and access to new services. The traditional, highly concentrated export-led model will struggle to deliver these. Matching the aspirations of an inclusive society requires adjusting the model, and finding new sources of growth to broaden society's participation in the economy and achieve shared prosperity. The youth are calling for free and better university education to ensure better prospects for all in the future. Chilean society has become more vocal in the last decade and is calling for trust to be rebuilt between large companies and citizens. Addressing these new demands for accountability and inclusiveness will be an essential component of the country's new growth and development agenda.

At the same time, the demand for more sustainable products and services is increasing globally. Greening the economy and developing inclusive and socially responsible businesses will be key drivers of competitiveness in the future (ECLAC, 2016). The global demand for sustainability limits the degree to which the current model can expand, but at the same time opens up new opportunities for Chile to partner with global players and identify new and sustainable solutions, for example to green the mining industry. The call for environmentally sustainable and "green" products and services could help to transform the Chilean economy, offering opportunities for innovative domestic entrepreneurs and research centres to generate new business opportunities along the whole value chain. This is true of traditional activities such as mining and agro-food, as well as in new enabling knowledge-based areas, including biopharma, solar energy, nanotechnology, big data and others. For example, solar energy widens business prospects to new, globally dynamic areas such as hydrogen, which has the potential to become one of the major future non-fossil fuels for industrial applications (for more information see Chapter 3). Through solar energy, hydrogen could be produced with almost zero environmental impact from renewables-based electrolysis at costs similar to those of traditional steam methane reforming or coal gasification technologies. This is an area of intense and growing technological research. For example, Eon's pilot plant in Germany is using renewable energy to produce hydrogen, which is then injected into the natural gas transmission system (IEA, 2017).

Global demand for lithium is expected to increase as its potential applications span many globally dynamic industries, especially those linked to electric-powered vehicles. Chile also hosts the largest world reserve of lithium (7.5 million of tonnes), corresponding to 52% of the world reserves. Electric cars require lighter inputs and more efficient and longer-lasting batteries. This is expected to increase the demand for lithium and for new solutions to generate energy from it. Currently, the global demand for electric vehicles is rising. In 2016, a record 750 000 electric cars were sold worldwide (IEA, 2017). Estimates suggest that the future global stock of electric cars will range between 9 and 20 million by 2020 and between 40 and 70 million by 2025 (IEA, 2017). Chile hosts the world's largest reserve of the metal at 7 500 000 metric tons (Mt), or 37% of total reserves. It is the second biggest world producer of lithium after Australia, with 12 000 Mt produced in 2016. Chile exports 70% of its high-grade lithium carbonate to China and Korea. Drawing on its natural resource asset and activating international partnerships to enter into more sophisticated parts of the battery value chain could enable Chile to increase the benefits from natural resources and to avoid being locked out from the experimentation and learning processes that are currently occurring. Being involved in the global research on lithium could enable Chile to combine the advantages of exploiting natural resources with upgrading in the value chain by participating in research and development (R&D) activities. This would increase the value capture for the economy by enabling Chile to upgrade its participation in global value chains (GVCs) from purely being a natural resource provider to being an innovation driver. Even though lithium processing has increased threefold in the past five years, the value share of lithium in the final value of a battery ranges between 1% and 3% of the total battery value added (depending on the design).

Figure 1.4. **Digitalisation is affecting all aspects of businesses, but at different speeds**

The Industry Digitisation Index of US industries, 2017

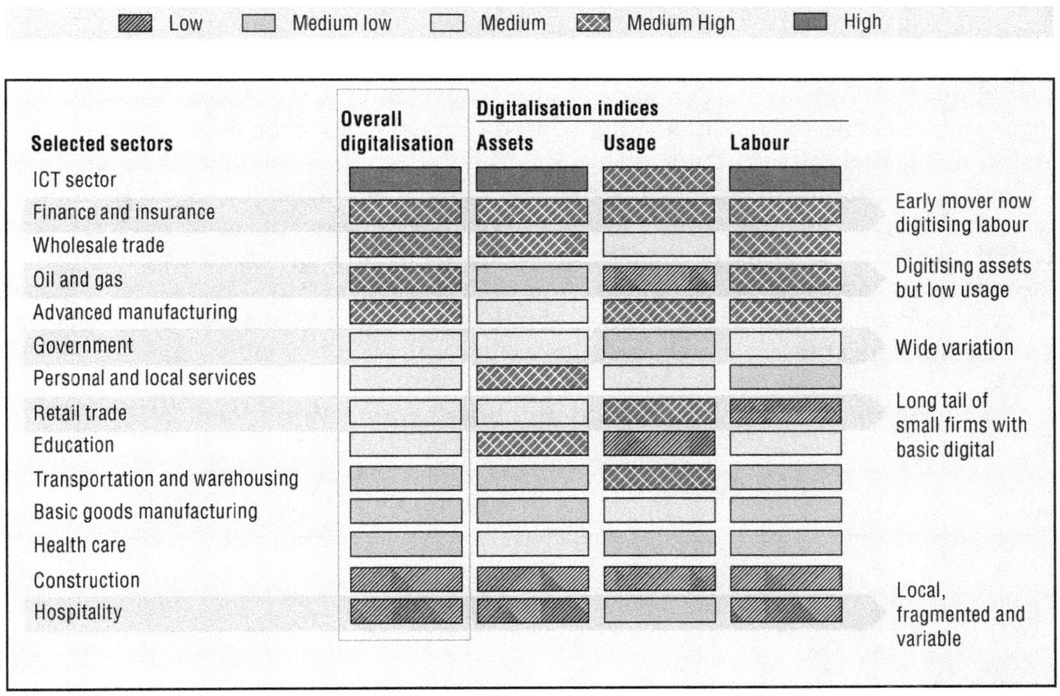

Note: The MGI Industry Digitization Index examines sectors across the economy through the lens of digital assets, digital usage, and digital workers, compiling 27 indicators to capture the many possible ways in which companies are digitizing. To measure digital assets the index considers business spending on computers, software, and telecom equipment, as well as the stock of ICT assets, the share of assets such as robots and cars that are digitally connected and total data storage. Usage metrics include an industry's use of digital payments, digital marketing, and social technologies, as well as the use of software to manage both back-office operations and customer relationships.

Source: Reames (2017), "Digital economy: snapshot of where we are today", McKinsey Institute presentation at the 9th Plenary Meeting of the OECD Initiative for Policy Dialogue on Global Value Chains, Production Transformation and Development.

The increasing demand for sustainability in business, coupled with the diffusion of new manufacturing techniques, big data and the internet of things (IoT), can help to increase productivity, and enhance innovation and learning (Cimoli et al, 2017). The current global landscape is characterised by the high-speed convergence and multiplicity in technologies and applications, transforming every aspect of the economy and of society. New technologies are changing the nature of manufacturing processes, service delivery and job creation. They will also have far-reaching consequences for employment, skills, income distribution, trade, well-being and the environment (OECD, 2017b). New technologies can increase productivity and enable the creation of new businesses. The technological complementarities and the simultaneous adoption of new technologies can have multiple impacts on productivity. In mining, for example, autonomous trucks could increase output by 15-20%, lower fuel consumption by 10% to 15% and reduce maintenance costs by 8% (OECD, 2017c). New technologies are affecting different industries in different ways and at different speeds, however. Figure 1.4 gives a United States example, where output and productivity for firms that adopt data-driven decision making are 5% to 6% higher than expected.

Structural weaknesses could hamper future progress

Exploring opportunities and synergies in solar, mining and electro-mobility could be a game changer for Chile, allowing it to be part of the next production revolution. However, there are two major agendas to be pursued if this is to occur. Firstly, the country needs to urgently close gaps in key enabling areas, especially in those that will determine the possibility of participating in the next production revolution. A major issue is linked with ensuring a resilient, redundant and high-speed Internet connection (Figure 1.5). A high-performing digital infrastructure is essential to fully reap the benefits of the digital era. Chile has increased the use of the Internet (the number of fixed and wireless broadband subscriptions per 100 inhabitants is 16 in 2017 compared to only 9 in 2008), but it still lags behind the frontier in terms of connection speeds. Chile's average broadband connection speed is 5 megabytes per second (Mb/s), four times slower than in Korea. Moreover, only 2% of broadband connections in Chile operate faster than 15 Mb/s, while in Sweden, Norway and Korea the share is above 35%.

Figure 1.5. **Chile lags behind in Internet connection speed, 2015**

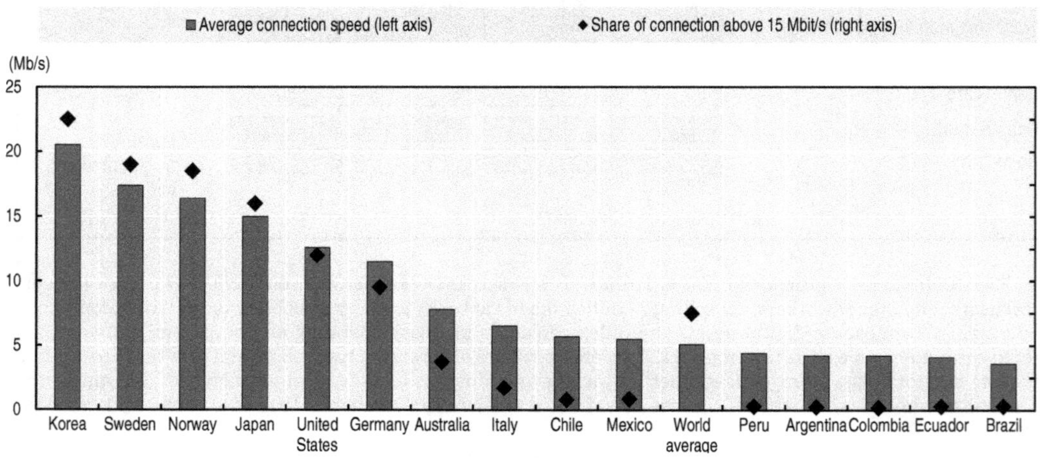

Note: Mb/s: megabytes per second.

Source: Authors' analysis based on Akamai (2017), "State of the Internet report, 2017", https://www.akamai.com/us/en/about/our-thinking/state-of-the-internet-report.

Secondly, the country needs to address some structural weaknesses that are hampering future inclusive and sustainable growth. There is no unique formula for taking advantage of the opportunities offered by the global landscape and to respond to the growing domestic demands for sustained progress, but there are some gaps that need to be closed to enable a positive transition and sustain the country's path towards prosperity. These include the productivity and skills required to operate in the new industrial ecosystems, and a narrow learning and production base. Addressing these structural weaknesses will help to strengthen the Chilean economy by opening up new opportunities for learning and upgrading and by increasing its interconnectedness, regionally and globally. Advancing in this direction will enable the economy to better anticipate future options, adapt to changing global circumstances and increase the value capture for the whole economy and society.

Higher productivity will be needed to compete in global markets

Chile faces a structural problem in terms of productivity growth. The total factor productivity (TFP) of the economy has remained stagnant since the beginning of the 1990s, mostly stemming from mining, where TFP dropped by 4.7% on average every year between 1993 and 2015 (Figure 1.6). The decline has also been linked to a decline in copper ore grades, forcing mining to shift underground and demanding that producers process more ore for the same quantity of refined copper (for more information see Chapter 3 of this report). A misallocation of factors of production, a higher level of employment in low productive and non-tradable activities, and the lack of efficiency within activities have also contributed to a slowdown in TFP. The negative contribution of TFP from the mining industry threatens Chile's path to sustainable growth and prosperity and may start to reverse the convergence in income per capita that Chile has experienced in recent decades with more advanced countries (Figures 1.6 and 1.7). This reinforces the importance of policies for economic transformation.

Figure 1.6. **Total factor productivity growth in Chile, 1993-2015**

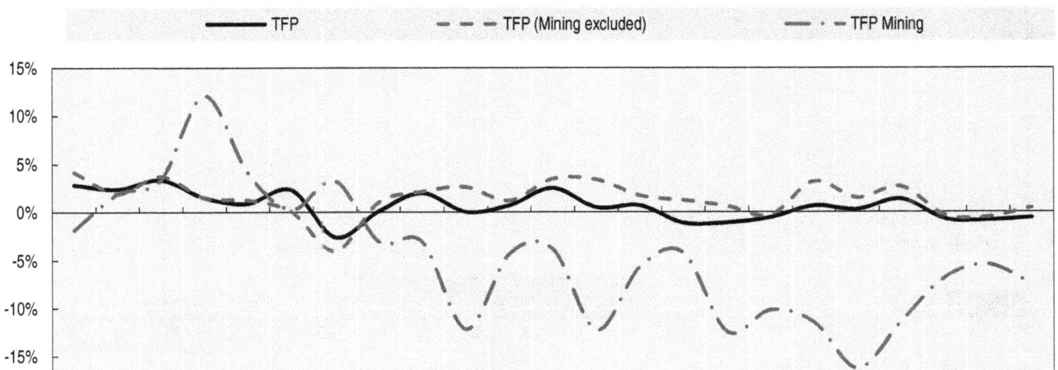

Source: Authors' analysis based on data from UAI/CORFO (2017), "Boletín trimestral Evolución de la PTF en Chile" (Quarterly Evolution of the TFP in Chile).

Most workers in Chile are employed in sectors that have low productivity and contribute little to GDP (Figure 1.8). Natural resource-intensive activities face a limit in terms of labour absorption, because of the characteristics of the production process and the move towards automated mining. Therefore, diversifying the economy by generating business opportunities for suppliers in related economic activities, and by enabling business development in new areas, would help to sustain growth and employment.

Figure 1.7. **Chile's growth is being held back by low total factor productivity**

Average percentage point contributions of factors to GDP growth, selected countries, 1990-2015

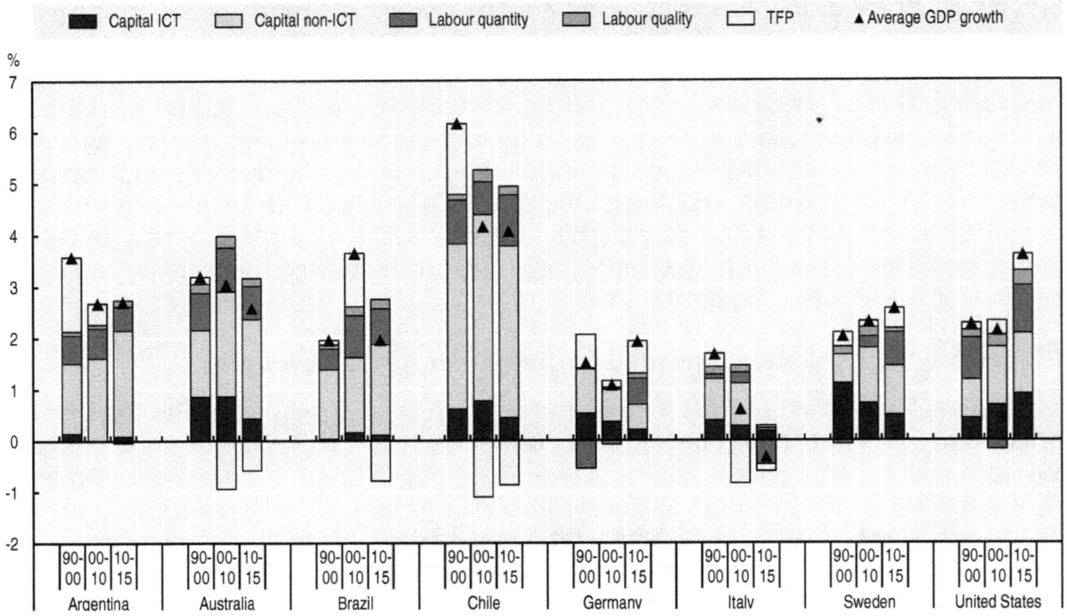

Source: Based on the Conference Board (2017), Total Economy Database™ (Adjusted version), https://www.conference-board.org/data/economydatabase/index.cfm?id=27762.

Figure 1.8. **Production structure and labour productivity gaps in Chile, 2015**

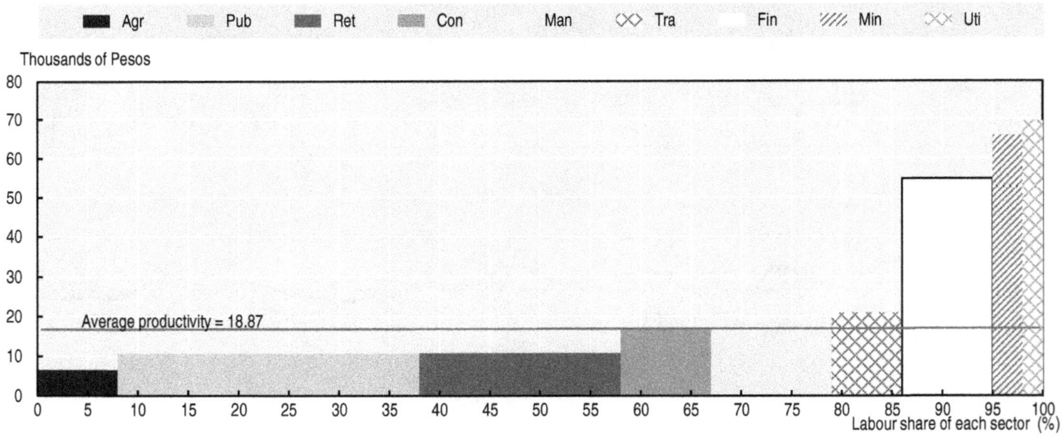

Note: Agr: agriculture; Pub: public administration; Ret: wholesale and retail; Con: construction; Man: manufacturing; Tra: transport; Fin: financial services; Min: mining; Uti: utilities.

Source: Authors' analysis based on ILO (2017), "ILO labour statistics", ILOSTAT, http://www.ilo.org/ilostat; and Central Bank of Chile (2017), http://www.bcentral.cl/en/web/central-bank-of-chile/statistics1.

Despite progress, the learning and knowledge base is still limited

There is increasing recognition that for sustained economic growth countries need to reduce the dependency on natural resources and invest more in innovation as a means of driving multi-factor and labour productivity growth across all sectors and as a driver of growth in new high value-added activities (ECLAC, 2016).

Since the 1960s, Chile has been progressively diversifying its export base. Mining still accounts for 52% of Chilean global exports, but the share is significantly lower than in the 1960s, when mining represented 80% of Chilean exports. Three main drivers of this diversification process can be identified:

4. The opening of the economy since the 1970s. This has facilitated exports, brought in FDI and created opportunities to learn from foreign companies. In the 1970s the country levelled import taxes to a single tariff, and since then has progressively reduced the tariff on multiple occasions. Today it applies a most favoured nation uniform tariff of 6%. Nevertheless, the investment in non-traditional export activities has remained below expectations. Over the years democratisation and the development of the financial system have helped to lower risk and encourage productive investment. In the 1990s, the country embarked on a liberalisation programme through an active trade policy directed by the Ministry of Foreign Trade through the General Directorate for International Economic Affairs (DIRECON), which facilitated exports and attracted FDI through non-discriminatory policies and state guarantees.
5. Public investment in the provision of public goods. Since the 1960s, Chile has strengthened the public institutions in charge of economic development. For example, the Chilean Economic Development Agency (CORFO), founded in 1939, has invested in infrastructure and human capital since its inception. CORFO initiatives have seen exports of fruits being sustained since the 1960s by the Fruit Plan, which invested in the provision of public goods such as sanitary surveillance and training. Human capital development was supported by fostering learning from international peers, for example through the Chile-California programme that enabled the development of agronomic schools in Chilean universities.
6. The capacity of public institutions to scan what is happening in more advanced countries. Chilean institutions have invested in learning from the experience of other countries, promoting co-operation programmes focusing on technology transfer, and implementing targeted policies for catching up, including export promotion for small and medium-sized enterprises (SMEs) through the Chilean Agency for Exports Promotion (PROCHILE). Foundation Chile, a public-private institution set up in 1976 to promote business activities, has scanned what was happening abroad and has been effective in bringing international experiences to Chile, including from the salmon industry in Scotland and Norway, and forestry in Finland – focusing on connecting science and business.

Nevertheless, the Chilean economy remains only modestly diversified (Figure 1.9). Its exports are mostly concentrated in natural resource-based and primary products, characterised by relatively low levels of sophistication and poor linkages with the rest of the economy (Chapter 3). Furthermore, 51% of Chile's exports are concentrated in China, the United States and Japan (Figures 1.10 and 1.11). Any contraction in demand by these countries could severely affect the entire economy.

Figure 1.9. **Commodities make up a high share of Chile's exports**

Share of gross exports by technology content towards selected regions, Chile and selected countries, 2016

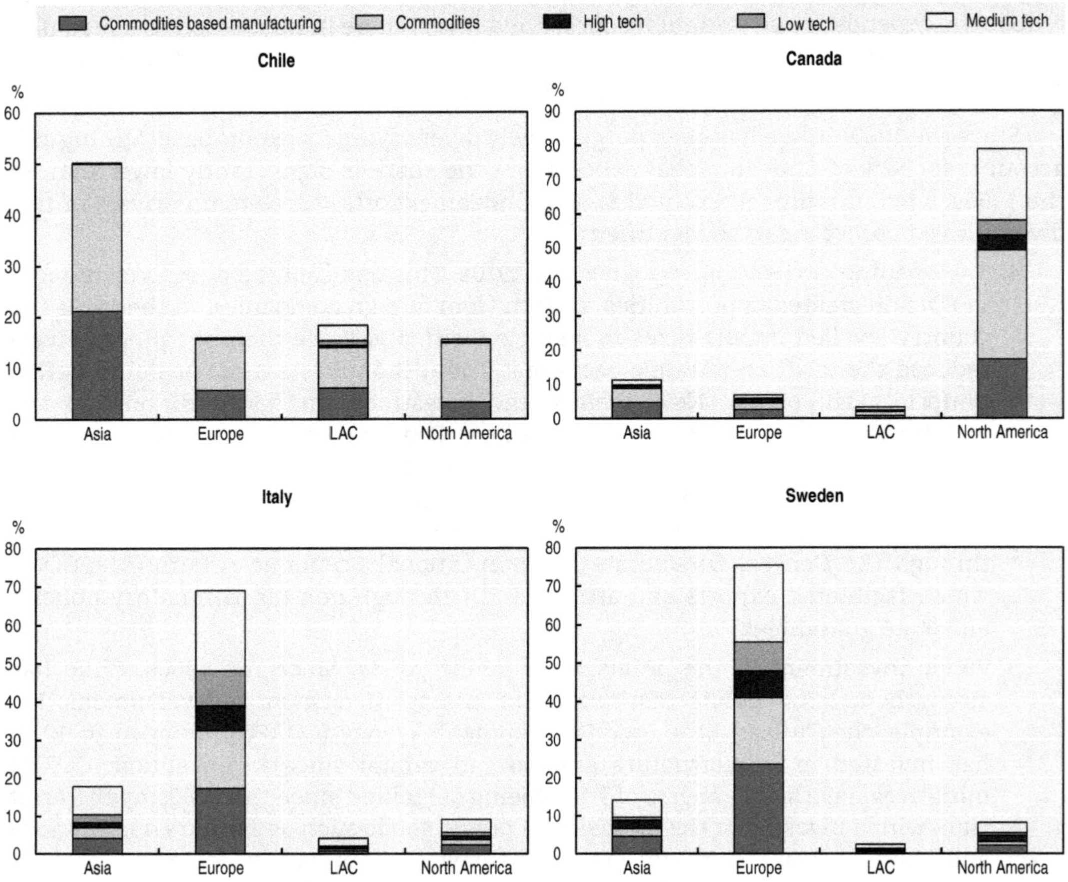

Notes: LAC: All Latin American and Caribbean countries.

The technological classification follows Lall, S. (2000) and Aboal et al (2015).

Source: Authors' analysis based on UN (2017), Comtrade Database, https://comtrade.un.org.

In mining, the shift towards extraction has intensified during the last 20 years. Between 1995 and 2014 China became the top export destination market for Chile (Figures 1.10 and 1.11), increasing its share in Chile's exports from 2% to 27%. A deeper look at the composition of trade in value added shows that the relative importance of mining increased, with copper ore increasing from 12% of exports to 21%. Meanwhile, refined copper remained stable, at around 23% of total exports. The growing specialisation in extraction and the consequent reduction in smelting and refining help to explain this pattern In fact, imports of smelting and refining products from China expanded five-fold between 2000 and 2015 (see Chapter 3).

Figure 1.10. **Decomposition of Chilean gross exports by origin and destination, 1995**

Value added of exports by origin and destination (%)

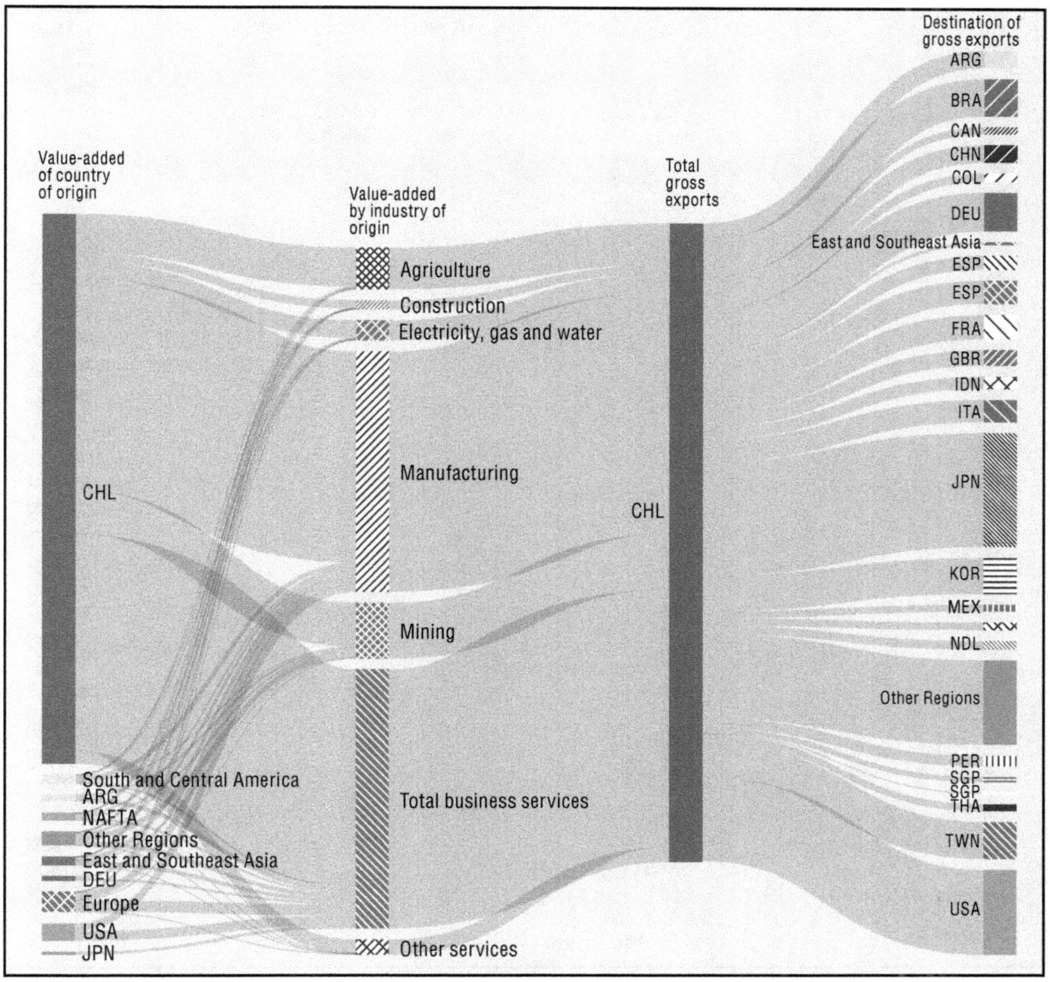

Note: Regional aggregates exclude member countries reported in the graph.

Source: OECD (2017d), TiVA Nowcast Database, http://stats.oecd.org/Index.aspx?DataSetCode=TIVA_NOWCAST.

Figure 1.11. **Decomposition of Chilean gross exports by origin and destination, 2014**

Value added of exports by origin and destination (%)

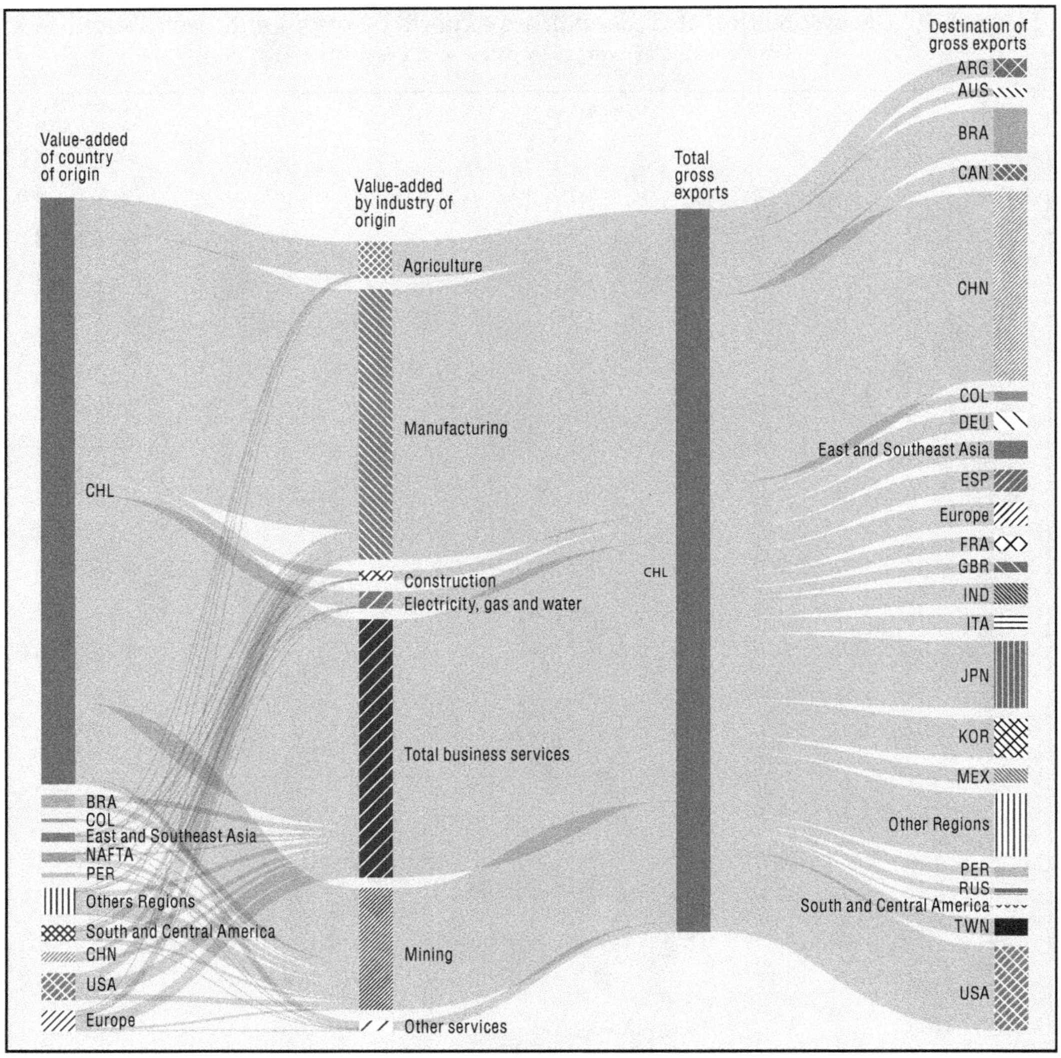

Note: Regional aggregates exclude member countries reported in the graph.

Source: OECD (2017d), TiVA Nowcast Database, http://stats.oecd.org/Index.aspx?DataSetCode=TIVA_NOWCAST.

Chile accounts for over one-third of the world's total copper reserves, and is among the top three producers of lithium. Mining will certainly be an important driver of growth and development in the future. However, there is a debate on the possibility – and the need – for the country to shift gears towards a new development model that builds on its natural resource assets to enable a more learning and knowledge-intensive development model (ECLAC, 2013). Achieving successful diversification in Chile would not mean dismissing mining, but instead transforming it and making it more productive. For example, the number of workers per unit of output in mining is three times higher in Chile than in Sweden. There are also opportunities to create the conditions for mining to become a learning platform for other industries and for new capabilities (such as solar and digital technologies), and to identify ways to enable the creation of new firms and develop new activities benefiting from global opportunities, unique local assets and new technologies.

The debate surrounding diversification is, of course, not new to Chile. The issue of diversification and the need to shift to a new development model surfaced in the political and economic debate at the end of the 1990s (Fajnzylber, 1990; Solimano, 2012; Ffrench-

Davis, 2010). However, it never became "the" key issue for the country's development because of an established policy approach that placed a premium on market forces as drivers of transformation. A booming mining sector, sustained by a growing Chinese appetite for raw materials and sound macroeconomic management, ensured high and stable economic growth over a long period of time. Coupled with more recent targeted policies to improve citizen well-being, the Chilean model was seen as a winning card, limiting the appeal of more transformative changes. In addition, the boom in copper prices in the mid-2000s significantly increased the profitability of mining, sustaining economic growth, but limiting the incentives to invest in other activities (Figure 1.12) (Correa and Stumpo, 2017).

Figure 1.12. **Return on assets (ROA) of biggest companies in Chile, 2003-16**

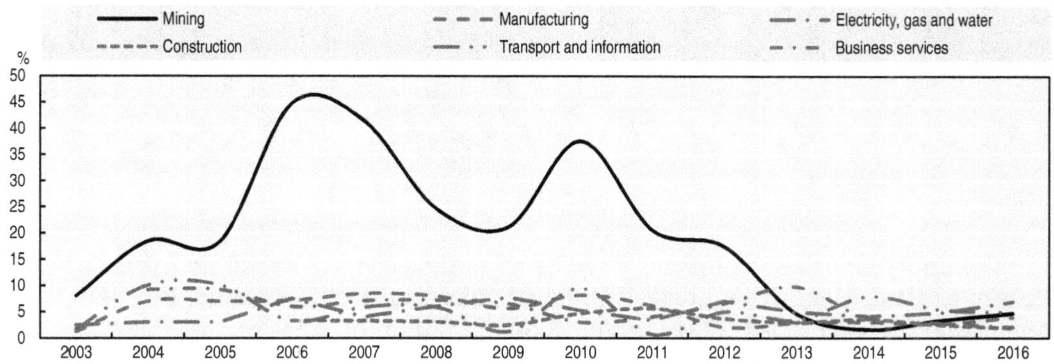

Note: Biggest companies are defined as the 500 largest companies in the region according to sales in each year, and includes state-owned, private national and private foreign companies that operates in the region, excluding the financial sector.

Source: Authors' analysis based on data from América Economía (2017), "Rankings", https://www.americaeconomia.com/rankings.

The limited diversification of the economy leaves Chile vulnerable to external shocks. Fluctuations in cooper prices have a major effect on the economy, despite effective mechanisms to maintain macroeconomic stability through the creation of the stabilisation fund in 2007 that manages the sourced from surplus revenues from Chile's copper exports. They also affect business and citizen perceptions, limiting pro-innovation, risky and long-term investments. In addition, specialisation patterns in Chile are associated with a highly concentrated economic structure. In 2015, large firms accounted for around 75% of turnover, SMEs for 20%, and microenterprises for 5% (Figure 1.13). Yet the contribution of large firms to total business R&D is only 57% (Figure 1.14).

Figure 1.13. **Large firms play a dominant role in Chile's economy**

Share of total turnover in business activities by firm size, selected countries, 2015

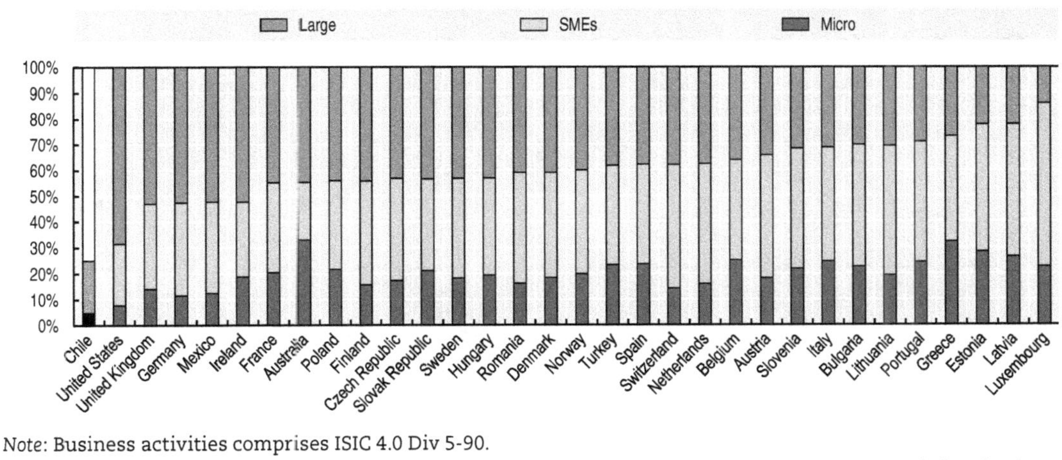

Note: Business activities comprises ISIC 4.0 Div 5-90.

Source: Authors' analysis based on OECD (2017g), *Structural and Demographic Business Statistics database*, http://stats.oecd.org; and SII (2017), "SII statistics and studies", www.sii.cl/estadisticas.

Figure 1.14. **Business enterprise R&D expenditure by firm size, 2015**

Share of total business R&D expenditure by firm size, 2015

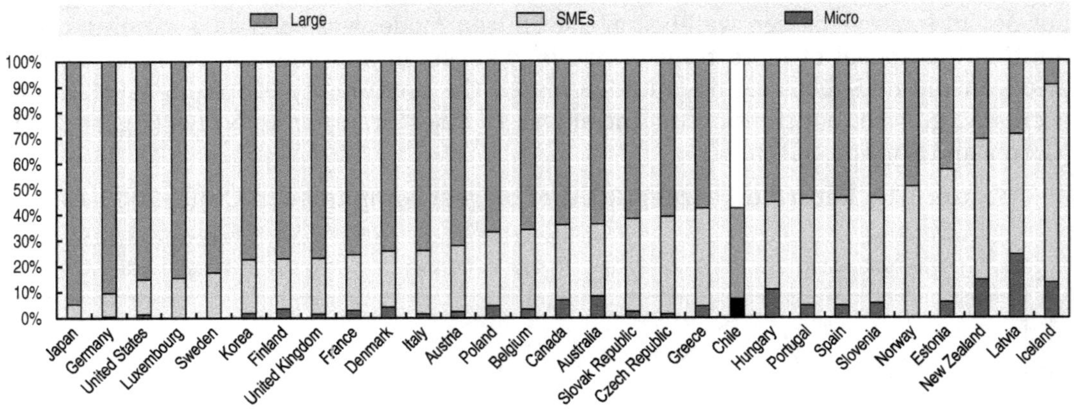

Source: Authors' analysis based on OECD (2017h), *OECD Science, Technology and Patents Database*, http://stats.oecd.org.

The limited innovation effort of large firms and the country's economic specialisation help to explain why Chile still lags behind frontier countries in terms of innovation and technological capabilities. With roughly USD 1.2 billion of gross domestic expenditure on research and development (GERD) (0.39% of GDP), Chile has one of the lowest R&D intensities of all OECD countries (Figure 1.15). Moreover, the private sector's contribution -at 33% of total R&D expenditure- is significantly below the OECD average of around 68% (Figure 1.15). Innovation output, particularly among SMEs; the quality of scientific publications; and science-industry collaboration patenting activity per capita are also well below most OECD countries (OECD, 2018). Recent studies on Chile suggest that the propensity for firms to co-operate is lower than in other OECD countries (OECD, 2013a; UNCTAD, 2017) and that the absorption of external knowledge increases the probability of developing R&D activities (González and Cristian, 2017).

Figure 1.15. **Public and private investment in R&D in Chile remain below average, 2015**

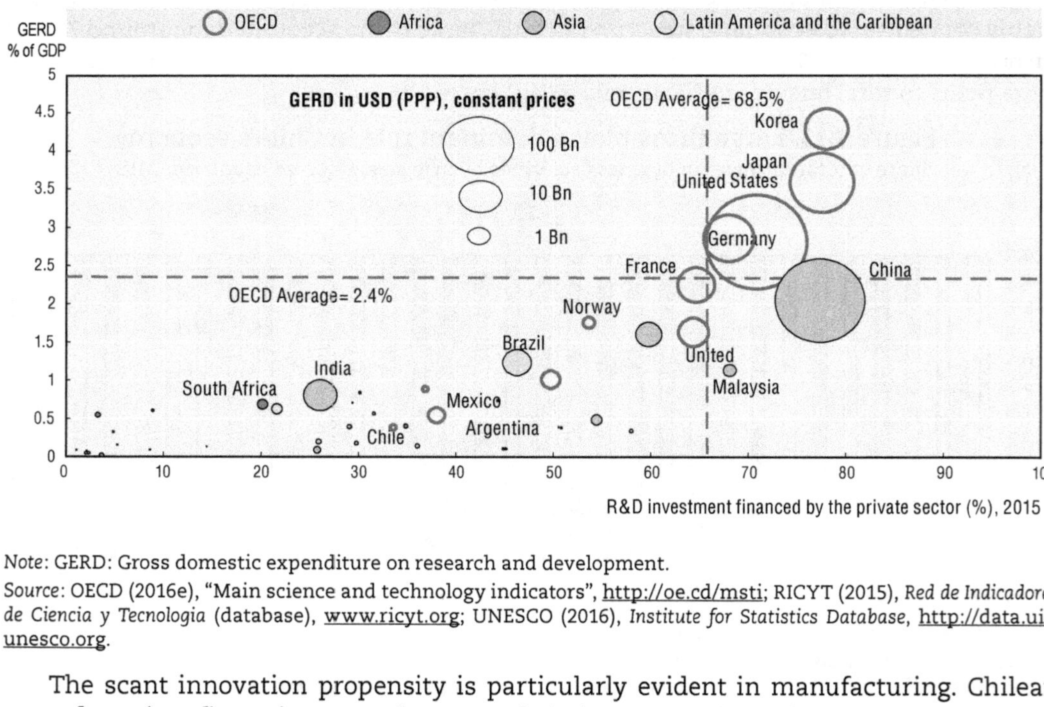

Note: GERD: Gross domestic expenditure on research and development.

Source: OECD (2016e), "Main science and technology indicators", http://oe.cd/msti; RICYT (2015), *Red de Indicadores de Ciencia y Tecnologia* (database), www.ricyt.org; UNESCO (2016), *Institute for Statistics Database*, http://data.uis.unesco.org.

The scant innovation propensity is particularly evident in manufacturing. Chilean manufacturing firms invest only 0.4% of their gross value added in research and development, which compares poorly to the 5% invested by Australian manufacturing firms, for example (Figure 1.16). Similar patterns emerge even when looking at broader measures of innovation, such as investment in software and other intellectual property products as defined in the 2008 System of National Accounts (Figure 1.17).

Figure 1.16. **Chile's manufacturing sector invests little in R&D**

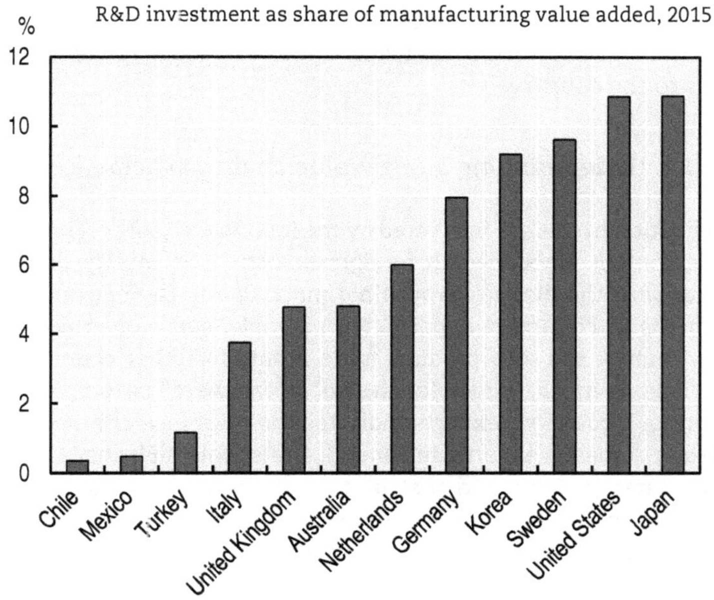

Source: Based on OECD (2017e), National Accounts Data, http://stats.oecd.org/; and OECD (2017i), Structural Analysis Statistics (TAN) Database, http://stats.oecd.org.

Figure 1.17. **Manufacturing investment in intellectual property (IP) products, 2015**

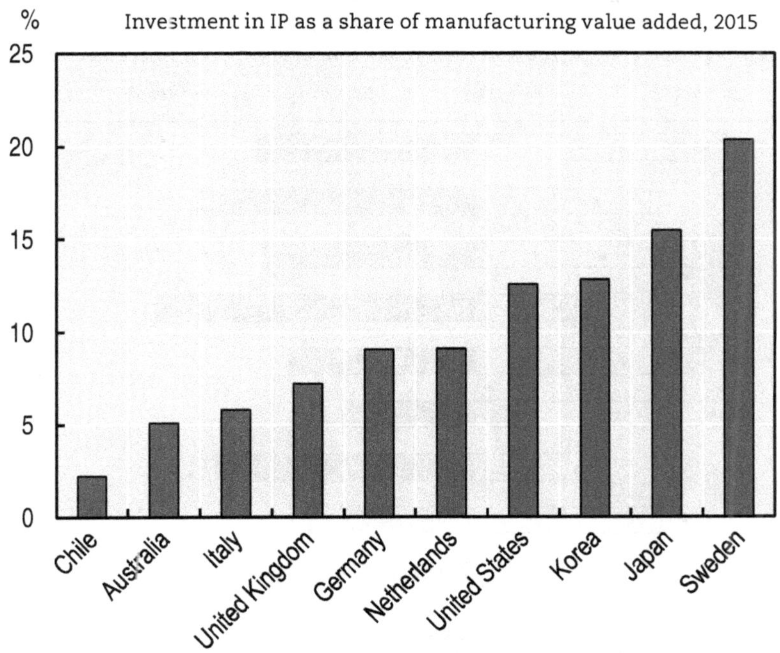

Note: Intellectual property products refer to the fixed capital formation (investment) in R&D and other IP products such as software and databases.

Source: Based on OECD (2017e), National Accounts Data, http://stats.oecd.org/.

There is room to maximise the gains from participation in the global economy

Chile is integrated into global value chains, but mostly as a commodity producer (Box 1.1). The country mostly provides inputs (raw materials, copper and lithium) that are then embedded in other countries' exports. The domestic value added embodied in foreign exports is 30% and the foreign value added embodied in domestic exports is 20% (Figure 1.18). China accounts for the largest part of Chile's upstream activities, with 9 USD billion of Chilean value added embedded in Chinese exports (Figure 1.19). The United States, with 3.21 USD billion embedded in Chilean exports, is the main provider of intermediary inputs to the country.

Box 1.1. Understanding global value chain participation

A country's participation in GVCs is measured by the foreign content of domestic exports and the domestic content embedded in foreign exports. It is mostly determined by the size of the economy, the distance from final markets and the relevance of natural resource endowments in countries' exports. For example, small open economies rely more on imported inputs and also produce more inputs for other countries' exports. This can be described as having larger "upstream" or "forward" participation in GVCs. The foreign content of a country's exports indicates the relevance of foreign goods and services embodied in domestic exports; in general, a relatively high share indicates that the country participates in GVCs and that it is specialised in downstream activities. A country's participation in GVCs can also be measured by the domestic value added embodied in foreign exports, thus indicating the extent to which the country is providing inputs to other countries' production processes.

Source: OECD (2013b), *Interconnected Economies: Benefiting from Global Value Chains*, OECD Publishing, Paris, http://dx.doi.org/10.1787/9789264189560-en.

Figure 1.18. **Chile's participation in global value chains**

Foreign value added embodied in domestic exports (backward) and domestic value added embodied in foreign exports (forward), as % of total gross domestic exports, 1995 and 2014

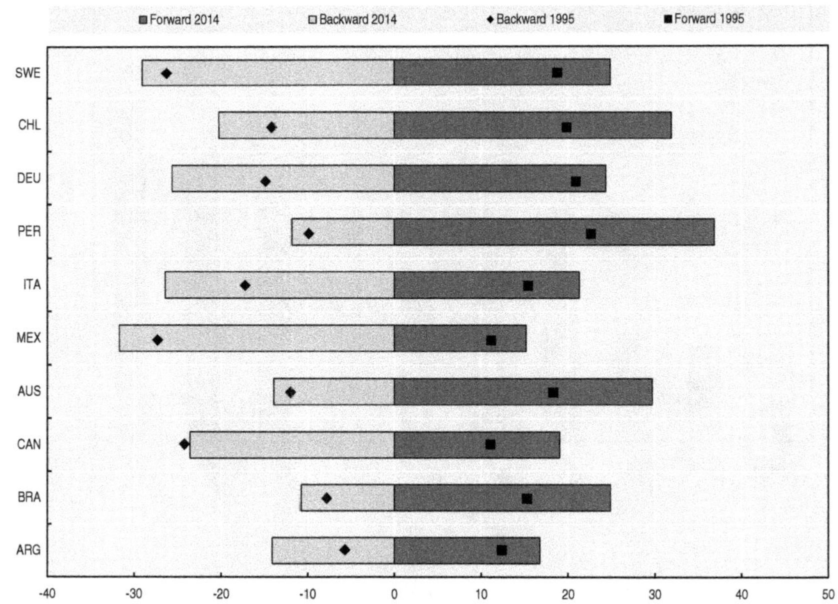

Source: Authors' analysis based on OECD-WTO (2017), Trade in Value Added database, http://stats.oecd.org.

Figure 1.19. **GVC participation by partner country, Chile, 2014**

Billion USD

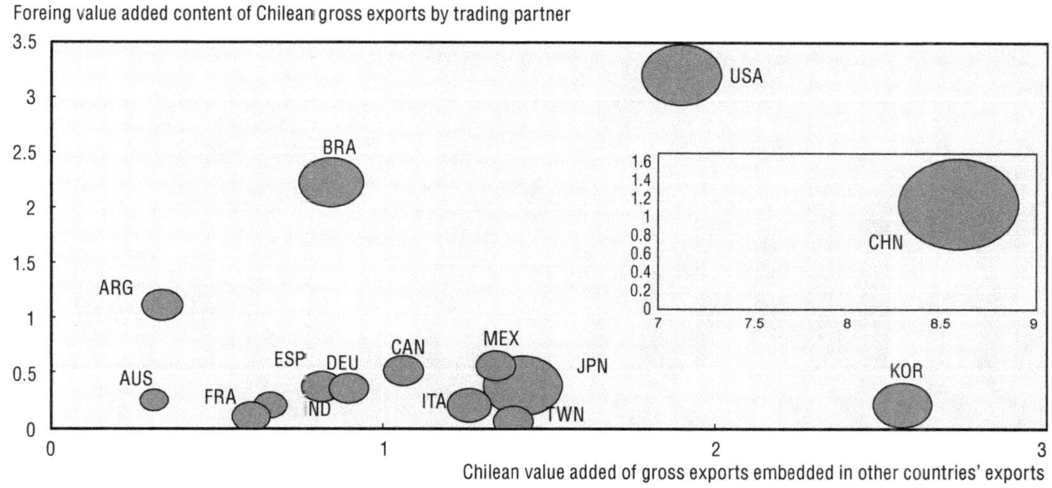

Note: Bubble size represents the share of Chilean exports to that country. Only countries that account for at least 2% of Chile's exports are displayed.

Source: Authors' analysis based on OECD-WTO (2017), Trade in Value Added database, http://stats.oecd.org.

Chile has the potential to benefit more from its openness and improve its participation in GVCs by seeking opportunities beyond mining, including in services. In 2014 the services value-added content of Chile's total exports was 38.4%, below the OECD average of 55.5% (Figure 1.20). This in large part reflects the country's relative specialisation in mining activities, which typically have lower services content than other activities. However, even looking at shares within sectors, Chile lags behind the OECD average in a number of activities (Figure 1.21 and see Chapter 3). Another channel for improving participation would be to activate learning in domestic firms and research centres and capitalise on knowledge spillovers and technology transfer offered by enhanced foreign partnerships and foreign direct investment (Box 1.2) (UNCTAD 2015). This could also help domestic SMEs to participate more in GVCs. In Chile, only 10% of SMEs are involved in export activities, one of the lowest shares in the OECD (OECD, 2018; UNCTAD/GDS/ECIDC, 2015).

Figure 1.20. **Services content of gross exports, Chile and selected countries, 2014**

Share of value added (VA) of services content in total gross exports

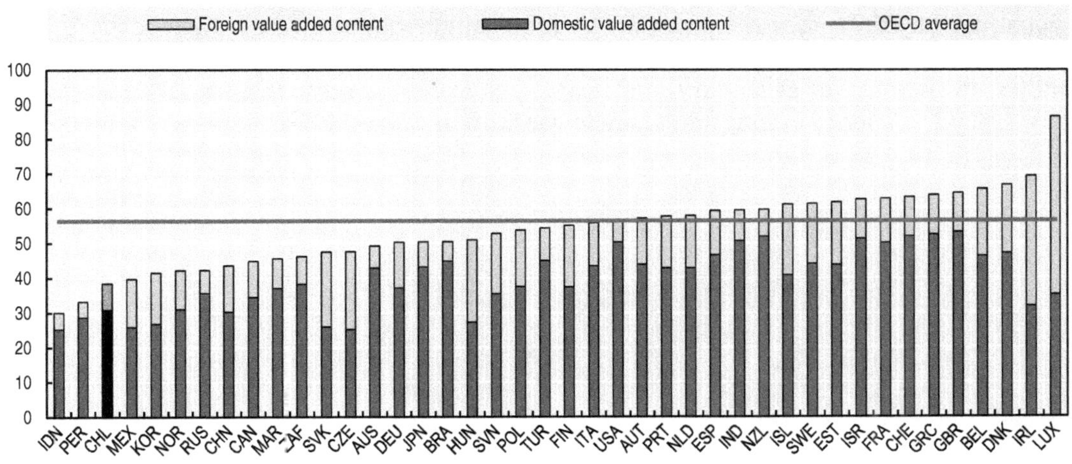

Source: Authors' analysis based on OECD (2017d), TiVA Nowcast Database, http://stats.oecd.org/Index.aspx?DataSetCode=TIVA_NOWCAST.

Figure 1.21. **Chile's services content of gross exports, by industry and service category, 2014**

Share of industry gross exports

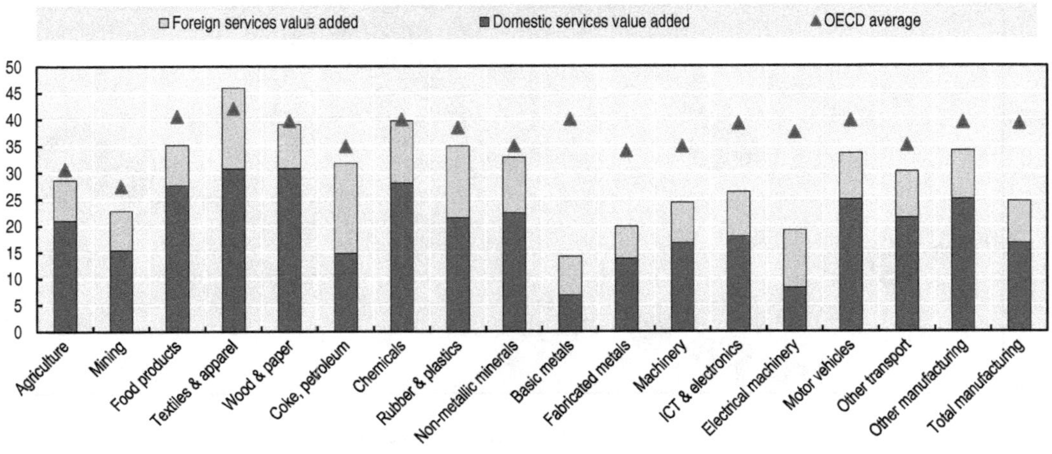

Source: Authors' analysis on OECD (2017d), TiVA Nowcast Database, http://stats.oecd.org/Index.aspx?DataSetCode=TIVA_NOWCAST.

To realise the potential of improving the participation of domestic firms in GVCs, Chile will need to address the issue of human capital. Despite having one of the highest shares of participation in tertiary education among OECD countries, Chile has gaps in several dimensions linked to skills development. The proficiency in literacy, mathematics and science of 15-year-olds in Chile is among the lowest in OECD countries; 28% of students lack the elementary skills required to read and understand simple texts, or to master basic mathematical and scientific concepts and procedures (OECD, 2017c). Graduate, post-graduate and vocational training are poorly connected to the needs of the private sector. Continuous updating of vocational programmes, as well as of university curricula, will be essential to close the gap between supply and demand in the labour market. At the tertiary level the highest shares of graduates are found in the fields of business, administration and law; and health and welfare (23% and 21% respectively). Only 3% of tertiary students graduate from information and communication technology (ICT), and only 1% from natural sciences, mathematics and statistics. The latter is the lowest share of all OECD countries and four percentage points below the OECD average. This skills gap is limiting Chile's opportunities to innovate in its strategic areas, such as earth science, natural resources and digital technologies. It is also hampering its capacity to be connected to global production systems, which will be increasingly dominated by digitalisation and new technologies. While the employment composition in terms of educational levels shows an increase of secondary and tertiary educated workers (Figure 1.22), levels of numeracy proficiency among adults are lower than in other OECD countries (Figure 1.23).

Figure 1.22. **Evolution of labour force by education level, Chile, 2000-15**

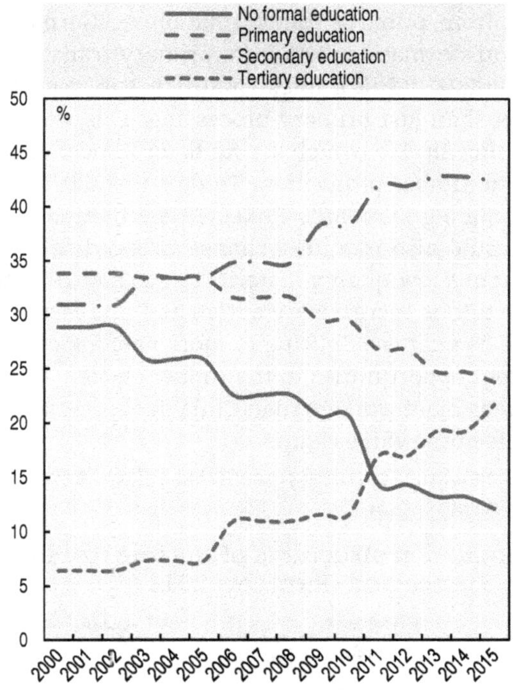

Source: Authors' analysis on CASEN and COFRO Information http://observatorio.ministeriodesarrollosocial.gob.cl/casen/casen_obj.php.

Figure 1.23. **Numeracy proficiency among adults, Chile and selected economies, 2015**

Percentage of 16-65 years old scoring at each proficiency level in numeracy

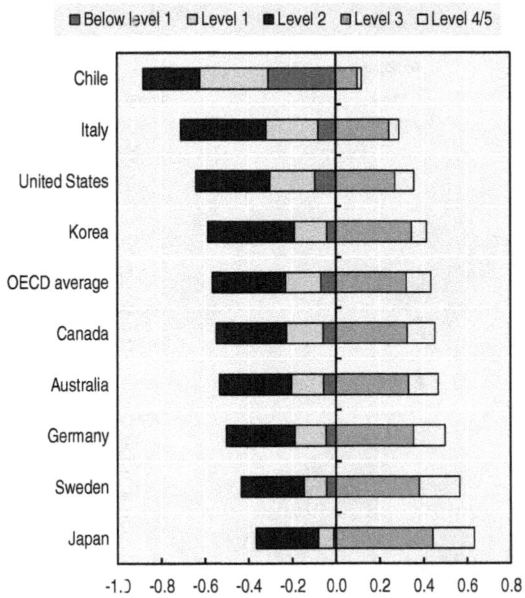

Note: Proficiency is described on a scale of 500 points divided into levels. Each level summarises what a person with a particular score can do. Six proficiency levels are defined for literacy and numeracy (Levels 1 through 5 plus below Level 1) and four are defined for problem solving in technology-rich environments (Levels 1 through 3 plus below Level 1).

Source: Based on OECD (2017j), Survey of Adults Skills (PIAAC) Database, www.oecd.org/skills/piaac/.

Box 1.2. Moving up the value chain to improve productivity and employment in Chile's timber industry

In Chile, 70% of the income generated by the timber industry comes from extraction, 16% from secondary transformation and 14% from primary transformation. In Germany, on the other hand, 59% comes from secondary transformation, 39% from primary transformation and only 2% from primary extraction (Figure 1.24). Chile's forest industry has opportunities to scale up and generate value in ways other than just primary processing. This would be particularly important for certain regions, including Bío-Bío, which accounts for almost 40% of the national forest resources and 60% of domestic timber production. To do so would require appropriate infrastructure; standard-setting, including standards linked to environmental sustainability; and targeted support for SMEs. It would also require a change in mind-set and branding: for example wood could be rebranded from a low-quality material to a future-oriented product that is sustainable and recyclable. Extraction is increasingly automated and less job-intensive and is normally managed by a few large companies. Shifting to more value-added activities would therefore help to increase employment opportunities in the timber cluster. The German timber industry employs, on average, 7.4 times more workers than Chile per processed cubic meter due to its specialisation in other segments of the value chain.

Source: OECD (2013b), *Interconnected Economies: Benefiting from Global Value Chains*, OECD Publishing, Paris, http://dx.doi.org/10.1787/9789264189560-en.

Figure 1.24. Different production structures of the forestry industry in Chile, France and Germany, 2013

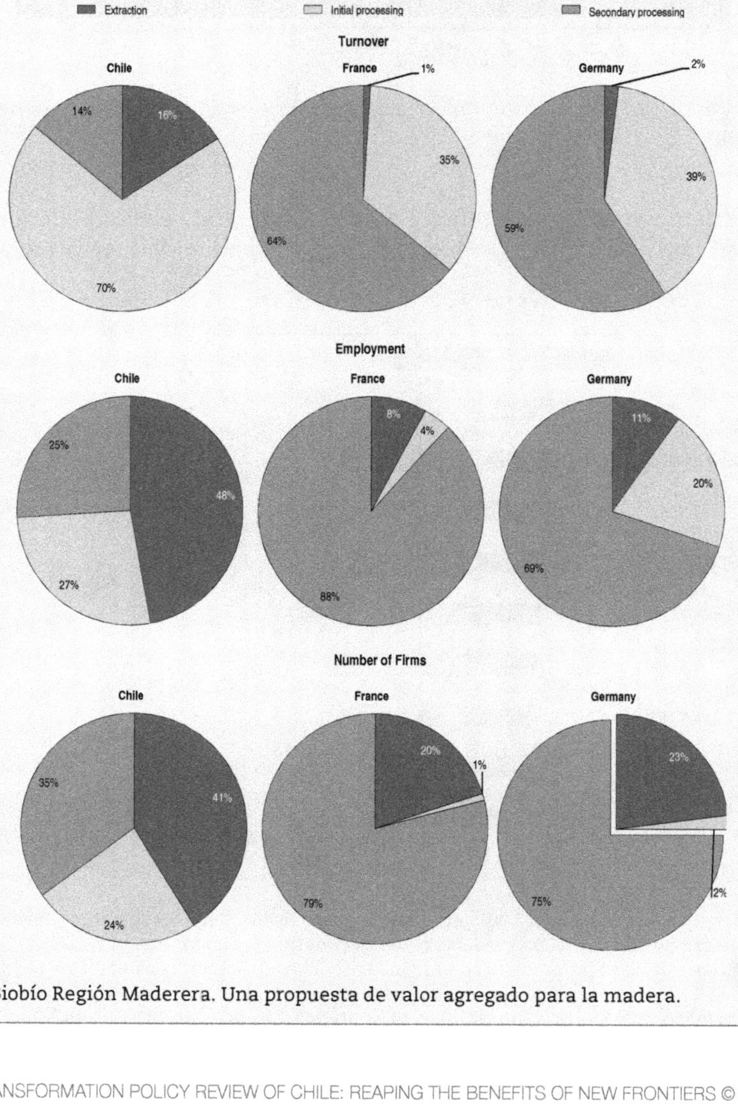

Source: Zilic (2014), Biobío Región Maderera. Una propuesta de valor agregado para la madera.

Economic opportunities are still unequally distributed between regions

Chile's population and GDP are highly concentrated territorially (OECD, 2016b). The Santiago Metropolitan Region (RMS) alone accounts for 30% of Chile's 18 million people and 44% of its national GDP (Figure 1.25). In comparison, the Paris region in France (Île-de-France) accounts for 18% of the national population and 30% of GDP. Three regions (RMS, Bío-Bío and Valparaiso) account for 62% of Chile's total population, and three regions (RMS, Antofagasta and Bío-Bío) account for 61% of total national GDP. Chile also shows pronounced differences in terms of GDP per capita among regions (Figure 1.26). The difference between the top and the bottom regions in per capita income is the second highest of all OECD countries (after Mexico). Only Antofagasta, Atacama, Tarapacá and the RMS have an annual income per capita that is above the national average of USD 22 000. The mining region of Antofagasta has the highest income per capita, three times the national average (Figure 1.25).

Figure 1.25. **Chile's population and GDP are concentrated in the Metropolitan Region, 2015**

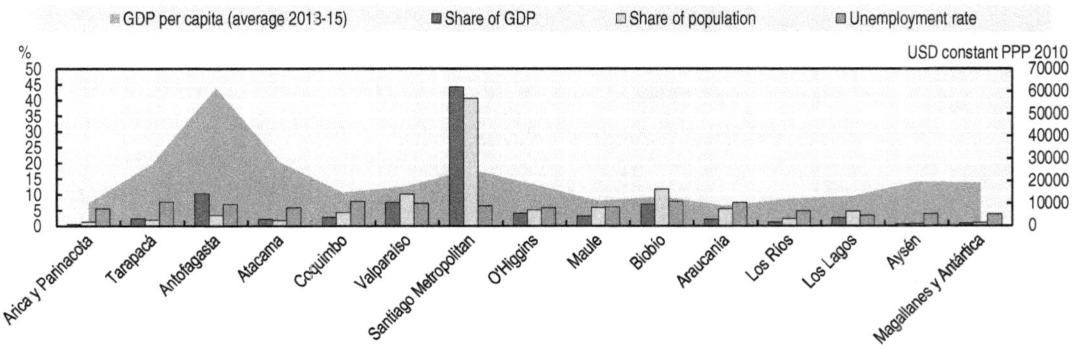

Source: Authors' analysis based on OECD (2017k), Regional Statistics Database, http://stats.oecd.org/; and Central Bank of Chile (2017), "Statistics", webpage, www.bcentral.cl/en/web/central-bank-of-chile/home.

How economic activities are distributed across the Chilean territory reflects its natural endowments. RMS generates more than half of the national GDP in financial intermediation (85%), retail (65%), and real estate, education, and health services (55% each). Manufacturing is also concentrated in RMS, which accounts for almost 50% of national GDP, followed by Bío-Bío and Valparaiso. Antofagasta alone accounts for 50% of national mining GDP, and fishery activities are clustered in the south, with Los Lagos, Aysen and Bío-Bío accounting for almost 90% of total national fishing GDP. Agriculture is mostly located in the central valley, with four regions accounting for 60% of national agriculture GDP.

Figure 1.26. **Chile's regional disparities in GDP per capita are the second highest of all OECD countries**

GDP per capita of top and bottom region as a % of national average, top and bottom OECD countries and selected economies, 2016

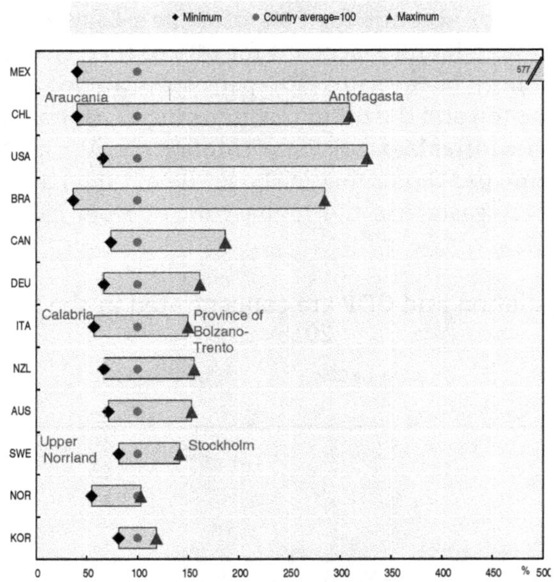

Notes: TL3 regions for Germany, Italy, New Zealand, Sweden, Korea and Japan.TL2 regions for Australia, Canada, Chile, Mexico and Brazil. Data refer to 2013 or latest available year. Brazil, Germany, Italy, and Sweden 2012.
Source: Authors' analysis based on OECD (2016d) Regional Statistics (database), http://stats.oecd.org/

RMS, Antofagasta and Atacama attract most FDI (Figure 1.27). The RMS is Chile's top region in terms of number of projects and jobs created (accounting for more than 40% of total green-field projects and 30% of jobs created), and comes second in terms of capital expenditures (17% of total capital expenditures in green-field projects in 2013-16). The mining regions of Antofagasta and Atacama are first and third in per capita expenditures (accounting for 22% and 16% respectively), attracting major investments in mining, and in solar energy in recent years.

Figure 1.27. **Foreign direct investment concentrates in Santiago, Antofagasta and Atacama**

Regional shares of total national number of projects, jobs created, and capital expenditures of greenfield FDI inflows to Chile

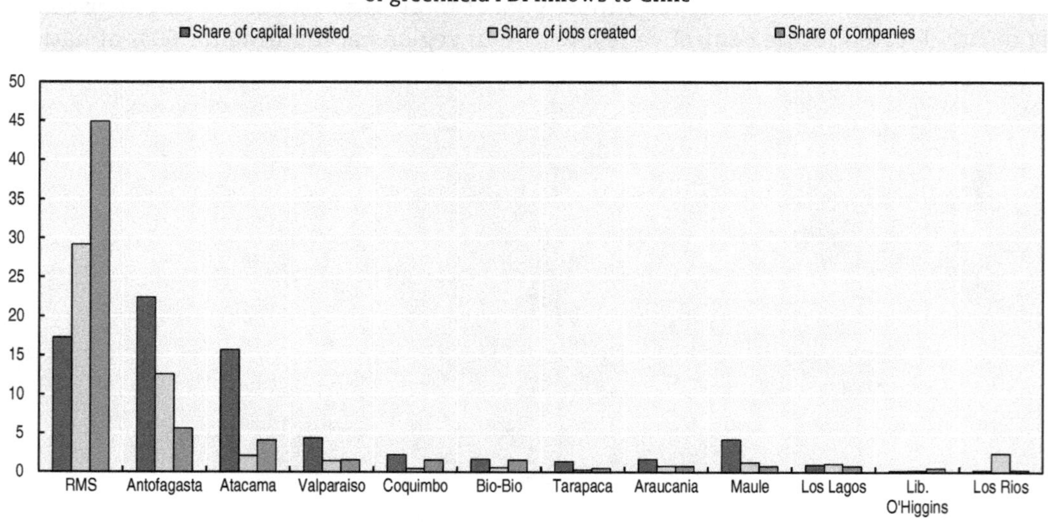

Source: Authors' analysis based on data from FDI Markets (2017), FDI Markets, database, a service from the Financial Times Ltd, https://www.fdimarkets.com/

The creation of new firms is concentrated in Chile's capital region. Estimates from AngelList – a database used by investors to find information on start-ups before making investment decisions – show that Chile ranks fourth in Latin America (after Brazil, Mexico and Argentina) for the number of start-ups. However, it is the country with the highest territorial concentration, with 80% of start-ups located in the RMS. In Colombia, by comparison, the capital region only accounts for 48% of total national start-ups (Figure 1.28) (OECD, 2016c).

Figure 1.28. **Santiago is the Chilean start-up hub, 2016**

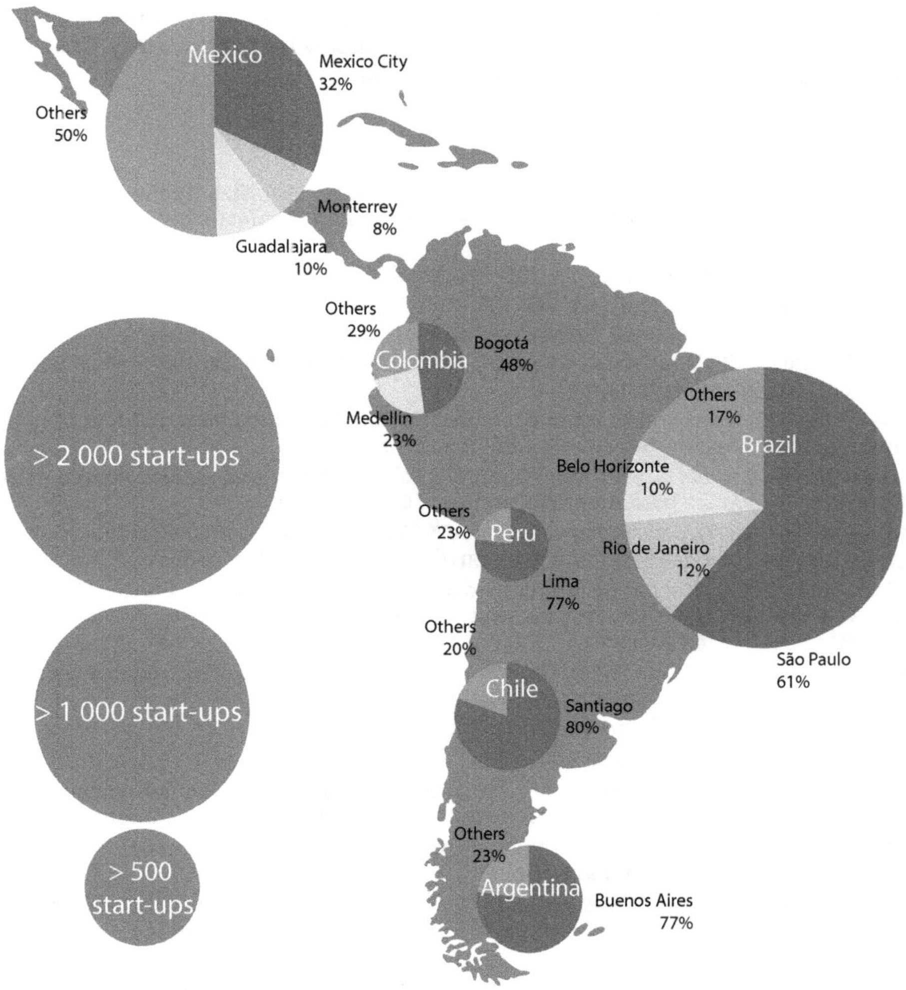

Note: The graph includes selected Latin American countries which had more than 200 start-ups as of October 2016, according to AngelList. Circle sizes represent the number of start-ups. The figure is meant to show an approximation of the size of the start-up landscape in the different countries and its distribution in the territory.
Source: OECD (2016c), Start-up Latin America 2016: Building an Innovative Future, http://dx.doi.org/10.1787/9789264265660-en, based on data from AngelList (www.angellist.com, accessed October 2016).

Conclusions

Chile's endowments offer it potential to be part of the next production revolution. Its natural resources could position the country in future green value chains. It has a sound reputation as a business partner and as a stable economy, and it counts on an extensive network of investors and trade partners. However, the speed of global change and the competition for lead positions mean that this window of opportunity will not remain open forever. Development is a moving target – successful countries are those that are able to seize opportunities at an early stage. Taking full advantage of global opportunities will require Chile to address the current structural weaknesses in its production ecosystem described in this chapter. This can be achieved only through investment and renewed and effective partnerships among government at all levels, businesses and society. Chapters 2 and 3 of this review provide suggestions in this direction.

References

Aboal, D., Garda, P., Lanzilotta, B. & Perera, M. (2015). "Innovation, Firm Size, Technology Intensity and Employment Generation: Evidence from the Uruguayan Manufacturing Sector." *Emerging Markets Finance and Trade* 51(1): 3-26.

Akamai (2017), "State of the Internet report, 2017", Akamai, available at https://www.akamai.com/us/en/about/our-thinking/state-of-the-internet-report.

América Economía (2017), "Rankings", https://www.americaeconomia.com/rankings.

Central Bank of Chile (2017), "Statistics", webpage, Central Bank of Chile, Santiago, www.bcentral.cl/en/web/central-bank-of-chile/home.

Cheyre, H., G. Larraín, G. Rivas and K. Schmidt-Hebbel (2016), "A common view and four proposals for promoting productive development in Chile", mimeo.

Cimoli, M., Castillo, M., Porcile, G. y Stumpo, G., (2017), *Políticas industriales y tecnológicas en América Latina*. Comisión Económica para América Latina y el Caribe (CEPAL).

Conference Board, The (2017), *Total Economy Database™* (Adjusted version), The Conference Board, https://www.conference-board.org/data/economydatabase/index.cfm?id=27762.

Correa, F., Stumpo, G. (2017), Brechas de productividad y cambio estructural, in Cimoli, M., Castillo, M., Porcile, G. y Stumpo, G., (2017), *Políticas industriales y tecnológicas en América Latina y el Caribe. Comisión Económica para América Latina.*

Corvalán Quiroz and D. Pezo Villar (2014), Growth and convergence in Chilean regions 1960-2010, Universidad de Playa Ancha, Valparaíso, Chile.

CPC (2016a), 109 Propuestas para la productividad.

CPC (2016b), Informe Anual de Productividad.

Crespi, G. et al. (2014), "¿Cómo repensar el desarrollo productivo? Políticas e instituciones sólidas para la transformación económica", Inter-American Development Bank, Washington, D.C.

ECLAC (2016), Horizons 2030: Equality at the centre of sustainable development. Thirty-sixth session of ECLAC. Mexico City: United Nations.

ECLAC (2013), Sustainable development in Latin America and the Caribbean. Follow-up to the United Nations development agenda beyond 2015 and to Rio+20. United Nations.

Fajnzylber, F. (1990), "Industrialization in Latin America: from the 'black box' to the 'empty box': a comparison of contemporary industrialization patterns", *Cuadernos de la CEPAL*, 60, ECLAC, Santiago.

FDI Markets (2017), *FDI Markets* (database), a service from the Financial Times Ltd, https://www.fdimarkets.com/

Ffrench-Davis, R. (2010), "Macroeconomics for development: from 'financierism' to 'productivism', *CEPAL Review*, 102, ECLAC, Santiago.

Frigolett, H. (2013), "Economías regionales en Chile: desigualdad y heterogeneidad", *Documento de Trabajo*, N°12, Serie Estudios Territoriales, Programa Cohesión Territorial para el Desarrollo, Rimisp, Santiago.

González U., Cristian. M. (2017), *Cooperar en I+D+i: Con quien y para qué? Evidencia Microeconométrica para Chile*, Dirección de Desarrollo Estratégico, CORFO, Santiago"

IDB-OECD (2010), "Strengthening institutional capacities for innovation policy design and implementation in Chile", *Inter-American Development Bank, Social Sector Science and Technology Division Technical Note*, No. IDB-TN-130, Inter-American Development Bank, Washington DC, http://services.iadb.org/wmsfiles/products/Publications/35166758.pdf

IEA (2017), *Global EV Outlook 2017: Two million and counting*, IEA, Paris, http://dx.doi.org/10.1787/9789264278882-en.

ILO (2017), "ILO labour statistics", *ILOSTAT*, International Labour Organization, Geneva, www.ilo.org/ilostat.

Lall, Sanjaya. (2000). The Technological Structure and Performance of Developing Country Manufactured Exports, 1985-98, Oxford Development Studies, Taylor & Francis Journals, 28(3): 337-369.

OECD (2018, forthcoming), *OECD Economic Surveys: Chile 2018*, OECD Publishing, Paris.

OECD (2017a), *OECD Services Trade Restrictiveness Index Database*, OECD, Paris, https://stats.oecd.org/Index.aspx?DataSetCode=STRI.

OECD (2017b), *The Next Production Revolution: Implications for Governments and Business*, OECD Publishing, Paris, http://dx.doi.org/10.1787/9789264271036-en.

OECD (2017c), "Chile", in *Education at a Glance 2017: OECD Indicators*, OECD Publishing, Paris, http://dx.doi.org/10.1787/eag-2017-42-en.

OECD (2017d), *TiVA Nowcast Database*, http://stats.oecd.org/Index.aspx?DataSetCode=TIVA_NOWCAST.

OECD (2017e), *National Accounts Data*, OECD, Paris, http://stats.oecd.org.

OECD (2017f), *International Direct Investment Statistics*, OECD, Paris, http://stats.oecd.org.

OECD (2017g), *Structural and Demographic Business Statistics Database*, OECD, Paris, http://stats.oecd.org.

OECD (2017h), *OECD Science, Technology and Patents Database*, OECD, Paris, http://stats.oecd.org.

OECD (2017i), *Structural Analysis Statistics (STAN) Database*, OECD, Paris, http://stats.oecd.org.

OECD (2017j), *Survey of Adults Skills (PIAAC) Database*, OECD, Paris, www.oecd.org/skills/piaac.

OECD (2017k), *Regional Statistics Database*, OECD, Paris, http://stats.oecd.org.

OECD (2016a), *OECD Compendium of Productivity Indicators 2016*, OECD Publishing, Paris, http://dx.doi.org/10.1787/pdtvy-2016-en.

OECD (2016b), "Chile", in *OECD Regional Outlook 2016: Productive Regions for Inclusive Societies*, OECD Publishing, Paris, http://dx.doi.org/10.1787/9789264260245-19-en

OECD (2016c), *Start-up Latin America 2016: Building an Innovative Future*, OECD Publishing, Paris, http://dx.doi.org/10.1787/9789264265660-en.

OECD (2016d), *Regional Statistics* (database), OECD, Paris, http://stats.oecd.org.

OECD (2016e), "Main science and technology indicators", OECD, Paris, http://oe.cd/msti.

OECD (2015), *OECD Economic Surveys: Chile 2015*, OECD Publishing, Paris, http://dx.doi.org/10.1787/eco_surveys-chl-2015-en.

OECD (2013a), *Perspectives on Global Development 2013: Industrial Policies in a Changing World*, OECD Publishing, Paris, http://dx.doi.org/10.1787/persp_glob_dev-2013-en.

OECD (2013b), *Interconnected Economies: Benefiting from Global Value Chains*, OECD Publishing, Paris, http://dx.doi.org/10.1787/9789264189560-en.

OECD (2012), Industrial Policy and Territorial Development: Lessons from Korea, OECD Publishing, Paris, http://dx.doi.org/10.1787/9789264173897-en.

OECD (2011), *Regions and Innovation Policy*, OECD Publishing, Paris, http://dx.doi.org/10.1787/9789264097803-en.

OECD-WTO (2017), *Trade in Value Added Database*, OECD, Paris, http://stats.oecd.org.

Reames, J. (2017), "Digital economy: snapshot of where we are today", McKinsey Institute presentation at the 9th Plenary Meeting of the OECD Initiative for Policy Dialogue on Global Value Chains, Production Transformation and Development, OECD, Paris.

RICYT (2015), *Red de Indicadores de Ciencia y Tecnologia* (database), www.ricyt.org.

SII (2017), "SII statistics and studies", SII, Santiago, www.sii.cl/estadisticas.

Solimano, A. (2012), *Chile and the Neoliberal Trap: The Post-Pinochet Era*, Cambridge University Press.

UAI/CORFO (2017), "Boletín trimestral Evolución de la PTF en Chile" (Quarterly Evolution of the TFP in Chile), Universidad Adolfo Ibáñez and CORFO, Santiago.

UN (2017), *Comtrade Database*, United Nations, New York, https://comtrade.un.org.

UNCTAD (2017), *Trade and Development Report 2017 - Beyond austerity: Towards a global new deal*, United Nations Publication, New York and Geneva.

UNCTAD (2015), *Global Value Chains and South-South Trade*, United Nations Publication, New York and Geneva.

UNCTAD/GDS/ECIDC (2015) *Global value chains and South-South Trade: economic cooperation and integration among developing countries*, United Nations Publication, Geneva.

UNESCO (2016), *Institute for Statistics Database*, UNESCO, Paris, http://data.uis.unesco.org.

World Bank (2017), *National Accounts Data*, The World Bank, Washington, DC, https://data.worldbank.org/indicator/NY.GDP.MKTP.CD.

Zilic, F. (2014), "Biobío Región Maderera. Una propuesta de valor agregado para la madera", Polomadera, Universidad de Concepción.

Chapter 2

Moving forward in Chile: A shared vision for the future

Most countries around the world are defining and implementing new strategies to reap the benefits and minimise the risks of the ongoing technological and geopolitical changes. Chile, in line with global trends, has updated its strategy to sustain productivity and enable a shift towards a more knowledge-based growth. Chilean firms, entrepreneurs and society are revealing a new openness to thinking long term and to identify a shared vision for the future. The current policy approach builds on previous experiences and, in a spirit of continuity, presents novel elements that contribute to make Chile advancing in its path towards prosperity. This chapter starts with a brief overview of global trends in strategies foreconomic transformation, with a focus on China, Germany, Sweden and Emilia Romagna (Italy). It assesses the current Chilean strategy focusing on its governance and its anticipation and adaptation capacity, propensity to foster learning and its interconnectedness and embeddedness potential. It concludes by identifying three game changers for Chile and its future development agenda.

The world is looking for new strategies to lead transformation

Globalisation is in transition. Despite some signs of recovery, the global economy has not yet recovered its dynamism and performance of the period before the 2008 economic and financial crisis. Most countries are facing fiscal constraints that challenge their spending capacity at a moment in which demand struggles to recover, and high and long-term investments are needed the most (OECD, 2013a; UNCTAD, 2017).

Major scientific, technological and production changes are revolutionising the economy and society at an unprecedented speed (OECD, 2017b). A high level of uncertainty characterises the global socio-economic landscape at multiple levels – from the kind of technology that will dominate in a given domain, to the forms of social contract that will be needed to regulate work in a platform-based economy, and the global race for leadership in the standards that will define the competitiveness advantage in the future. This socio-economic revolution is happening in a context where there is growing discontent over the capacity of the first wave of globalisation to deliver on its promises of more opportunities and higher wealth for all (OECD, 2017a,c; UNCTAD, 2016).

These macroeconomic, geopolitical and technological changes, coupled with stronger demands for shared prosperity and more sustainable and inclusive economic development models, are calling all countries – at different levels of development and wealth – to revise their strategies and to define new policy approaches (Box 2.1).

Most countries are defining visions for the future, scanning potential options and planning for the long term (OECD, 2017; Bitar, 2013). Awareness of the potential disruptive impacts of the ongoing technological change is growing, and most countries are taking steps to shape the future. Each country is following a unique approach, but three common characteristics emerge (Table 2.1):

1. **Planning for the long term and anticipating the future.** Most countries and regions have invested time and resources in defining long-term strategies to cope with the growing technological uncertainty and to set the basis for their production ecosystems to lead or at least benefit from the major global technological transformations. For example, the People's Republic of China has a vision to 2025, Italy's Emilia Romagna region and Germany have an industrial plan to 2020, and Sweden has a vision to 2030.
2. **Generating consensus to embrace change.** The ongoing technological and production transformation, coupled with growing demands for environmental sustainability and social inclusiveness, call for new forms of partnerships and agreements among all parties involved. The strategies for industry 4.0 are requiring new forms of dialogue and pacts to agree on shared responsibilities and actions. The Labour Pact signed in Emilia Romagna by all social, business and government parties is an example of how constructive dialogue can align different stakeholders on a modernisation path while at the same time preserving the values of a specific territorial reality (Emilia Romagna, 2015). In Sweden, the government has set up a bottom-up approach through an advisory board with the participation of industry, academia, government and civil society. China, Emilia Romagna in Italy, Germany and Sweden have different strategies, but they all count on high-level political support for bringing about consensus.
3. **Setting up tailored actions to enable transformation in each production ecosystem.** Digitalisation, the Internet of Things, big data, automation and new manufacturing techniques affect different activities and production ecosystems in different ways. Most governments, including regions like Emilia Romagna in Italy, and China and Germany, are implementing tailored roadmaps to enable each ecosystem to benefit from the changes and to minimise the potential downsides. Sweden is supporting specific pilot projects to test options that could then be viable in multiple contexts.

These actions focusing on specific ecosystems enable to better address the opportunities and challenges and foster a constructive dialogue among different stakeholders on issues linked to interoperability and sustainability standards, new social contracts, and new forms of business and societal organisation.

Table 2.1. **Most countries are taking steps to shape the future**

		China	Emilia Romagna	Germany	Sweden
Strategy		Made in 2025	Industria 4.0	Industrie 4.0	Produktion 2030
Time horizon		2015-2025	2014-2020	2010-2020	2013-2030
Budget		USD 10 billion	USD 2 billion	USD 250 million	USD 35 million (2014-2017)
Governance		Cross-ministerial, multi-level	Cross-ministerial, multi-level & participatory	Cross-ministerial, multi-level & participatory	Cross-ministerial, multi-level & participatory
Prioritisation	Horizontal	Automation & robotics, new materials, renewable energies	Nine enabling technologies	IoT, automation & robotics	Digitalisation, automation, resource ; energy efficiency, green technologies
	Sectoral	Aerospace and aeronautical, transport equipment, biopharma and advanced medical products	Five value chains (agro-food, construction, mechatronics, health industry, creative industry)	Machinery, electronics	Horizontal

Note: IoT: Internet of things.

In 2014, the Emilia Romagna region developed an industry 4.0 initiative in line with the national strategy (Table 2.1). The initiative is structured around nine enabling technologies that sustain industrial upgrading in five value chains: agro-food, construction, mechatronics, the health industry and the creative industry. It aims to stimulate the transformation of regional manufacturing services through three levers: digitalisation of production, global competitiveness and the circular economy. The initiative is governed through the participation of regional public authorities, industrial representatives, academia and labour unions in a Piloting Committee. This supervises the implementation of the plan and verifies that it complies with objectives. Programme implementation is coupled with a clear communication and promotion plan to secure the highest possible participation, along with a publicly available monitoring and evaluation system (see Chapter 3 for more details). The programme is funded by national, regional and European Union structural funds and private financing, amounting to a total of USD 2 billion for the period 2014-2020.

In Sweden the Minister for Enterprise and Innovation defined a long-term strategy – labelled *Produktion 2030* – in 2013. Sweden's industrial and services activities are responsible for one-fifth of the country's gross domestic product (GDP) and together account for 77% of the total value of Swedish exports. The strategy focuses on improving companies' chances of dealing with the rapid technological transformation. It is built on four pillars: 1) exploiting the potential of digitalisation in all companies and activities; 2) greening the economy and improving resource-efficient production; 3) adapting industrial skills for the future; and 4) creating attractive innovation environments through pilot projects. For the period 2014-2017, 30 pilot projects have been financed with the involvement of 150 firms. Each project has obtained private sector co-financing of at least 50%. The total public budget for this period is USD 35 million.

There is no unique best approach for getting ready for the future and enabling the sustainable and inclusive transformation of the economy and society. But the ongoing industrial revolution, which is wider and deeper than a purely technological one, is requiring an "update" of the state, of its governance mechanisms and tools (Box 2.1). Chile's current approach is outlined in the following section and in Chapter 3 of this report.

Box 2.1. Production Transformation Policy Reviews: five pillars of successful transformation strategies

The Production Transformation Policy Reviews (PTPRs) are a policy assessment and guidance tool elaborated in response to countries' demand in the framework of the OECD Policy Dialogue Initiative on Global Value Chains, Production Transformation and Development. The PTPRs respond to the need of designing and implementing better strategies to cope with the opportunities and challenges offered by globalisation and digitalisation by identifying reforms that enable cities, regions and countries to succeed in a changing world.

The PTPRs are a 15-18 month process based on peer-learning and multi-stakeholder dialogue to enable policy makers to better plan and act for the present and the future. The PTPRs assess the economic structure, the upgrading potential and the governance for economic transformation, identify lessons learned and clarify priorities for reform. They rely on peer review mechanisms through the participation of international peers and through a Peer Learning Group that steers each PTPR process.

The PTPR framework rests on three main assumptions:

- Growth is necessary for development, but there is a need to take into account not only the rate of economic growth, but also the qualitative dimensions (in terms of the capacity of this growth to be job-rich, to be inclusive and environmentally sustainable).
- Production structure matters for development. What countries produce and trade shapes not only economic growth but the capacity of economic systems to generate and redistribute rents and determines overall development outcomes.
- Policies and institutions, in the form of formalised strategies or multiple initiatives, play an important role in shaping development trajectories and in supporting the transition towards superior development stages characterised by the accumulation and diffusion of organisational, production and technological capabilities.

The PTPRs propose an interpretative framework that assesses countries' capabilities and potential in five domains (Anticipation capacity, Adaptation Capacity, Learning and Upgrading Potential, Interconnectedness Propensity and Embeddedness Potential). These derive from the recognition that there is no unique model of development and that there are common features that determine the capacity to succeed in the fast changing global landscape (Figure 2.1).

Figure 2.1. **The five pillars of the PTPRs**

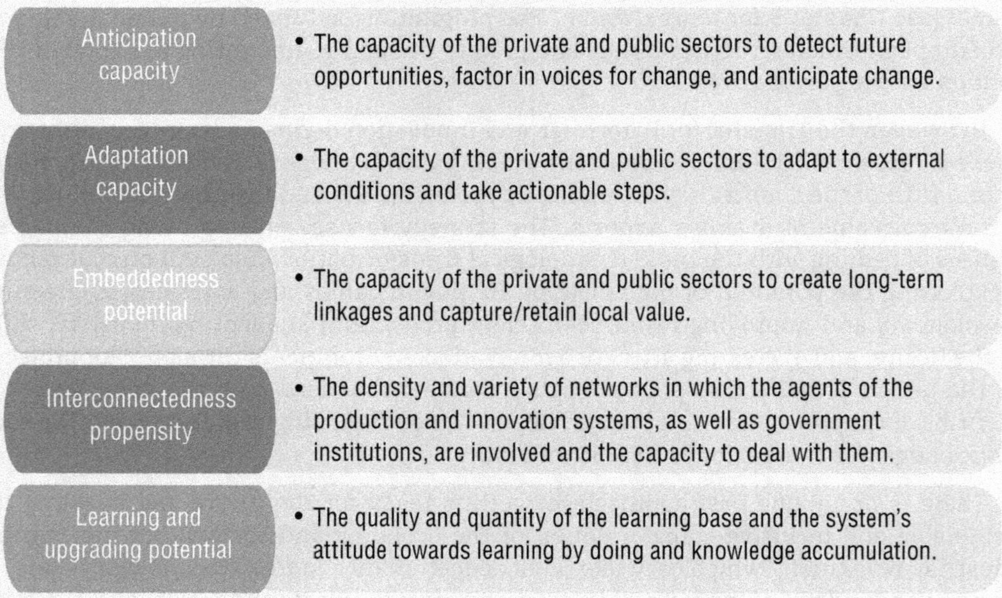

Source: OECD (2017), *Production Transformation Policy Reviews: Actions to Succeed in a Changing World*, OECD Publishing, Paris, http://dx.doi.org/10.1787/9789264276628-en.

Chile is updating its strategy to transform the economy

Awareness about the opportunities that global trends could offer Chile is growing. The country – its businesses and society – are revealing a new openness to thinking long term, and finding new ways to bring all stakeholders together to identify a shared vision for the future. Over the last decade, Chile has seen some of its large companies grow and become regional leaders in forestry, retail and the airline business. At the same time, society is strengthening its demands for environmental and social sustainability and for inclusiveness. A new pact between the business community and society is needed to allow Chile to embark on its path to prosperity. Being a stable and open economy will not be enough to sustain business development or respond to societal demands. The world is moving fast, and for Chile to be part of the global wave of change, a renewed approach to policy making and government-business-society relationship is needed. Going beyond ideological divides and finding a common ground to mobilise private and public actors is of critical importance to avoid marginalisation in the changing global context. It will also help to identify national development challenges – such as greening the economy – that can align interests and enable change in the economy and society alike.

Since the mid-2000s, Chile has aimed to foster diversification through innovation

By the beginning of the 1980s Chile was already a fairly open economy. Until 1982, the country had a fixed exchange rate regime and then shifted to a floating exchange rate with bands up to 1999. In the 1980s Chile established a reserve system to control capital flows to favour the stability of the economy. In the 1990s it started to set up a wide network of bilateral and multilateral trade agreements that supported the country's consequent export growth. For example, the free trade agreements with Canada, the EU, the United States and China were signed in 1996, 2002, 2003 and 2006 respectively. In parallel, the National Fund for Science and Technology (FONDECYT) was established in 1981 to promote basic scientific research, and the Fund for Scientific and Technological Development (FONDEF) was set up in 1991 to finance joint and applied research projects between academia and the business sector. *Fundación Chile*, a public-private entity set up in 1976, played a key role in the 1980s and 1990 in identifying new economic opportunities for business development in Chile and fostering technology transfer and business creation. In 1992, the Chilean Economic Development Agency (CORFO) established the National Technology Fund (FONTEC) to promote business innovation through matching grants. In 1998, Chile introduced a fund to support the development of venture capital in the country, with a contribution of USD 2 from the public sector for each dollar invested by the private sector (OECD, 2013b). In 1999, CORFO financed the creation of incubators to support the creation of innovative, high-growth firms.

In the mid-2000s, Chile started to roll out targeted reforms to foster innovation and enable the creation of new firms, with a view to identify strategic opportunities and improve the country's position in the global economy. The sustained demand from China for Chilean copper (see Chapter 1) contributed to a high increase in the prices of raw materials which created a favourable climate for thinking about production development. At that time, the government had a plan, based on three key reforms, which represented a positive step forward (IDB/OECD, 2010):

1. The introduction of a royalty on mining, to enable multi-annual financing of innovation in the country.
2. The setting up of the Fund for Innovation and Competitiveness (FIC), administered by the Ministry of Economy.
3. The creation of the National Council for Innovation and Competitiveness (CNIC) (renamed National Council for Innovation and Development, CNID in 2016), an

advisory body answering to the Presidency and in charge of identifying strategic priorities for the innovation and competitiveness policy and for the FIC.

Of that original design, the bridge between the mining tax and the financing of innovation and competitiveness programmes (through the FIC) has not materialised due to a constitutional impediment that does not allow taxes to be earmarked as the common practice is to pool all fiscal revenues in the national budget. Nowadays, the FIC is operating and receives resources from the annual budgeting process. Currently, 30% of the FIC goes directly to the regions to implement the actions defined in their development programmes, and 70% is allocated by the two implementing agencies, CORFO and the National Commission for Scientific and Technological Research (CONICYT), through performance-based contracts. Although the CNID has been set up, it has not become a key space for ensuring co-ordination across ministries and agencies because of governance arrangements that reduce its convening and decision-making powers.

The National Innovation Strategy for Competitiveness, developed by the CNIC in 2007-08, identified strategic options for diversifying the Chilean economy. The strategy prioritised 13 areas of strategic importance to Chile, including mining, agro-food and global services. In those years, in addition to a targeted policy to strengthen human capital, reforms were implemented with a view to fostering innovation in firms. In 2008, the government introduced a law to give a research and development (R&D) tax incentive for firms, and CORFO started a programme to develop clusters of industrial excellence linked to the 13 strategic areas. This programme aimed at fostering investments in technical skills development, innovation in firms, and infrastructure in these areas. In 2011, the Agenda for Competitiveness laid out a new strategic vision to unleash the country's growth potential through the simplification of red tape and the promotion of start-ups. The well-known Start-up Chile programme was introduced as part of that agenda (OECD, 2013b; 2016b).

Chile is implementing reforms to address long-term challenges

The evolution of the Chilean strategy for economic transformation shows a relative continuity over time, with the exception of the acceptance or not for more strategic and selective approaches. Since 2014, the government has embarked on an ambitious programme that included an educational reform to respond to the demand of young people for better and more inclusive education, targeted efforts to promote environmental sustainability, reforms to increase decentralisation and autonomy in the regions, and reforms for enhancing productivity, innovation and growth.

The Productivity, Innovation and Growth Agenda, started in 2014, builds on past experiences. It includes a large number of reforms in multiple areas and has a budget of roughly USD 1 billion (CLN 700 billion) for 2017; Figure 2.2). The public investment in areas linked to economic transformation – notably science, technology, innovation and entrepreneurship – has risen from 0.2% of GDP in 2007 to 0.4% of GDP in 2017. Most of the increase is explained by skills development and training programmes, such as *Becas Chile,* which provides scholarships for study abroad (see Figure 2.8 later in the chapter). Of the USD 1 billion planned for 2017, almost 45% goes to the National Council for Science and Technology (CONICYT), 29% to the Ministry of Economy, and the rest is executed by other ministries, including Foreign Affairs, Agriculture and Energy (Figure 2.3). Despite the fact that public investment has increased two times in real terms since the mid-2000s, it is still limited in absolute and relative terms compared to global trends. For example, Chile's annual investment in productivity and innovation represents one-third of the annual investment in R&D by a multinational company: in 2016 Chile invested USD 1 billion in actions linked to the productivity agenda, while Fiat-Chrysler invested USD 2.9 billion in R&D (JRC, 2017).

Figure 2.2. **National budget for economic transformation (STI and entrepreneurship), 2007-17**

Millions of current Chilean pesos

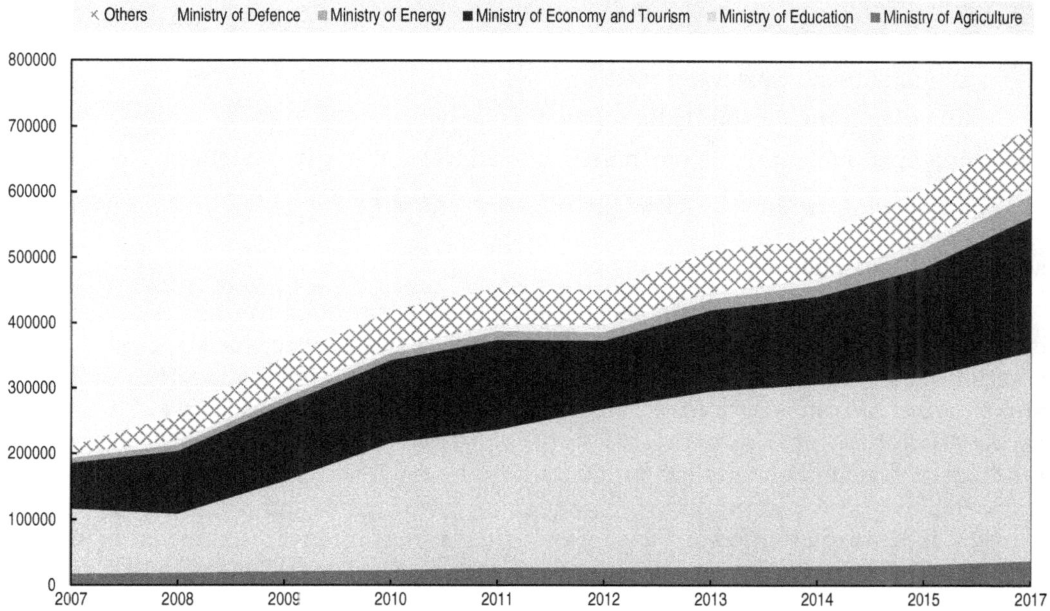

Note: STI: science, technology and innovation.

Source: Authors' analysis based on data from the National Directorate for Budgeting, Ministry of Finance, 2017.

Figure 2.3. **Breakdown of budget for economic transformation, Chile, 2017**

Share by ministry/agency

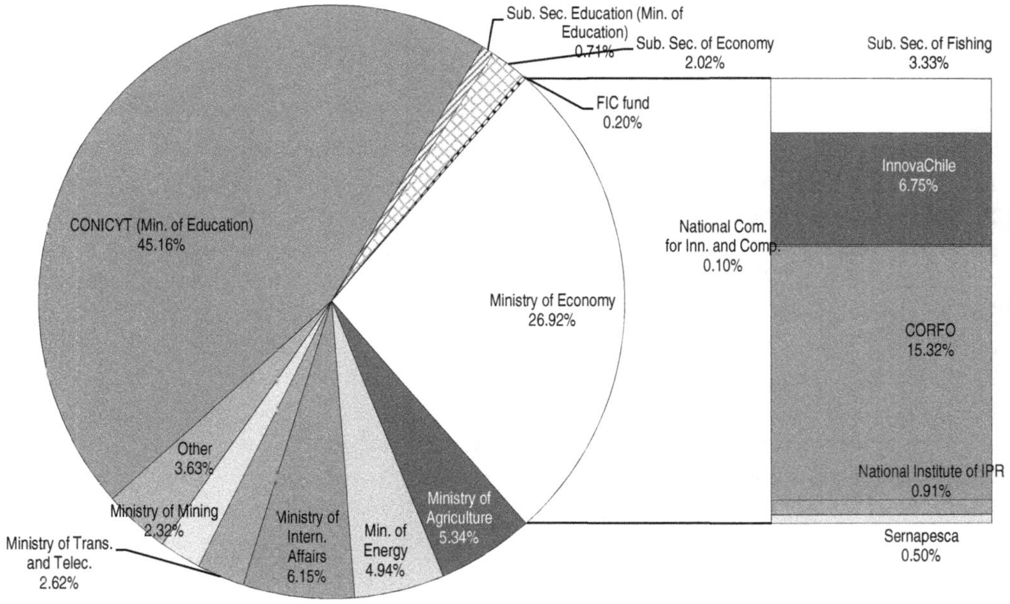

Note: CONICYT: National Council for Science and Technology; CORFO: Chilean Economic Development Agency; FIC: Fund for Innovation and Competitiveness.

Source: Authors' analysis based on National Directorate for Budgeting, Ministry of Finance, 2017.

The current agenda for sustaining growth and productivity can be categorised into four main areas:

- modernising the state for greater impact;
- enabling business development;
- fostering human capital and innovation; and
- enabling public-private partnerships to address strategic challenges.

The following sections describe the main actions in each area.

Modernising the state for greater impact

The government has been active in reforming institutions to increase impact and deliver more effective results. The main actions in this respect have included: i) The creation of the National Productivity Commission (CNP) to facilitate strategic co-ordination and to better prioritise actions. The CNP was set up by national decree in 2015, inspired by the Australian experience that tracks back to 1998. The CNP is a consultative body for production development and pro-productivity reforms. It is composed by representatives from the business community, the academy, government and well known national experts; ii) Reforms to increase the role of regions in economic transformation and the creation of three CORFO regional pilot projects; iii) A proposal for creating a Ministry for Science and Technology, responsible for financing the training of advanced human capital and research, to which CONICYT would respond to as an implementing agency; and iv) The creation in 2016 of Invest Chile to attract strategic FDI. The agency replaces the previous Committee on Foreign Investment and has the mandate to attract FDI into Chile in areas that could be strategic for the future development of the country (Box 2.2). Invest Chile has a strong focus on emerging partners for Chile, including China.

Box 2.2. **Leveraging on FDI to strengthen new business activities**

The openness of the country has helped to attract foreign capital. Between 2003 and 2006, mining and quarrying absorbed 77% of total capital and 60% of total jobs from greenfield FDI, mainly from Canada and Australia. Between 2013 and 2016, electricity, gas and water supply absorbed 45% of total capital and 12% of jobs and mining accounted for 20% of the capital and 11% of the jobs. Wholesale and retail activities absorbed 5% of capital and 33% of jobs (Figure 2.4, Panels A and B). In 2017 the Ministry of Economy, through CORFO, opened a call for proposals to expand the exploitation of lithium in the Atacama Salar. The winning tender will deliver royalties, and a share of the production will be sold at FOB prices in the country. Moreover, CORFO along with InvestChile are currently calling on companies willing to expand their lithium business activities in Chile to bid for a tender. Together tendering together aim to explore the possibility of entering into a new value chain by leveraging on Chile's abundant metal resources (52% of world reserves).

Box 2.2. **Leveraging on FDI to strengthen new business activities** *(Cont.)*

Figure 2.4. **Green field FDI by sector and country of origin, Chile 2003-16**

Share of jobs by country of origin (left axis) and share of total investment (right axis)

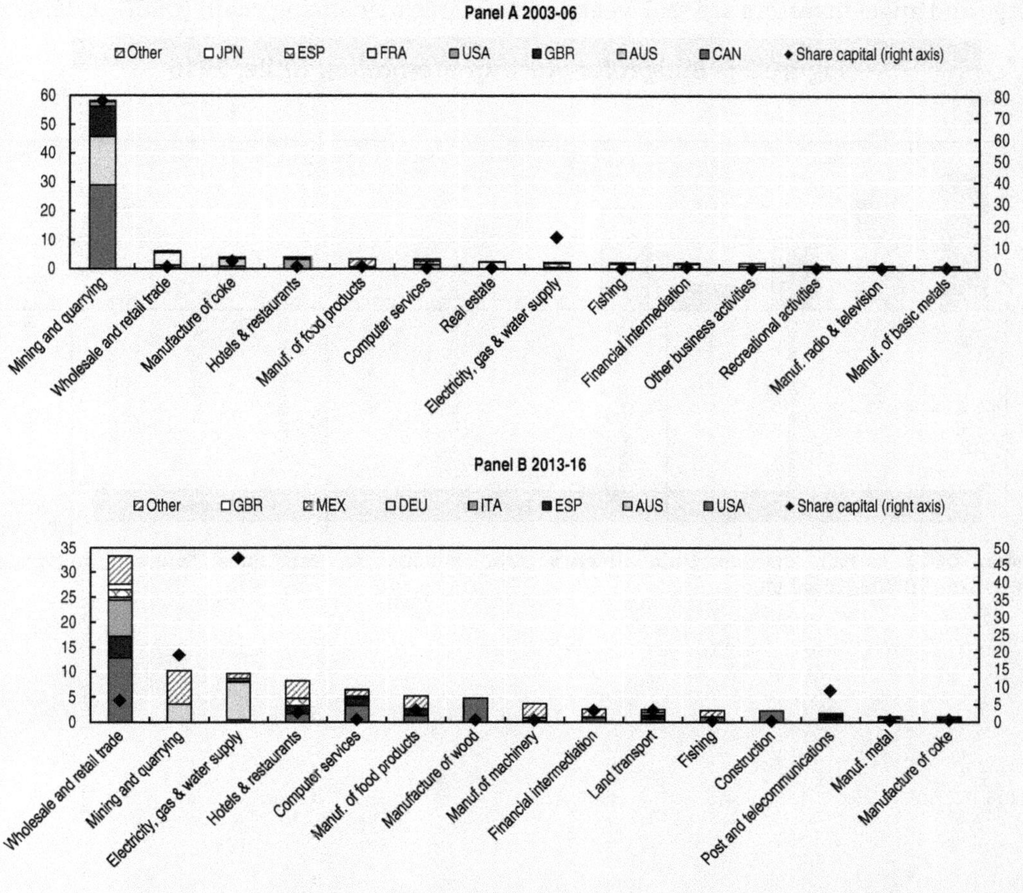

Source: Authors' analysis based on data FDI Markets (2017), FDI Markets, database, a service from the Financial Times Ltd, https://www.fdimarkets.com.

Enabling business development

In the spirit of continuing the efforts at the end of the 1990s, and with the more recent emphasis on start-up creation since 2010, the country is continuing to update its policies to favour business development by reducing red tape and fostering start-up creation and expansion. The policy for start-ups focuses on: 1) financing for start-ups (61% of the total budget for start-ups in 2016); 2) ecosystem development (25%); 3) support to high technology start-ups (8%); and 4) start-ups for social inclusion (6%) (Figure 2.5) (OECD, 2016b). Since the launch of Start-Up Chile in 2010, the country has moved from a pilot phase of pro-start-up programmes to a more structured start-up policy linked to its national production transformation strategy. Chile has reformed the policy based on the results of its monitoring and evaluation, and the country now prioritises retaining more talent and businesses in the country (Figure 2.6). Chile also promotes the creation of start-ups in the regions outside Santiago, and supports the founding of firms that offer innovative solutions to social problems in the country's strategic sectors (smart mining, the food industry and engineering, for instance). The country has closed the financing gap at the early stage; it has modernised services to entrepreneurs through more flexible mechanisms tailored to the needs of start-ups, such as collaborative workspaces and mentoring networks; and it has simplified the regulations for starting a business (a new law allows people to start a business in a single day). Private investment at the expansion stage and angel investors are still weak links in Chile's financing chain (OECD, 2016b).

Figure 2.5. **Budget for start-up promotion, Chile, 2016**

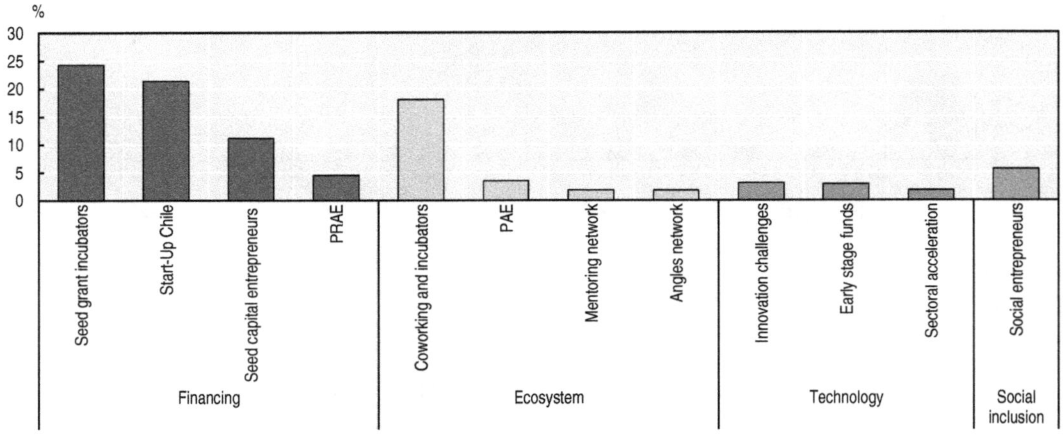

Source: OECD (2016b), Start-up Latin America 2016: Building an Innovative Future, http://dx.doi.org/10.1787/9789264265660-en.

Figure 2.6. **The policy mix to support start-ups in Chile is becoming more sophisticated, 2012-16**

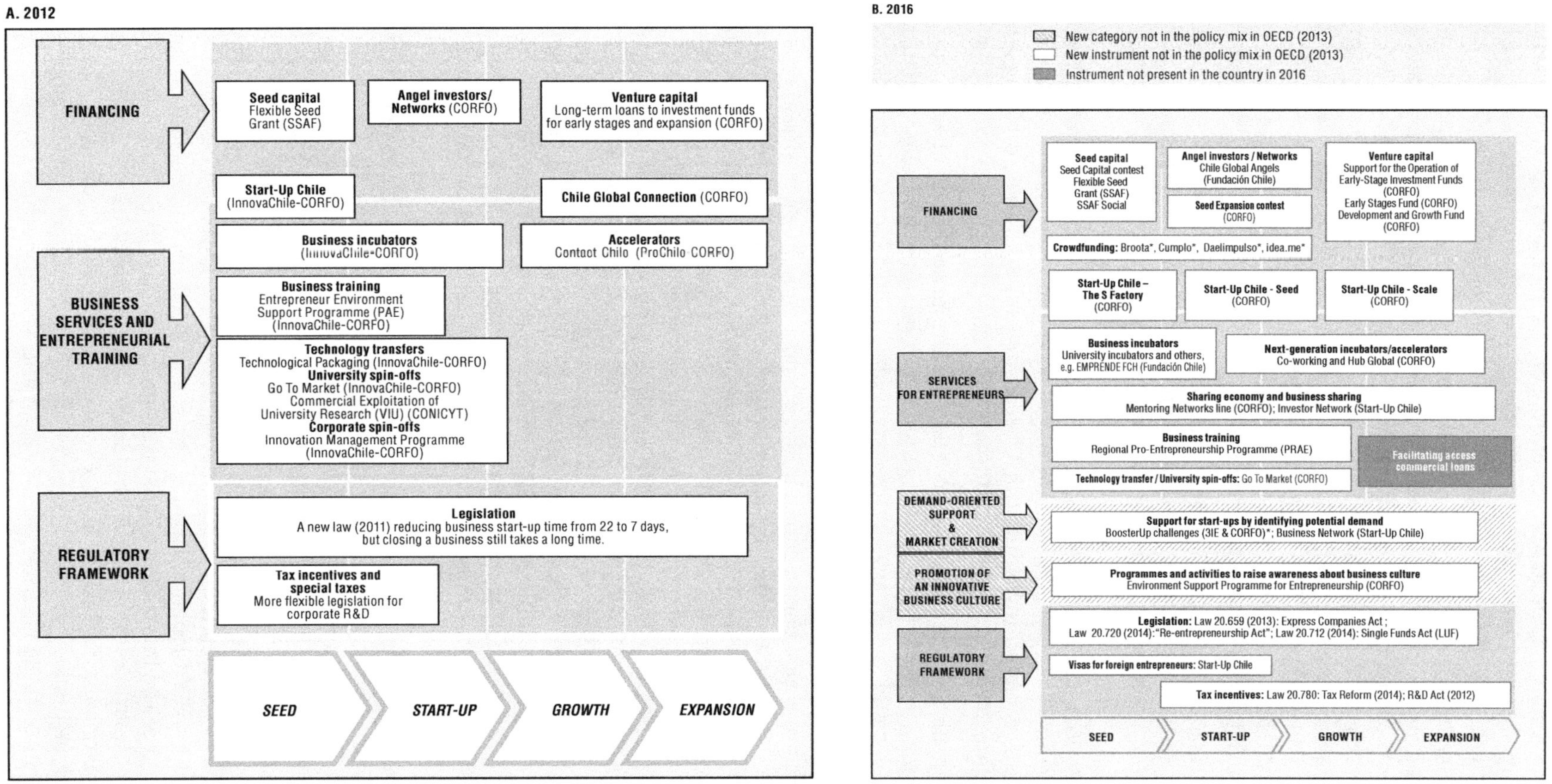

Source A: OECD (2013), Start-up Latin America: Promoting Innovation in the Region, http://dx.doi.org/10.1787/9789264202306-en.
Source B: OECD (2016b), Start-up Latin America 2016: Building an Innovative Future, http://dx.doi.org/10.1787/9789264265660-en

In particular, Chile has made it easier to start a business and has facilitated entrepreneurship. In 2014, the country introduced three reforms in line with the recommendations of the first review of start-up policies in Latin America (OECD, 2013b):

1. Law 20 659/2014 (*Ley de Empresas en un Día*, or Express Companies Act) simplified procedures for incorporating, amending or dissolving commercial companies. The act also introduced the "once only principle", meaning that businesses only need to register once through a subscription to an online portal to all the government administrative sites. This has reduced the cost and time involved in starting up a business. Today almost 70% of all new businesses in Chile are registered through that portal. Until 2014, an average of 6 400 businesses were registered monthly; today this figure is up to 8 500 per month.
2. Law 20 720/2014 (*Ley de Re-emprendimiento*, or Re-entrepreneurship Act) facilitated swifter negotiations between creditors and debtors for unsuccessful enterprises and made it easier to start a new business thanks to the rapid discharge of the debtor.
3. Law 20 712/2014 (*Ley Única de Fondos*, or Single Funds Act) sought to make investment in the country's investment funds bigger and more diverse, introducing tax incentives for foreign investment in Chilean investment funds, creating a single tax, and simplifying tax payment procedures.

Nevertheless, Chile's science and innovation performance remains below the OECD average (Chapter 1), and start-ups are not emerging or growing naturally. In addition to the barriers they would face in any country, start-ups in Chile face systemic difficulties resulting from the low propensity for business risk within society and among investors; the low density of the science and technology system; and logistical barriers. However, even if start-ups are a new phenomenon in the country and Chile's business ecosystem is not nearly as dynamic as those of more advanced countries, they are a reality, and one that is growing. As of early 2016, the Chilean ecosystem for start-ups included more than 1 000 start-ups supported by public policy, and 34 facilities across the country specialising in start-ups (co-working spaces, incubators and accelerators). According to CORFO data, the first five years of the Start-Up Chile programme saw the mobilisation of capital amounting to USD 420 million and the creation of more than 5 000 jobs (OECD, 2016b). Estimates by CORFO for the end of 2015 showed that Chilean start-ups included one unicorn (i.e. a start-up worth at least USD 1 billion), seven centaurs (worth between USD 100 million and USD 1 billion) and 32 little ponies (worth between USD 10 and 100 million) (Figure 2.7). These figures are comparable with those of more developed start-up ecosystems, such as in Singapore, which has around 1 000 start-ups, including 2 unicorns, 12 centaurs and 27 little ponies (OECD, 2016b).

Chile also supports university tech spin-offs. In a first phase, it provides financing for innovation workshops and covers the cost of presenting projects. In a second phase, it finances a one-month stay in the country or market chosen for the sale of the product, as well as the development of a practical programme in that country or market. In recent years, Chilean universities have increasingly been supporting start-ups. Some university incubators have received international recognition. Two appear in the ranking of the University Business Incubator, an annual list of the top 25 university incubators in the world, produced by UBI Global, a consultancy that specialises in analysing university business incubators. The International Business Innovation Institute (3IE) at Universidad Técnica Federico Santa María is ranked 17th globally, and Chrysalis at Pontífica Universidad Católica de Valparaíso is ranked 24th. At Pontífica Universidad Católica de Chile (UC), the science and technology research agency DICTUC focuses on the development of technological spin-offs. DICTUC created SIRVE, an anti-seismic technology firm, in 2003.

It also created Eduinova in 1995, a company dedicated to research and development in educational innovation and technology. Universidad de Santiago de Chile has the INNOVO centre, an incubator specialising in tech firms that has given rise to several successful spin-offs, including VoZE, a firm that began operating in 2013 and designed Chile's first prototype electric vehicle.

Figure 2.7. **Unicorns, centaurs and little ponies in Chile, 2017**

Number of start-ups

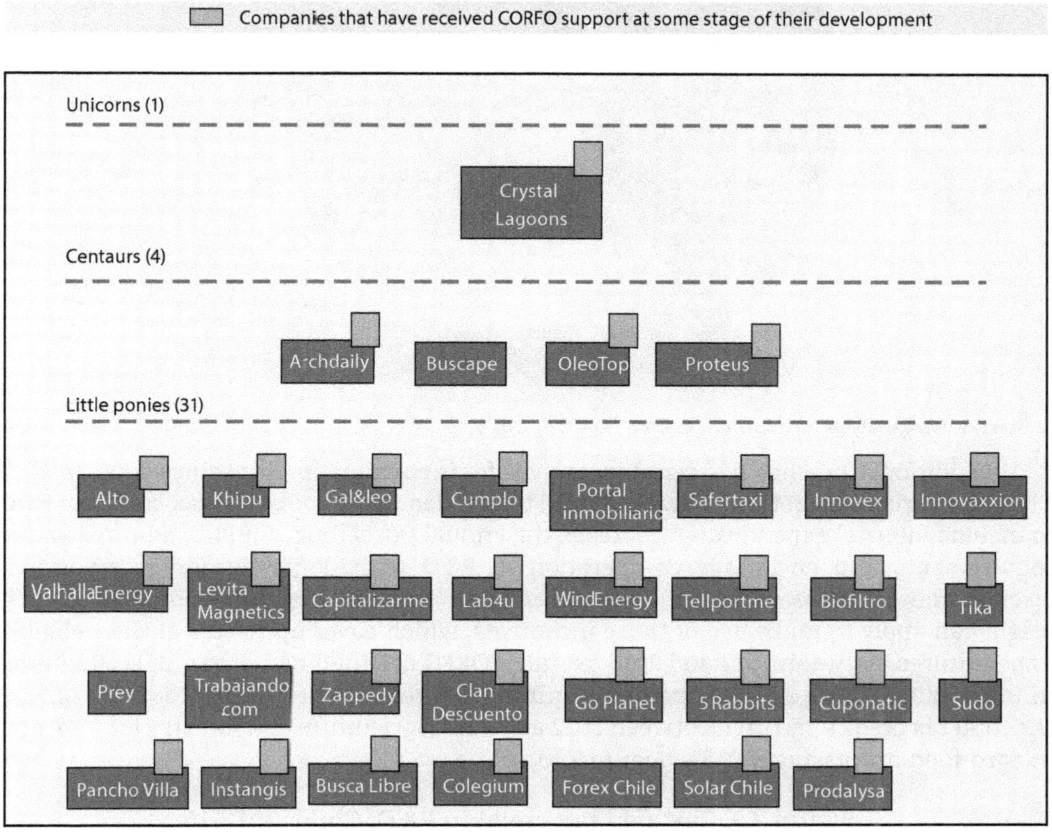

Source: Authors' analysis based on CORFO data, 2017.

Fostering human capital and innovation

CORFO and CONICYT foster innovation using several tools. CONYCYT fosters human capital development, including through *Becas Chile* which finances post-graduate training abroad. Between 2009 and 2014, 2 300 students participated in the programme, with (41%) in social sciences (Figure 2.8). CORFO manages several lines of financing, fostering innovation in firms from pre-competitive research to piloting and scale up. Some instruments specifically target SMEs. CORFO also promotes applied research by financing the creation of Technclogy Transfer Offices (TTOs) in co-operation with international partners, for example Fraunhofer-Germany and CSIRO, Australia.

Figure 2.8. **Doctoral graduate students in the *Becas Chile* programme by area of study, 2009-14**

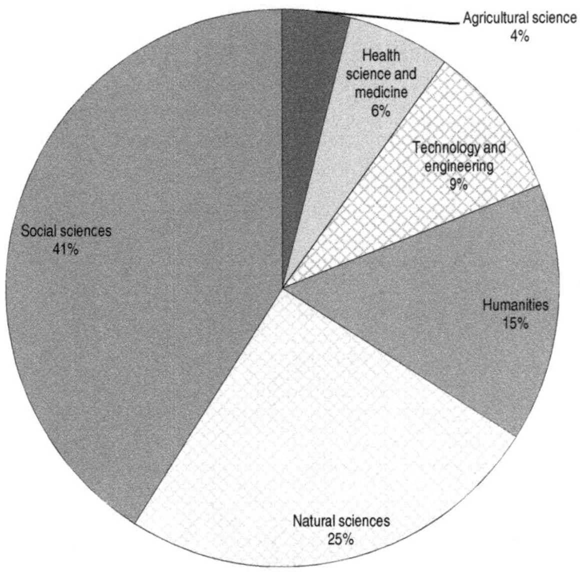

Source: Authors' analysis on information from CONICYT, 2017.

In addition, Chile has had fiscal incentives for innovation in place since 2008. In 2012 Chile implemented a reform (Law N° 20.659) to broaden the scope of the tax credit for R&D to include internal expenditures, increase the annual tax ceiling, simplify administrative requirements and encourage co-operation in R&D with domestic and international science and business partners. Companies of all size and regardless of their capital origin can apply to make use of these incentives, which cover up to 50% of their eligible expenditures. Between 2012 and 2016 overall, CORFO certified more than USD 60 million in tax credits (Figure 2.9). Companies in mining and related activities account for 50% of the total tax credits certified between 2012 and 2017; agriculture and forestry for 35%; and in agro-food processing for 18% (Figure 2.10).

Figure 2.9. **Certified tax credit in R&D, Chile, 2012-16**

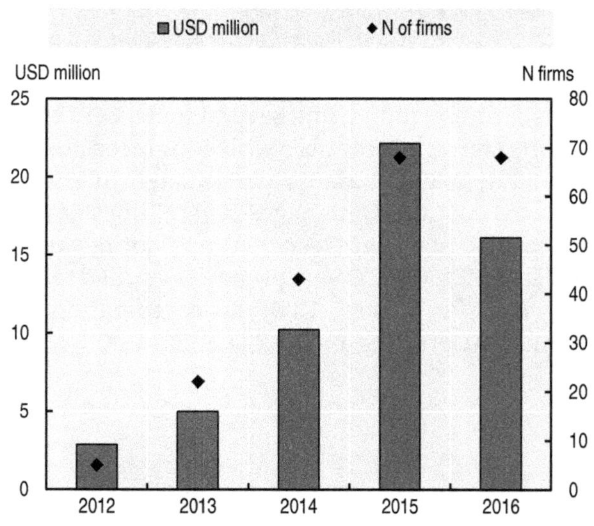

Source: Authors' analysis based on information provided by CORFO.

Figure 2.10. **Certified tax credit in R&D by economic activity, 2012-16**

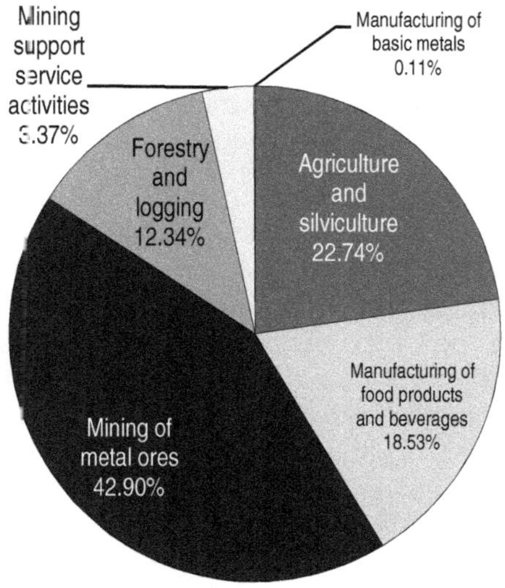

Note: The classification used is Isic 4.0.
Source: Authors' analysis based on official information provided by CORFO.

Enabling public-private partnerships to address strategic challenges

The 2014 Productivity, Growth and Innovation Agenda seeks to identify the most significant co-ordination failures between the government and the private sector in order to get the country ready to operate in the emerging global digital context (Government of Chile, 2014). The agenda calls for greater progress to ensure a resilient, redundant and safe Internet connection; to define standards for interoperability and digital trade; and to modernise training at all levels – from vocational to post-graduate – to endow the next generation of workers and managers with the skills needed for the future.

While on average Chile is not quite ready to operate in the digital world, some initiatives at the micro-level are noteworthy as they represent positive steps forward. The University of Development (*Universidad del Desarrollo*) has strengthened its teaching collaboration with the private sector to bridge the gap between training and work, and is working on shortening the training cycle to increase students' employability. CORFO is financing the training and certification of workers in programming and ICT skills. A major challenge for skills development is the system of career accreditation and certification, which requires an update to bring it into line with the demands of the digital age, for example by shortening the training cycle.

In 2015, Chile created the Strategic Investments Fund (FIE). The FIE has a budget of approximately USD 160 million for 2015-18 to finance mid-term, high-impact innovative and strategic projects jointly selected by the government and the private sector. The FIE is administered by the Ministry of Economy. Its board is chaired by the Minister of Economy and comprises the Ministers of Finance, Energy, Mining and Agriculture and three leading representatives of the business community. The FIE's original aim was to provide a long-term financing for strategic projects jointly selected by the public and the private sector. In practice, its long-term financing capacity is limited as it has been constituted as a treasury fund with a time limit of 2018. At the end of 2016 the FIE adopted a monitoring and evaluation system led by an external advisory panel to increase accountability.

Since the mid-2000s, in line with the renewed willingness to shift gears and embrace innovation-driven growth, Chile has started to experiment with different approaches to enable diversification. The country adopted a "cluster" approach in 2008, with a view to nurture ecosystems in key economic areas (including mining, global services and agro-food). The "cluster" approach built on the previous experiences in managing competitiveness programmes in specific industries such as forestry and salmon. In 2011, the programme was reformulated, eliminating the specific industry focus, in response to a logic that privileged horizontal rather than strategic approaches in policy making and public investment.

In line with global trends, Chile is now focusing on identifying key future challenges and it is working on setting up public-private partnerships to enable change in its industrial ecosystems. Based on the lessons from previous experiences, including the importance of early partnerships with key actors in the private sector and the need to mobilise government support beyond financing, including infrastructure and standards, the new approach focuses on strategic national and regional programmes. These have three objectives: i) promoting the diversification and sophistication of the Chilean ecosystem; ii) developing world-leading suppliers of higher value-added products and services; and iii) enabling a shared vision for the future in key industries through the co-ordination of public and private stakeholders.

The strategic programmes focus on: mining, agro-food, construction, health services, tourism, creative industry, fishing and aquaculture, and is based on three horizontal enablers of future competitivenes: logistics, solar energy, and smart industries and advanced manufacturing (Figure 2.11). These priority industries represent around 65% of Chile's GDP. In each area, the government has facilitated a process of multi-stakeholder self-discovery. This has resulted in the definition of road-maps with a 10 to 15-year time horizon, and has clarified gaps in areas such as human capital, physical and digital infrastructure, R&D, supply chain development, and standards and norms. These strategic programmes are articulated in national, regional and meso-regional actions. The total expected public investment for 2015-26 is expected to be USD 230 million. For 2015-18 the total approved public budget amounts to USD 160 million, or 0.1% of Chile's GDP in 2016 (Figure 2.12). The programmes are managed by CORFO with co-financing from FIE and FIC. Chapter 3 contains an analysis of the strategic actions in solar energy, mining and agro-food.

Figure 2.11. **Chile's strategic programmes, 2017**

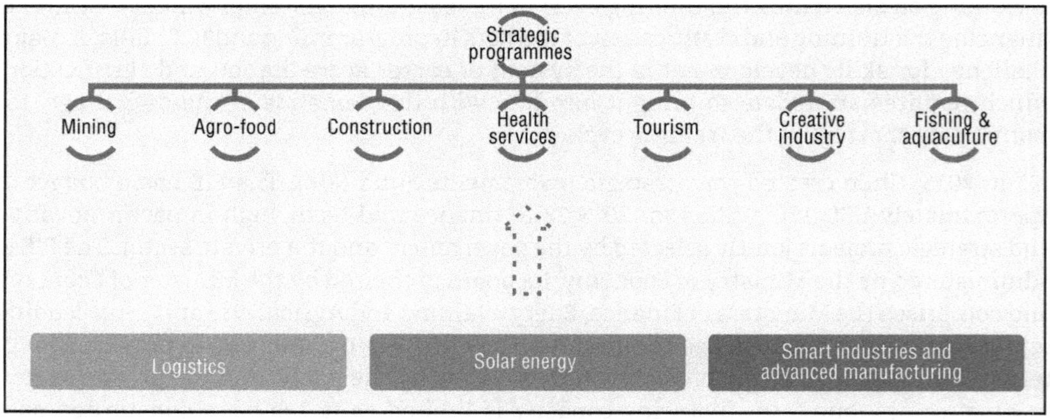

Source: Authors' analysis based on the information provided by CORFO, 2017.

Figure 2.12. **Public investment in strategic programmes, Chile, 2015-26**

USD million

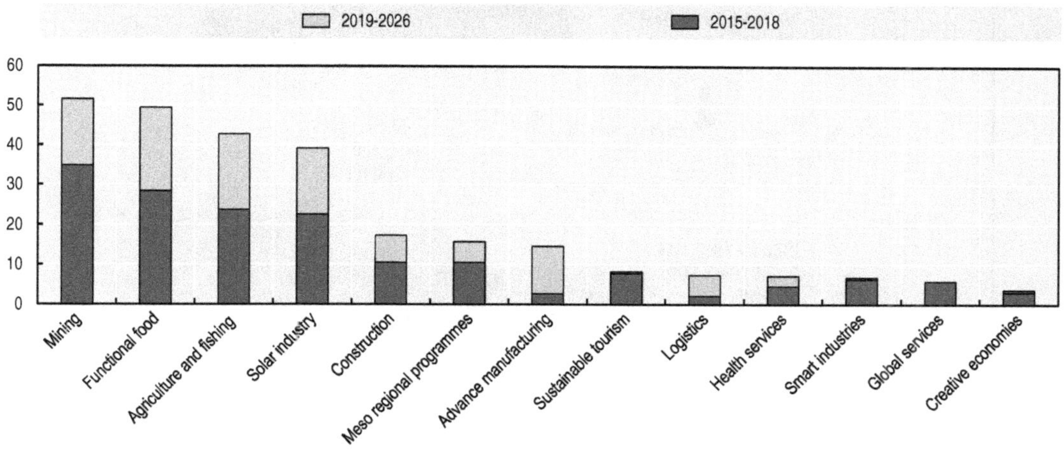

Source: Authors' analysis on information provided by CORFO and DIPRES, 2017.

The strategic programmes include a monitoring and evaluation system that follows the indications of the Interamerican Development Bank (IADB) (Boneu et al., 2016). It uses ad hoc surveys and considers four impact areas: 1) enterprise performance; 2) diversification and sophistication; 3) investment; and 4) governance and social capital (Table 2.2). The strategic programmes are in their initial phase of implementation, and it is therefore too early to assess their impact; however, comparing the governance and the planned actions with international experience reveals some good practices and possible areas for improvement (Table 2.3).

Table 2.2. **Monitoring the impact of Chile's strategic programmes, 2017**

Impact evaluation areas	Indicators
Enterprise performance	Share of exporting firms Employment Firms' turnover
Diversification and sophistication	R&D personnel New innovative products and process Entry of new firms
Investment	Share of private and public funds Number of innovative projects
Governance and social capital	Number and share of public and private representatives in each programme Governance satisfaction

Source: Authors' analysis based on information from CORFO; and Boneu et al. (2016), The Impact Evaluation of Cluster Development Programs: Methods and practices.

While it is globally recognised that different industries face specific opportunities and challenges, there is less consensus on: 1) which governance, transparency, and accountability mechanisms are best placed to enable policies to take into account and respond to these industry-specific challenges; and 2) how to design and manage a policy mix that attends the needs of each specific ecosystem and maximises the synergies among different industrial needs. Sectoral and industry-focused programmes are difficult to manage. The public sector lacks specific knowledge on scientific, technological and market opportunities, and incumbent actors often pursue their individual strategies without necessarily including the public good dimension in their utility function. In general, effective sectoral or industry focused programmes need to: 1) define needs with a long-term vision; 2) identify the policy mix for action; and 3) mobilise investment (Figure 2.13). To do it in an effective way, they need to rely on multi-stakeholder dialogue and mobilise private as well as public funding.

Figure 2.13. **What actions for economic diversification and prioritisation?**

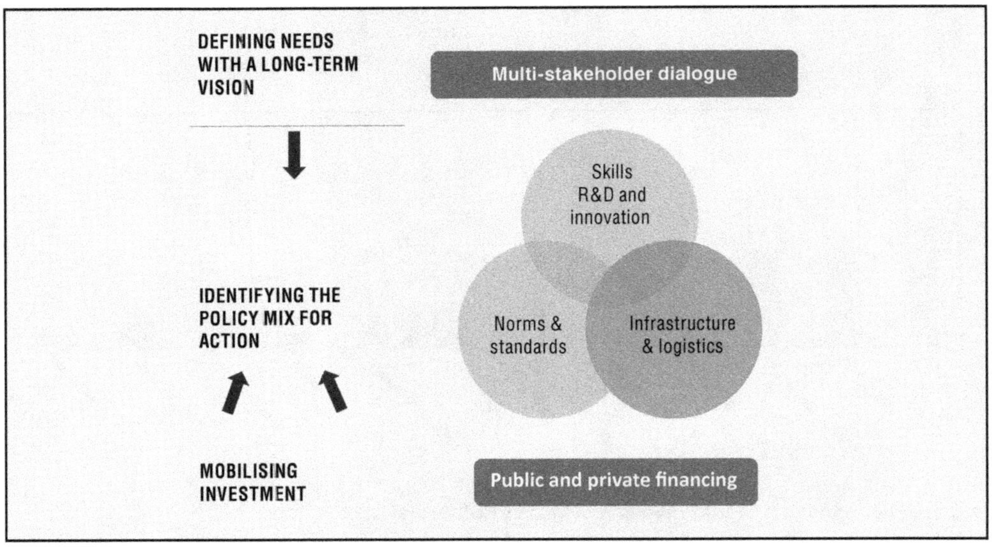

Source: OECD (2017d), Key Outcomes of the Peer Learning Group (PLG) Meeting of the PTPR of Chile, hosted by the OECD in Paris, May, 2017.

Chile seems to have found an effective policy approach by identifying enabling areas that are relevant for all industries (i.e logistics, solar energy, smart industries and advanced manufacturing) and by creating opportunities for the actors operating in different industries to share visions and challenges and define future specific needs in terms of skills, infrastructure, supply chain development, R&D and standards. This process, set up by CORFO, is a step forward in consensus building and in fostering public-private co-operation for economic development. In going forward, key priorities, drawn from the lessons learned from Chile and international good practices, include:

1. **Start small, experiment, and identify quick wins**. Legitimising state intervention in specific industries needs particular attention, as the risks of capture and corruption are high. Industry-specific programmes need to be technically feasible, yet they also need to be politically acceptable. Transparency mechanisms and bargaining capacities with multiple stakeholders are needed. In Colombia, for example, the Production Development Policy (PDP) started with by piloting some actions to gain credibility and increase trust.
2. **Generate synergies between industry-specific actions**. Future-oriented public-private dialogue in existing industries can be an effective way to reveal missing public goods and horizontal needs that could boost competitiveness across all industries, both existing and future ones. When governments are engaged in multiple industry-specific programmes, establishing formal mechanisms for comparing the results of industry specific consultations to identify common gaps can help to better prioritise public intervention in the creation of public goods.
3. **Go beyond pure economic assessments,** and analyse the impact on jobs and the environment. This will require new sets of indicators to assess transformation strategies according to a more comprehensive framework.
4. **Understand the needs of the buyer as the first step in developing a local supply chain**. The Japanese International Cooperation Agency (JICA) supports private sector development loans, technical assistance and services for firms in developing countries (Box 2.3). JICA scans the local economy, identifies potential suppliers, and sees how to link them up with buyers. JICA provides support for skills development, product development, and overall enhancement of the capacities of local firms, and links these activities with the needs of buyers located in special economic zones.

5. **Ensure local ownership.** Even when some targeted or sectoral programmes are initiated through international partnerships, ownership by local communities should be built and maintained. In the European Union, the Smart Specialisation approach relies on a bottom-up process of identification of territorial opportunities for the future, and in Colombia, the National Production Development Policy (PDP) starts with the identification of industrial development opportunities in specific industries linked to regional strengths.
6. **Avoid capture by incumbents and explore the potential to create medium-sized firms upfront.** Sectoral programmes require spaces for dialogue with multiple stakeholders, and mechanisms are needed to avoid the public interest simply being aligned with the strategic orientations of large and dominant firms. Strategic investors and big players are important, but it is also paramount to ensure that the sectoral programmes avoid responding to the agenda of monopolistic powers to the detriment of the development opportunities of other firms, especially in a sector characterised by wealthy medium-sized firms.
7. **Set up incentives to manage the extra rents earned by big winners.** Effective transformation programmes will result in new market structures, products and services. When significant public resources are invested, it is important to set up mechanisms that ensure the productive re-investment of the extra rents earned by certain economic agents through the creation of new market opportunities.
8. **Closely monitor implementation and evaluate impact.** Monitoring on a continuous basis and establishing feedback mechanism between strategy planning and monitoring to ensure fine tuning of policy design are good practices that increase accountability and effectiveness of policy action.

Box 2.3. **Fostering private sector development: lessons from the Japanese International Cooperation Agency (JICA)**

JICA is active in fostering private sector development. This box summarises some key lessons learned from project implementation in different countries.

Promoting multi-stakeholder dialogue in Ethiopia. Ethiopia's vision is to be the leading nation in Africa in light manufacturing. To achieve this, the whole industrial and technological system needs to be transformed. For this, JICA invested in creating a multi-stakeholder policy dialogue to align the visions of multiple stakeholders. These dialogues should have high political leadership to ensure impact.

Strengthening the quality and image of Ethiopian leather. Japanese buyers had a preconceived, negative image of the quality of Ethiopian leather. The uniqueness and the qualities of the Ethiopian leather were not recognised by consumers and the price premium that they were ready to pay was very low. In addition, designs did not reflect the preferences of potential Japanese buyers. JICA set up a branding programme for Ethiopian highland leather. It developed high-quality products to show the quality of domestic production and promoted international awareness through participation in Japanese trade fairs. JICA also worked with Japanese designers to develop new design patterns for the local leather that match buyers' demands.

Strengthening the automotive supply chain in Thailand. The Thai government wanted to enhance local domestic capabilities in this sector. JICA mobilised the private sector and foreign investors to train and share good practices to enhance the capabilities of local suppliers.

Building a tier 2 automotive supply chain in Mexico. Japan has a long history of co-operation to strengthen the competitiveness of local suppliers in Mexico. JICA collaborated with tier 1 providers to scan and identify potential tier 2 suppliers. Japanese experts were then assigned to the potential tier 2 suppliers to increase their local capacities. As a result of the programme, the sales between tier 1 and tier 2 providers increased.

Source: OECD (2017), Key Outcomes of the Peer Learning Group (PLG) Meeting of the PTPR of Chile, hosted by the OECD in Paris, May 2017.

Table 2.3. **Progress overview of Chile's strategic programmes, 2017**

Governance dimensions		
Anticipation capacity	√	Having road-maps with a long-term horizon (to 2025-30) takes Chile a step forward in line with international good practices. Aligning financing with the time-line of the road map will be an additional step forward.
Adaptation capacity	≈	In the fast changing technological environment the time for design and validating road-maps could be shortened from the current 13 months, while adaptability could be increased by introducing periodical revision of road-maps.
Learning and upgrading potential	√	The public-private consultations led to an effective identification of gaps in skills needed to compete in the future and of priority actions to bridge them. Growing cooperation between businesses, training centres and academia is a positive step. Overcoming barriers, including aligning educational accreditation processes with emerging needs, will be important to getting the right skills for tomorrow.
	≈	Setting up mechanisms to generate synergies between the different programmes and to enable learning and cross-fertilisation could align multiple-stakeholders to take actions and provide public goods which would act as competitiveness enhancers across all industries and firms, including digital infrastructure and skills. The creation of the Solar Research Institute, if endowed with a broader science base and mission could contribute to enhance learning opportunities in the whole economy.
Interconnectedness propensity	√	**Within government**. The programme benefits from multi-agency co-ordination.
	≈	**Private sector**. Businesses participated in the road-map process, but enhanced. participation of start-ups and SMEs would be needed as well as increased commitment by lead firms and investors would be needed in going forward.
	√	**Academia**. The programme benefits from commitment and co-operation mechanisms with academia and international research centres.
	√	**Civil society**. There is room to increase the participation of civil society in the process, and to identify new mechanisms to strengthen business-community relationship.
	x	**Regional.** Strengthening regional ties could help to scale up investments and reach the critical mass needed to compete effectively at the global level.
	√	**International**. Scaling up on international cooperation could help closing knowledge and technology gaps.
Embeddedness potential	≈	There is a need to clarify procedures and standards to ensure environmental and social sustainability.
	×	There is a need to increase the role of regions & territories in planning, implementation and monitoring.
	≈	Open government and effective monitoring and evaluation are needed to track progress and performance and identify areas for reform.

Future challenges
Ensuring the long-term commitment of the private sector. Mechanisms to avoid rent seeking and capture need to be in place to ensure that publicly-financed actions benefit all stakeholders and deliver public and club goods not available otherwise
Aligning the budget with the strategy's objectives. Chile has an initial budget of USD160 million for three years (0.1% of 2016 GDP). In comparison, the Emilia Romagna region (Italy) has a USD 700 million budget for the period 2014-2020 in the context of the European Union Smart Specialisation Strategy
Avoiding the overlap of programmes and actions and foster synergies among the different sectoral programmes. It is important to convey resources towards economic activities that have the greatest spill-over effects for the economy and society
Ensuring high-level political ownership. The programmes are designed, implemented and revised within the Ministry of Economy through CORFO and with the financial support of FIE and FIC. In order to scale-up and foster production transformation it will be important seek higher political commitment

Note: √: positive progress; ≈: margin for improvement; x: reform needed.

Three game changers to ensure future policy impact

This section concludes the chapter by highlighting three game changers for the future of Chile. It focuses on one issue that emerged as a priority for reform in the short-term during the activities of consensus building carried out in the framework of the PTPR process: the need to "update" the public institutions and governance to cope with the broader and more sophisticated roles that the state is called to play in the future. The section also discusses two areas for reform that are key in the medium and long term for Chile and that have been addressed during the Peer Learning Group (PLG) Meeting of the PTPR of Chile, hosted by the OECD in May 2017 (OECD, 2017). These include: a) the importance of scanning for possible futures to design better policies and to endow the state with a capacity to do so in a structured way; and b) the need to advance in shifting towards a place-based approach in policy making as a key component of an inclusive and sustainable economic transformation of Chile.

Modernising the state to cope with a high-speed, uncertain and complex landscape

Chile's current institutional arrangements, funding mechanisms and policy mix for economic transformation (Figure 2.14) are the result of a long-term, cumulative process of trial and error, successful experimentation, and subsequent reforms to policy making (Griffith-Jones et al, 2017). Most of the institutions in charge of promoting Chile's industrial and scientific development have a long history (Figure 2.15). The Chilean Economic Development Agency (CORFO) was set up in 1939. This agency answers to the Ministry of Economy and is in charge of implementing policies for industrial and technological development. The agency in charge of promoting the development of micro and SMEs (SERCOTEC) was established in 1952; and CONICYT – the National Council for Science and Technology, the other major implementing agency responding to the Ministry of Education – was founded in 1967.

Over the years, several institutional reforms have been implemented within and across organisations. In some cases these changes have improved the governance, in others they created several institutional layers and a high level of complexity in the bureaucracy. In the future it would be important to preserve the state's modernisation agenda and making it more agile, effective and capable of responding to future needs. "Updating" the state includes an agenda on several fronts:

- **Leadership and co-ordination.** Ensuring high-level leadership for the transformation agenda would help to achieve consensus and mobilise actions across ministries. In going forward it would be desirable to reduce the multiplicity of co-ordination bodies (National Productivity Commission, National Council for Innovation and Development and Ministerial Committee for Innovation) and aim for a unique, but empowered and strengthened, body directly answering to the President. Co-ordination at the ministerial level on economic transformation also needs to be strengthened. The current negotiation process for annual budgeting between finance and each line ministry, coupled with weak co-ordination at the strategic level, weakens the capacity to prioritise actions in a more effective way.
- **Long-term financing.** Enabling long-term financing for strategic investment is also important. The creation of the Strategic Investments Fund (FIE) is a positive step forward, even though its nature as a treasury fund limits the long-term perspective in practice. To simplify the procedures it could be shifted to the responsibility of the implementation agency (CORFO), rather than being directly managed at the ministerial level.
- **Policy co-ordination.** As the challenges of global, digital, inclusive and environmentally sustainable economies are multidimensional and complex, increased co-ordination among the production, investment, trade, education and regional development agendas would be desirable. Increased co-ordination is needed to better harness the potential of key enabling areas for the future, such as the digital agenda and the definition of skills, standards and norms for the future.
- **Public-private partnerships.** Ensuring inclusive public-private partnerships is important to consolidate the recent progress of consensus building among business, government and society. Chile now has well-established consultation capacity with leading domestic and international firms. The next step would be to enlarge

the consultation base and increase the capacity for dialogue with entrepreneurs and small businesses. In the new technological paradigms, disruptive innovations increasingly come from start-ups and small firms. Having a governance structure capable of interacting with them will increase the capacity to design better policies.

Figure 2.14. **Chile's governance of economic transformation, 2017**

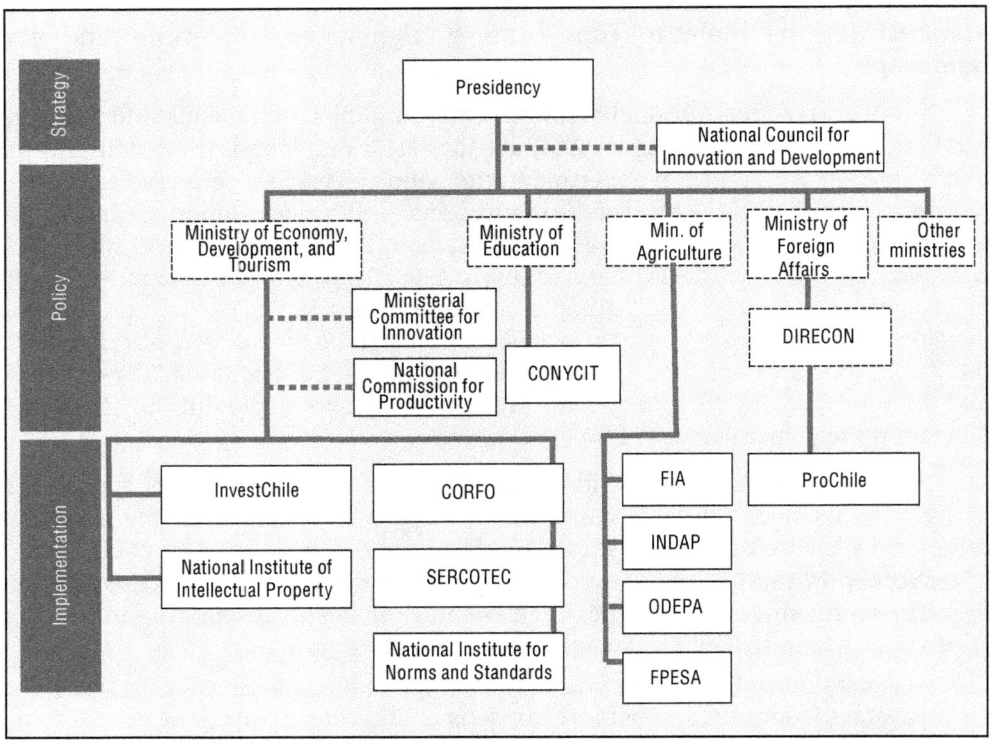

Note: CORFO: Chilean Economic Development Agency; CONICYT: National Council for Scientific and Technological Research; DIRECON: General Directorate for International Economic Affairs; FIA: Agriculture Innovation Foundation; SENCE: National Service for Training and Employment; SERCOTEC: National Service for Technical Cooperation. The organigram only includes ministries with implementing agencies at the national level.

Source: Authors' analysis based on official information from CORFO and DIRECON.

Figure 2.15. **A chronology of Chile's main institutions, funds and programmes for production development and innovation, 1939-2017**

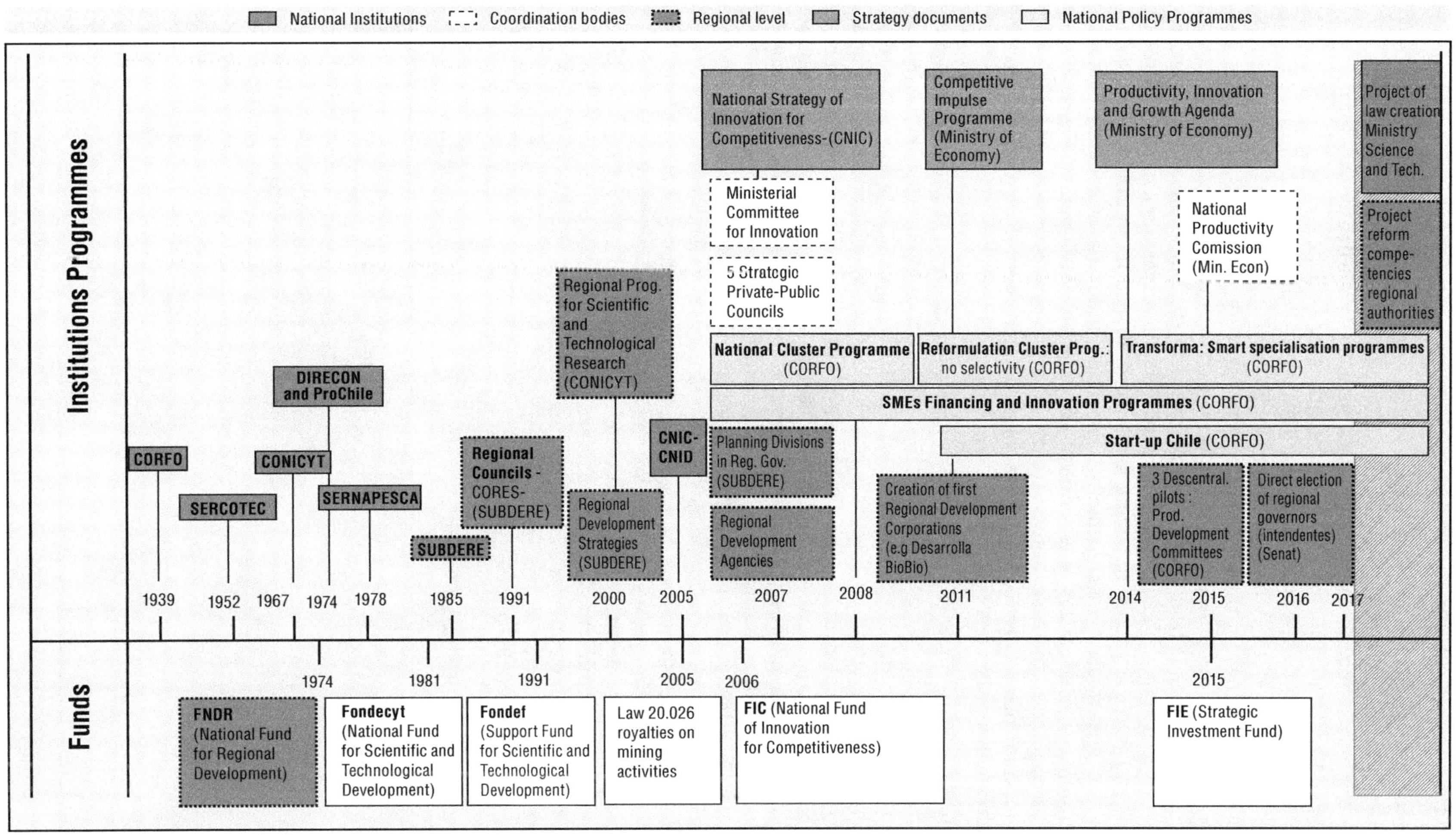

Note: CORFO: Chilean Economic Development Agency; CONICYT: National Council for Scientific and Technological; DIRECON: General Directorate for International Economic Affairs; SERCOTEC: Technical Cooperation Service; SERNAPESCA: National Fishing Service; SUBDERE: Under-secretary for Regional and Administrative development CNIC-/CNID: National Council for Innovation and Competitiveness/ Development.

Source: Authors' analysis based on official information from CORFO and DIRECON.

Scanning for possible futures to achieve consensus

As Chile looks into the future, there are many proposals for going forward. On the one hand, there is a call for advancing the simplification agenda, building on successes such as the 2014 Express Companies Act for creating a business in one day, enhancing support for starting and scaling up businesses, and strengthening skills, especially in technical and vocational training. On the other hand, there is an open debate on what Chile could do beyond improving productivity in its existing industries. This implies a more ambitious agenda with key priorities for the medium and long term (as the one put forward by the Ministry of Economy in the 2014 National Agenda for Productivity, Innovation and Growth). To be effective, this agenda needs to take into account potential scenarios for the future; ensure buy-in from all stakeholders, including local communities; domestic and foreign companies; and make adequate financing available. It is also important to ensure co-ordination among several policies, including innovation, industrial development, trade, infrastructure, energy, education, environment and regional development. The strategic programmes could form the base for this stronger, shared vision for the future. However, the vision for transformation is not yet mainstreamed among all stakeholders, within the government and across society (Table 2.4).

Identifying priorities is a challenging task, and even more so in the fast-changing global landscape in which we currently live. Selecting the areas on which to focus and mobilise resources is a major challenge for all countries (Figure 2.16). Some countries prioritise by enabling bottom-up processes of regional discovery in areas of potential advantage; others select key industries of relevance for the country based on current and potential advantages; and others prioritise by investing in scientific and technological development. Governments are not known for being at the forefront of mechanisms and tools for scenario building, nor for using scenarios and foresights in strategic planning. However, the complexity and uncertainty of the current global economic landscape, characterised by high-speed change, major global political shifts, and technological and digital revolutions, are increasingly calling for more sophisticated and forward-looking strategies. There is no unique way to increase the anticipatory capacity of governments (such as the capacity to detect future opportunities, to factor in voices for change, and to anticipate potential shifts in global and domestic dynamics). Much can be learned by looking at the various instruments some countries are putting in place to increase their forward-looking perspective and to enable effective prioritisation and co-ordination of actions for economic transformation (Box 2.4).

Figure 2.16. **A shared vision is needed for effective prioritisation**

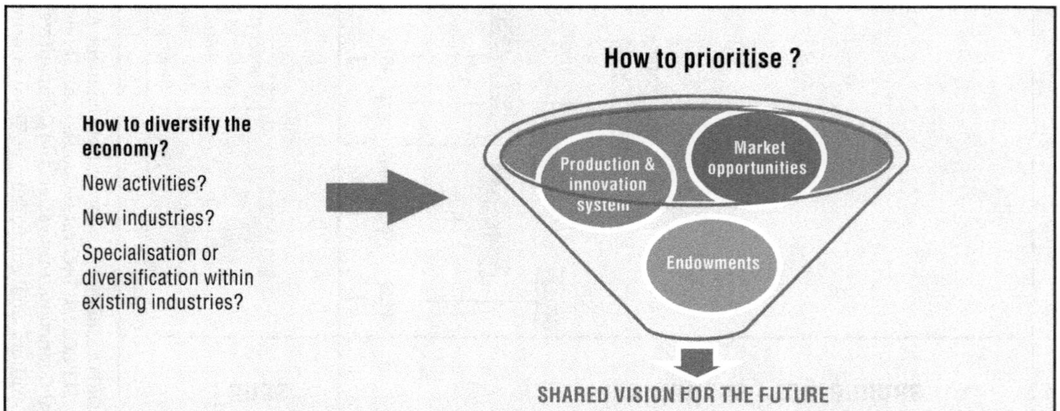

Source: OECD (2017), Key Outcomes of the Peer Learning Group (PLG) Meeting of the PTPR of Chile, hosted by the OECD in Paris, May 2017.

Table 2.4. **Diversifying the Chilean economy: opportunities and challenges**

Consensual issues	**Controversial points**
Need to reduce copper dependency The history of sound macroeconomic management, good governance and trade openness could be an asset for managing the more complex policies needed for diversification in an industry 4.0 & GVCs global landscape Need to identify mechanisms to better learn from FDI, and increase knowledge & technology spillovers from foreign talents and firms Banks are perceived as conservative and having limited interest in backing up innovative ventures and projects	Identification of priorities through: 1. Sectors/economic activities approach 2. Challenge-driven approach 3. Market signals & economic openness
Opportunities & challenges of the current approach to prioritisation	
+ Existing initiatives (mostly led by CORFO) to create opportunities for change (creation of new companies, incentives for changing the behaviour of firms and technology centres & universities) + Scenarios and future scanning capabilities in the ministry of Energy and Energy Agenda 2050 + Creation of a Productivity Commission favouring public-private dialogue for identifying priorities for actions	- Political polarisation might have a negative impact on planning and execution - Lack of a shared vision for the future => little commitment to high-impact-long-term projects, little patience in allowing diversification projects to deliver results, and difficulty in scaling up successful experimentations (e.g. cluster policies) - Excessive reliance on documents & plans instead of creating the foundations for the plan to be implemented (e.g. having a sound STI and trade infrastructure, an ecosystem of companies and technology centres, and a mind-set that values innovation and change)
+/- Existence of spaces for forward-looking thinking (e.g. Future Commission in the Senate and National Council for Innovation and Development) but no mechanisms to translate future perspectives into a shared vision for action	

Source: OECD (2017), Key Outcomes of the Peer Learning Group (PLG) Meeting of the PTPR of Chile, hosted by the OECD in Paris, May 2017.

Effective prioritisation needs to be based on scanning for potential futures. And it needs to ensure the commitment of all actors (private sector, academia and local communities) from its inception. This means having mechanisms in place to engage all actors in defining strategic priorities, not only in the implementation of specific programmes and tools. In the case of Emilia Romagna, the competitiveness strategy follows a three-track approach: 1) it prioritises value chains with the consolidated local industrial and technological system; 2) it identifies two additional areas in which the region could excel in the future, based on shared perceptions of all the actors in the regional production and innovation system: cultural and creative industries, and life sciences; and 3) it directs investments to enabling areas that have cross-industrial implications, especially services and technology transfers for firms, with a specific emphasis on SMEs.

Box 2.4. **Good practices to increase anticipation capacities for planning and prioritisation: lessons from the Peer Learning Group (PLG)**

What is strategic foresight?

Strategic foresight is a structured, systematic approach to thinking about the future. It is not forecasting; it is about exploring and preparing for a range of plausible alternative futures. Most of the work done in public policy is on the expected possible outcome of existing events; the role of strategic foresight is to provide decision makers with an analysis of potential future scenarios to enrich the strategy setting process and define better policies for today and tomorrow. Why strategic foresight now? The pace of change at the global level is so rapid and uncertain that it is impossible to do responsible policy making without preparing for a range of alternative possible futures.

Box 2.4. Good practices to increase anticipation capacities for planning and prioritisation: lessons from the Peer Learning Group (PLG) *(Cont.)*

Good practices in strategic foresight for policy planning and prioritisation

There is no single best way to carry out strategic foresight. Several countries have invested heavily in developing these capabilities: Canada, Finland, Sweden and Singapore. From their experiences it is possible to identify six key features required of any effective strategic foresight exercise:

1. Political demand. High-level political demand is a precondition, because engaging policy making in foresight requires a cultural change in the approach to policy making. In Finland, for example, it is the Parliament that requests the development of future scenarios. In the US, potential scenarios are developed and given to the new President at the beginning of each mandate.
2. A dedicated centre of expertise. There is no unique ideal institutional arrangement, and each country needs to identify the solution that best fits its institutional governance and culture. But a common principle is to identify and empower a dedicated centre of expertise in charge of strategic foresight.
3. Co-ordination of foresight exercises across the whole government. From the experience of countries that have advanced the most in the elaboration and use of scenarios for public policies, the most interesting potential changes (and solutions) usually come from interactions of actors across different institutions, not only within institutions.
4. Targeted training both for experts in charge, and as part of the overall training of public officials.
5. Multi-stakeholder dialogue. Strategic foresight cannot be done behind closed doors and in isolation. There is a need to bring unusual stakeholders and disruptive voices on board. Strategic foresight can also be a powerful tool to reach alignment and shared visions across different groups – often views that are ideologically polarised tend to smooth out when thinking about medium- and long-term perspectives.
6. Integration of strategic foresight into national strategy setting. There should be a mechanism to ensure that the results of the strategic foresight processes are embedded into the national strategy and that they trickle down to each policy area.

Source: OECD (2017), Key Outcomes of the Peer Learning Group (PLG) Meeting of the PTPR of Chile, hosted by the OECD in Paris, May 2017.

Scanning for possible futures and defining scenarios is not an easy task. On the one hand, civil society can be resistant to this exercise. Engaging in strategic foresight implies the recognition that future outcomes are uncertain. This conflicts with the generalised expectations of society that the policy makers in charge know what the future will look like, and that they are well prepared for it. On the other hand, the exercise is useful when it can go beyond the predictable, when weak signals are detected and transformed into potential game changers. Achieving these types of results is not often easy as most people tend to be conservative when identifying potential futures. In Canada, for example, the first results were not much different from the expected future. Therefore, the government changed its method of work and challenged the strategic foresight group into looking at options that could be more disruptive. Some of these changes may look plausible, or they may not. But the point here is that there is a benefit to thinking about what foresight means to policy, and to be better prepared for whatever radical alternative does happen.

In some cases, the anticipation of disruptive changes comes from the private sector. In these cases, the government needs to be able to react quickly and become a key enabler of transformation. For example, in Sweden the state-owned steel manufacturing company decided to shift towards carbon-neutral high-performance steel in 2015. The company wanted to get a head-start in the future of the auto-industry, in which one of the future plausible scenarios is dominated by electro-mobility and sustainability. Today, steel production uses old furnace technology that has high energy consumption. The company scanned for a number of alternatives, including the use of hydrogen gas. Shifting towards hydrogen gas would affect the whole supply chain and require the buy-in of all stakeholders, including science and technology institutes, universities and the overall supply chain network. In the Swedish case, the transformation could happen because the science, technology and innovation system works together on problem solving. The national energy company recognised that the production of hydrogen gas was feasible, and the private sector shared the costs with universities and research centres that were challenged by businesses to address this issue and provide alternative solutions. In this context – a dense and well-functioning innovation system that uses trust and incentives to work towards common goals, combined with a generalised pro-innovation mind-set – the small isolated vision of one agent (shifting towards carbon-neutral steel production) was transformed into a massive opportunity for diversification in multiple industries.

In Chile, there is no formal process or institutionalised space for scenario building and foresight to inform strategy setting. Back in the 1960s, Chile had a Ministry of Planning which to a certain extent played the role of scanning for possible futures to define scenarios and plan economic development policies. However, over time, that ministry was assigned to social development, and its incipient capability of scenario setting has been lost. Since 2005 the country has taken steps to rebuild this forward-looking capability, including a first analysis in 2008, led by the National Council for Innovation and Competitiveness and the Boston Consulting Group. Since 2014 the strategic programmes co-ordinated by CORFO explored future trends in key areas relevant for the country (e.g. digitalisation, IoT, electro-mobility, solar energy, and the emergence of new consumer demands that give a premium to healthy and sustainable food products). These steps served as basis for identifying key road-maps for the future. In its turn, the National Productivity Commission, a public-private consultation body created in 2015, is looking for options to scale up and increase value added from mining. The Future Commission of the Senate, set up in 2012, discusses future trends and identifies ways to better inform policies with national and foreign experts. The Chilean National Council for Innovation and Development (CNID) advises the Presidency on innovation opportunities by developing a strategy for the future (currently with a time horizon to 2030), focusing on big national and global challenges where Chile can draw on its unique assets (water management, solar energy, and smart and green mining, to name a few). Other initiatives include the Agenda for Energy 2050, the Engineering Agenda 2030 and the analysis implemented by the Council for Future Perspectives and Strategies. While these initiatives are looking into future trends, there is no systematic way to integrate these visions into a shared vision and concrete policies.

As Chile makes progress to foster dynamic change in its economy and society, government will need stronger internal institutional capabilities to scan and identify potential futures. Stronger anticipatory capacities could increase the ability to identify needs, prioritise actions and generate consensus on what actions are needed in the short and medium. These capabilities could play multiple roles, especially to:

- **Build consensus on Chile's future options and needs.** Strategic foresight can be a powerful tool to align visions for the future, to generate consensus, and create the required buy-in from all actors, necessary for its economic transformation to become a reality (Box 2.4).

- **Identify key needs so as to compete in the future.** Chile faces a challenge in training people in a way that matches the demands of a very dynamic international market. Scanning for possible futures might help identify specific skills gaps in unusual areas. For example, scenarios on the global functional and healthy food industry reveal that in addition to sophisticated agro, chemical and digital skills, modelling and predicting skills to better understand consumer behaviour are needed to compete globally.

Shifting towards a place-based approach to policy making

Chile has experimented with different ways of increasing the role of regions in economic transformation

Chile is the most territorially unequal country in the OECD. Indicators of population, GDP growth and productivity are concentrated in the capital city (Chapter 1). This is not unique to Chile – some OECD countries, such as France and UK, show the same pattern. However, Chile's situation is more extreme, as regions are not catching up in terms of productivity growth. Even mining regions, such as Antofagasta, are reaching their limits of labour-productivity growth, and future scenarios for mining are not the brightest for these regions.

Chile is highly centralised, though it has a recent history of gradual decentralisation (OECD, 2016a). On average, globally, convergence in income per capita is correlated with growing decentralisation. However, there are notable exceptions, such as New Zealand, which despite its high income per capita maintains a high level of centralisation in public policies. In Chile, regions account for 13% of general government expenditures (compared to an OECD average of 40%) and 27% of government staff expenditure (compared to the OECD average of 60%). The persistently high level of centralisation is perceived as a barrier to identifying new sources of growth.

The country has been gradually implementing reforms to increase the decision-making and financial autonomy of its regions. The national body in charge of decentralisation – SUBDERE (Under-Secretary for Regional and Administrative Development) – was created in 1985. In 1991 elected Regional Councils (COREs) in charge of co-operating with SUBDERE were created to develop regional development strategies. The decentralisation process has advanced slowly, with the election of the head of regional governments (*intendentes*) only approved in 2016. The draft law that regulates the competences of these locally elected governors is currently pending approval. However, most of these efforts have had limited impact due to poor capacity in regional governments, scant support to increase this capacity, and a lack of clarity in the mechanisms for resource transfer and budget management. There is growing consensus over the limitations of an excessively centralised approach, which not only contributes to reinforce the existing specialisation pattern (retail and finance in the capital region and extractive industries in the mining regions), but also limits the possibility to identify new opportunities for innovation, for the creation of new firms and the participation in regional and global value chains in different areas. Excessive centralisation therefore limits Chile's ambition to achieve an inclusive growth strategy.

However, much less consensus exists over how to advance in the decentralisation process. There are large variations across regions in terms of government capacity and the readiness of local actors to actively engage in transformation strategies. When consulted, local actors tend to reveal valuable information about opportunities and challenges for production development in their territory, and are eager to be more actively involved in national and regional strategies (Box 2.5). Institutional and professional capacity at the sub-national levels of government influence its ability to design and implement effective policies. Usually lower levels of government suffer from capacity gaps relative to the central government, and there are often large differences among regions and provinces. Investing in institutional capacity at the local level will be crucial for realising the potential for production development in Chile's territories.

The first efforts to build capacity in the regions to support production development and innovation date back to 2007, with the creation of Regional Development Agencies (RDAs) (IDB-OECD, 2010). The RDAs were created with strong support from the national administration, which was supposed to be gradually reduced over time. In 2011, the RDAs were closed and transformed into private corporations in charge of regional development, thus increasing their relationship with the Regional Councils and reducing their dependency on CORFO. Each Regional Council decides on the composition and governance of its corporation. As of 2017, 10 of Chile's 15 regions have a production development corporation (such as "Desarrolla Bío-Bío", "Agencia Araucania" and "Regional Production Corporation of Coquimbo"). The corporations are regional entities financed by regional governments and the private sector. These corporations perform mixed functions, from advisory in strategy setting to the implementation of production development policies.

Since 2014, Chile has given renewed impetus to the decentralisation agenda: it aims to increase the autonomy of regional authorities and the budget allocated to regional development, as well as the share of the budget directly executed by regional governments. The agenda, which is accompanied by a plan to transfer competencies for production development to regions, includes:

1. A constitutional reform allowing for the direct election of regional governors (*intendentes*). This was approved in 2016; however the reform on the effective power of these regionally elected governors is still pending approval.
2. A reform for transferring competencies and budget from the central to the regional governments (currently under discussion in Parliament).
3. Targeted financing for capacity building in regional and local governments.
4. The regionalisation of policies for production development. CORFO is planning to decentralise 40% of its budget and it is now piloting this decentralisation process in the regions of Antofagasta, Bio-Bio and Los Rios. It plans to expand the experiment to three additional regions in 2018 and to all regions by 2021. The pilot projects include the creation of a Production Development Committee in each region. These committees co-ordinate the implementation of CORFO and SERCOTEC policy tools in the regions. While these pilot projects are perceived as way to increase the space for regional voices in Antofagasta and Los Rios, in Bío-Bío the pilot project is not unanimously considered as an advance in regional autonomy. This is because Innova-Bío-Bío has been operating in the region since 2001 as a kind of decentralised CORFO unit. Additionally, under the strategic programmes initiative, 5 meso-regional and 20 regional sub-programmes are under implementation. Each programme is associated with a specific economic activity that aims to reduce co-ordination gaps undermining the development of existing sectors in the regions; incorporate and foster innovation in the sectors with a clear competitive advantage; and increase productivity through highly qualified human capital.

Box 2.5. **Moving forward: Three scenarios for the Bío-Bío region in 2030**

Bío-Bío is the third most populous region in the country (accounting for almost 12% of the national population) and comes fourth in terms of its share of national GDP (7%). At present it is divided into four provinces (Ñuble, Concepción, Bío-Bío, and Arauco), with Concepción hosting 46% of the population. Ñuble will become an additional region in 2018. It hosts a large number of universities and has a good track record in patenting and in collaborative processes between universities and the private sector. Bío-Bío is a manufacturing region (representing 23% of regional GDP, compared to a national average of 10%). The region is currently the second manufacturing region in the country, accounting for 16% of national manufacturing value added (after the Metropolitan Region of Santiago, which accounts for 45% of total national manufacturing value added).

Bío-Bío is quite diversified. It has a mining sector (which is declining), activities linked to fishing and agriculture, a growing agro-food and fresh fruit industry and a strong manufacturing tradition, linked to the wood and pulp and paper industries. Half of the planted forests in Chile are in Bío-Bío. The region mostly exports commodities linked to unprocessed wood and fresh and frozen fruit. Its major export destinations are the United States, China and Japan, which account for 19%, 18% and 10% of its exports respectively (National Statistical Institute - Bío-Bío Regional Direction, accessed December 2016).

During the PTPR review process a scenario-setting exercise was carried out with representatives from the regional government, CORFO, the private sector, professional associations, opinion leaders and regional counsellors (COREs). This led to key strengths, weaknesses, opportunities and threats being identified (Table 2.5), as well as several scenarios (outlined below the table).

Table 2.5. **Strengths, weaknesses, opportunities and threats for the Bío-Bío region**

Strengths	**Weaknesses**
• Relatively diversified production matrix • Natural resource abundance (in the timber industry and agro-food production) • Strong university and research base, human capital formation • Incipient attempts to increase co-ordination between universities and the private sector	• Limited regional autonomy • Wage differentials with the metropolitan region leading to brain drain • High inequality in the distribution of income and wealth • Poor connectivity (ports, roads, etc.) • Low cultural propensity for cooperation and sharing (low interpersonal trust and social capital) • Ineffective implementation of the corporate social responsibility framework • Persistent specialisation in commodities and low- value adding activities • Few and weak linkages across economic activities • Stop and start approach to policy making • Weak linkages between universities and the private sector & lack of applied research on regional strategic economic sectors • Lack of an appropriate definition of SMEs
Opportunities	**Threats**
• Grasping the opportunities of sustainable economy (e.g sustainable agro-food production; exploiting wood potential as a recyclable, renewable and durable raw material) • Capitalising on youth talent and young entrepreneurs • Increasing local voices through the recent administrative reform of the election of the regional governor (intendente), despite the limitations of the reform itself • Increased investments from China and linkages with Chinese investors and consumers	• High market concentration leading to excessive market power and rents • Challenging conditions for medium-sized firms • Lack of policies addressing functional regions • Relatively low attention to global economic trends • Increased competition with China in domestic manufacturing activities • Growing conflict with indigenous population

Box 2.5. **Moving forward: Three scenarios for the Bío-Bío region in 2030** (*Cont.*)

Scenario 1: Bío-Bío Green: The region is able to take full advantage of its endowments (forestry, which is renewable-recycling-durable) given the rising demand for sustainable production. The regional government is increasingly autonomous in strategy and budgeting and effective mechanisms for accountability are in place between the national and regional governments. Medium-sized enterprises are successfully operating in the market and region, and produce and export increasingly sophisticated and value-added products and services. Some big enterprises are moving their headquarters to Bío-Bío. Universities and technological centres are innovating on the frontier and train people in line with the needs of industry 4.0. Global and regional connectivity is reinforced.

Scenario 2: Bío-Bío Drained: The human capital is drawn towards other regions. Production is limited to natural extraction and oriented towards the export of unprocessed commodities. Top quality universities leave the region, limiting the growth opportunities of local firms and entrepreneurs. Regional autonomy remains low. Climate change raises regional vulnerabilities through various channels.

Scenario 3: Bío-Bío in Transformation: The region is not yet autonomous but governance reforms enable local voices to be better heard in national/regional negotiations. Successful co-ordination between universities and the private sector enables some firms to upgrade their production. Universities attempt to improve their innovation capacity. Relative infrastructure modernisation and increased investment from China enable technological transfers and increase productivity.

Source: Collective results of the scenario-setting exercise for the region of Bío-Bío. The exercise took place in Concepción on January 11th 2017 in the context of the first fact-finding mission to Chile of the PTPR process. Participants included representatives from the regional government, CORFO, private sector, professional associations, opinion leaders and regional counsellors (COREs).

The start-up policy has been reformed to enable innovation in regions

One of the areas in which Chile has achieved remarkable impact is in facilitating the creation of start-ups (OECD, 2016b). In line with the national priority of fostering territorially and socially inclusive development, the policy mix for start-up promotion was modified in 2014 with the introduction of new conditions and tools to promote start-ups in regions. In fact, ensuring equal opportunities has become a priority in start-up promotion. Start-Up Chile's first assessments in 2015 had revealed the limits of a "space-blind" start-up policy. Most of the beneficiaries were located in Santiago, the capital city, meaning that opportunities were being missed to link start-up creation to existing production ecosystems outside Santiago's metropolitan area, such as the agro-food industries, mining, fishery and forestry, to name but a few. Start-ups in these regions face higher barriers in accessing finance and services. In response to the need for greater inclusiveness, Chile introduced new programmes and reformed the conditions of existing programmes:

- Regional Pro-Entrepreneurship Programmes (PRAEs): Introduced in 2014, the PRAEs co-finance start-ups with high growth potential and specifically those with the potential to reach growth of above 20% during the first three years. CORFO provides non-repayable contributions covering up to 75% of the total cost of the project with a maximum of CLP 25 million (USD 34 000). Applications are submitted via one of CORFO's approved sponsors.
- The Environment Support Programme for Entrepreneurship and PAEI-Regional Innovation: Introduced in 2015, this programme aims to create a more business-oriented culture and raise business skills in the regions. It co-finances programmes

that have a substantial regional impact and that promote entrepreneurship and innovation. CORFO subsidises up to 70% of the project costs, up to a maximum of CLP 50 million (USD 68 000).

- Start-Up Chile has opened regional offices in Valparaíso and Concepción, and in 2015 it began to offer the Go-Regional incentive, which consists of a CLP 5 million (USD 6 800) non-repayable contribution – in addition to the CLP 20 million (USD 27 500) under its Seed Programme – for start-ups to locate in regions. As of 2016, after two editions of Start-Up with this additional incentive, 23 start-ups had benefited from the Go-Regional incentive by moving into the regions: 15 in Valparaíso, 8 in Concepción.
- The Support for Operating Collaborative Workspaces for Entrepreneurship programme also has a regional focus. Created in 2005, the programme supports the opening of collaborative workspaces – co-working spaces, laboratories and accelerators – in regions with few incubators or accelerators. It covers 75% of the project costs in the form of a non-repayable capital contribution, up to a maximum of CLP 200 million (USD 145 000). The first stage of the programme focuses on turning the cities of Antofagasta, Valparaíso and Concepción into new innovation hubs. By the end of 2015, Chile had 30 collaborative workspaces for entrepreneurs in the regions. One example is the CoWork Espacio Atacama centre in Antofagasta, which was formed by a partnership between CORFO, Chrysalis and the Pontífica Universidad Católica's business incubator in Valparaíso, along with Fundación Mi Norte, Universidad Católica del Norte, and Corporación Incuba. The centre has air-conditioned rooms for meetings and spaces for training, and provides mentoring, training, legal and accounting services.

Since the instruments to support start-ups in the regions began operating as recently as 2014, it is still too early to assess their impact. However, there are signs that they are having positive results. According to information released by CORFO's Entrepreneurship Division in 2016, thanks to instruments such as co-working, the concentration of start-ups in Santiago has fallen from 75% to around 50%. Temuco, for instance, is positioning itself as a dynamic area for the creation of technology based firms.

The place-based approach to economic transformation is still in its infancy

The current national agenda for economic transformation is accompanied by an explicit concern for the territorial dimension. This marks a departure from earlier industrial policy efforts, in which the regional dimension was only taken into account as a way of compensating for the agglomeration effects of industrialisation. Today, the rationale for addressing the regional dimension is broadening; compensation remains crucial for certain areas and aspects, but territories are increasingly seen as new sources of innovation and growth. At the global level, regions and cities are becoming key units for the planning and implementation of actions to support economic transformation. The city of Paris, for example, is active in promoting start-up creation, while the Italian region of Emilia Romagna has a dedicated ministry for employment, development and education. Despite its initial efforts in 2007 to create the RDAs, Chile is still at an incipient phase.

As in other countries, the role of the regions is shaped by Chile's institutional framework (Table 2.6). In Brazil and India, subnational governments enjoy a significant role in mobilising industrial and innovation policy. In China, the central government maintains strong control over local authorities by appointing them, but in practice local authorities have ample room for manoeuvre in policy planning and implementation (Xu, 2011). The role of regions in transformation strategies also changes over time. In Korea, for example, during the catching-up phase regional authorities were directly appointed by the central government and had little autonomy. From the late 1990s, the country engaged in successive reforms to strengthen the role of regions by increasing the allocation of resources to regional development (OECD, 2012).

Table 2.6. The variety of institutional frameworks for "place-based" transformation strategies, selected economies

Degree of planning and financing responsibilities in industrial and innovation policy of sub-national governments	National multilevel governance setting		
	Federal countries	Unitary countries	
		Elected regional authorities	Non-elected regional authorities
Significant	Brazil, Canada Germany, India Switzerland United States	Italy, Spain	China
Medium	Argentina, Malaysia Mexico The Russian Federation	Colombia, France, Netherlands, Poland, Korea	---
Limited	---	Chile, Denmark, Japan, Peru, South Africa, Turkey	Finland, Ireland, Indonesia, Morocco

Note: China, India and Indonesia have multiple relevant institutions at different sub-national government levels with responsibilities for industrial, scientific and technological development with non-elected authorities. Significant responsibility in industry and innovation does not imply better performance, or a judgement of value; it refers to a different organisation and it implies different policy options. The degree of devolution of competences in innovation-related matters is subject to change. Information reported in this table refers to the first semester of 2010 for OECD countries, and to the second semester of 2011 for non-OECD economies.

Source: OECD (2013), Perspectives on Global Development 2013: Industrial Policies in a Changing World, http://dx.doi.org/10.1787/persp_glob_dev-2013-en. Draws on and updates OECD (2011), Regions and Innovation Policy, http://dx.doi.org/10.1787/9789264097803-en; and OECD (2012), Industrial Policy and Territorial Development: Lessons from Korea, http://dx.doi.org/10.1787/9789264173897-en.

Economic transformation never happens in a balanced way within countries. But successful economies tend to put in place mechanisms to ensure that territories' potential is enhanced by national strategies and that excessive disparities within nations are avoided. Often, growth, investment and innovation take place in specific locations within countries, while most of the territories tend to lag behind. If not counterbalanced by "place-based" policies, this trend may create social tensions and undermine potential future growth by neglecting new sources of growth and contributing to decreasing returns in large-urban agglomerations. Some countries are backing up national transformation strategies with regional policies. Regional actors, if empowered with responsibilities and resources, can be powerful allies in implementing policies for industrial development.

To increase the voice of regions in strategy setting, highly centralised countries need to change their way of functioning. Effective transformation strategies require governance mechanisms that take into account territorial perspectives. This goes beyond territorial planning, to view the territory and local communities as repositories of the knowledge, know-how and capabilities that help to define the uniqueness and the competitive advantage of nations. The government needs to learn how to work with its territories, its constituencies and its population to reveal their priorities and identify a shared vision for the future (Figure 2.17). This means creating effective spaces for dialogue with regional stakeholders and accepting that these processes do not happen overnight – they require time and continuous effort. Regional development policy debate is shifting to a new paradigm: initially it was focused on the equalisation of regions. In the 1990s/2000s the emphasis was on the competitiveness of regions. Today, the debate in the OECD is shifting towards a more comprehensive approach that takes into account the overall wellbeing of citizens (OECD, 2016a). This requires recognising and taking into account the specific needs of low-density regional ecosystems.

Figure 2.17. **Enabling territories to be agents of change**

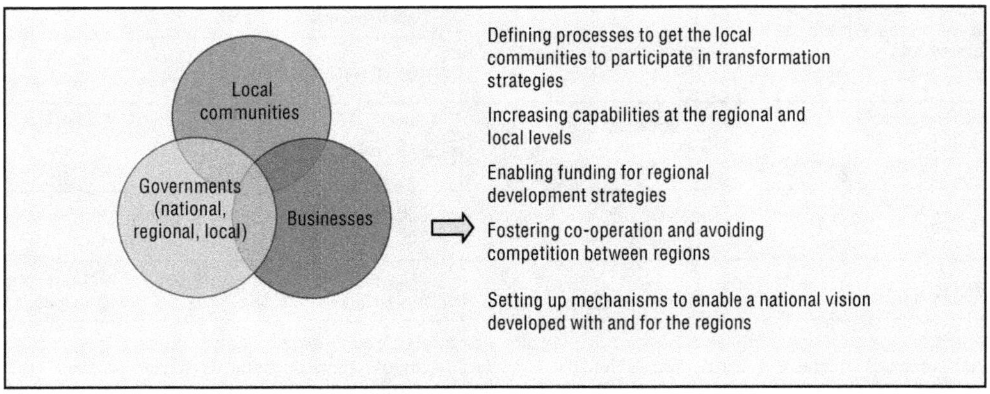

Source: OECD (2017), Key Outcomes of the Peer Learning Group (PLG) Meeting of the PTPR of Chile, hosted by the OECD in Paris, May 2017.

The international experience offers lessons and good practices for economic transformation and regional development:

- **Production transformation strategies need to take territorial perspectives into account as a starting point, regardless of the level of centralisation of the country.** For example, Slovenia is a fairly centralised country, yet it has developed a system to involve and work with regional stakeholders to foster competitiveness and industrial development. A key dimension is creating the right environment for business development. In Slovenia, for example, regions are central actors in the promotion of interactions and co-operation among firms and the technological system, including incubators, accelerators, technology transfer offices, and creative economy centres.
- **Avoid focusing on innovation only**: everything needs to be provided at the same time. Competitive territories offer dense and trust-rich environments in which education, standards and norms, infrastructure, financing and services are available. In the 2000s, there had been too much emphasis on solely promoting innovation and/or human capital, while successful experiences show the need for a more comprehensive approach. In particular, it is important to create spaces for aligning norms, infrastructure and services to the priorities of the strategy. This is a systematic effort that requires trust and social capital across the whole production and innovation system. For example, in promoting smart specialisation in Emilia Romagna (an already substantially developed and industrialised region of Italy), incentives for R&D, support to entrepreneurship, efforts to attract FDI, training, and export promotion are all coordinated under a vision of the region and for the region. The policy mix is included in a seven-year framework and endowed with an initial public investment of USD 700 million, complemented by private funds for investments up to at least 50% of the initial public investment.
- **Redefining the "regions"**. On the one hand, it is important to look beyond administrative borders to identify economic and functional regions. This can avoid duplicating efforts and can increase impact. Often, a production and innovation ecosystem spans administrative boundaries; transformation strategies need to take economic, social and geographical realities into account. This is particularly relevant for tradable activities for which the value chain often passes through several regions. Another issue is to refine the definition of rural areas. The OECD is already exploring better ways to define rural areas through criteria such as remoteness and/or proximity to given economic and functional regions.

- **Implementing effective mechanisms for resource transfers.** Setting up mechanisms for resource transfers and checks and balances between the national government and the regions through contract plans will avoid duplicated effort and wasted resources.

The EU's smart specialisation strategy is one of the most relevant and recent experimental efforts for enabling diversification and industrial development. The strategy rests on the principle that territories are repositories of knowledge and know-how. It has mobilised EUR 65 billion to enable the definition and implementation of regional specialisation strategies in EU regions, fostering dialogue and knowledge-sharing among actors in local production and innovation systems. The strategy enables actions from a bottom-up perspective at the regional, national and EU levels, with a view to identifying needs and opportunities, and to then provide support in the form of financing, services and infrastructure at the most appropriate level (Box 2.6).

Box 2.6. **Place-based transformation policies: lessons from the EU smart specialisation strategy**

While it is too soon for a comprehensive impact assessment of the EU Smart Specialisation strategy, four key success factors can be identified:

- **Triggering the interest of regions to participate.** The interest of regions in these policy changes cannot be taken for granted. Some systems might simply want to preserve their current position or resist change. In addition, not all regions will be proactive in the same way, so investment is needed to explain the strategy and clarify the potential benefits.
- **Shifting the focus from document development to action.** A key element of the EU approach is to enable a constructive dialogue among businesses, the government, academia and civil society. The regions that have managed to implement this approach effectively did so not in a bureaucratic way, but by identifying actions that could trigger change in the region. The development of the regional strategy document was considered as a means, not an end.
- **Taking history into account.** Within and between countries, regions differ greatly in terms of their institutional setting, history and culture. The EU strategy needs to value and recognise these differences if it is to be effective. Some regions focus on strengthening their historical richness, while others used the smart specialisation to reinvent themselves in light of potential future opportunities.
- **Achieving strong political commitment.** A capable and determined public administration is needed to translate interactions among businesses, academia and civil society into actionable strategies and policy tools.

Source: OECD (2017), Key Outcomes of the Peer Learning Group (PLG) Meeting of the PTPR of Chile, hosted by the OECD in Paris, May 2017.

To advance in a place-based approach in production transformation, Chile will need to (Table 2.7):

- Advance in its decentralisation process by finding the approach that best suits its historical and overall institutional arrangement.
- Set up mechanisms for resource transfers and define contract plans between the central government and the regions. These are essential components of the effective implementation of Chile's decentralisation strategy.
- Explore meso-regional approaches in strategy setting and implementation, and take into account the specific needs of remote and low populated areas.
- Explore international cross-regional co-operation. This will also be important for certain production ecosystems, especially in the north and in the south of the country.

Table 2.7. **Increasing the "place-based" approach in Chilean policies: priorities and challenges**

Priorities
• Advance in the decentralisation of industrial and territorial policies by enabling effective regional autonomy and intensifying the dialogue with local actors.
• Create mechanisms for identifying local priorities based on territorial assets and visions and to create spaces for allowing these priorities to be part of the process of priority setting at the national level.
• Identify mechanisms to implement actions that go beyond each region's strengths and that exploit the synergies and complementarities among regions.
• Shift from experimentation to effective and well-funded regional strategies, with clear strategic objectives and good governance and support.
Current challenges
• Increasing the involvement of the local community in national territorial planning and economic diversification strategies.
• The centralised tax collection system, which hinders the fiscal capacity of municipalities and limits possibilities to create more diversified local economies.
• The mechanisms to support lagging/less developed regions, which would benefit from revisions.
• The concentration of political and economic powers in the capital city, which might translate into diseconomies of scale and mega-urbanisation challenges for Santiago, and in growing social tensions and underutilisation of the growth potential in other areas of the country.
• Weak capacity at the regional and local level, which hinder the capacity of the state to act as an effective planner and implementer.

Source: OECD (2017), Key Outcomes of the Peer Learning Group (PLG) Meeting of the PTPR of Chile, hosted by the OECD in Paris, May 2017.

References

Bitar, S. (2013), "Why and how Latin America should think about the future", *Global Trends and the Future of Latin America*, Inter-American Development Bank, Washington D.C.

Boneu, F., D. Alfaro Serranc, A. Maffioli, C. Pietrobelli, R. Stucchi, G. Casaburi and A. Matta (2016), "The impact evaluation of cluster development programs: Methods and practices", Inter-American Development Bank, Washington DC, https://publications.iadb.org/handle/11319/7605.

Cheyre, H., G. Larraín, G. Rivas and K. Schmidt-Hebbel (2016), "A common view and four proposals for promoting productive development in Chile", mimeo.

Corvalán Quiroz, Pezo Villar, D. (2014), "Growth and convergence in Chilean regions 1960-2010", Universidad de Playa Ancha, Valparaíso, Chile.

CPC (2016), Informe Anual de Productividad.

Crespi, G. et al. (2014), ¿Cómo repensar el desarrollo productivo? Políticas e instituciones sólidas para la transformación económica, Inter-American Development Bank, Washington, D.C.

Emilia Romagna (2015), Patto per il lavoro (labour pact), Bologna.

FDI Markets (2017), *FDI Markets*, database, a service from the Financial Times Ltd, https://www.fdimarkets.com.

Frigolett, H. (2013), "Economías regionales en Chile: desigualdad y heterogeneidad", Documento de Trabajo No. 2, Serie Estudios Territoriales. Programa Cohesión Territorial para el Desarrollo, Rimisp, Santiago, Chile.

Government of Chile (2014), "Productivity, Innovation and Growth Agenda" (agenda de productividad, innovación y crecimiento), http://www.agendaproductividad.cl/sobre-la-agenda/, Santiago, Chile.

Griffith-Jones, S., M. L. Martínez Sola and J, Petersen (2017), "The role of CORFO in Chile's Development: Achievements and Challenges", BNDES and CAF Project on Development Banks.

IDB/OECD (2010), "Strengthening institutional capacities for innovation policy design and implementation in Chile", *Social Sector Science and Technology Division Technical Note*, No. IDB-TN-130, Inter-American Development Bank, Washington D.C., http://services.iadb.org/wmsfiles/products/Publications/35166758.pdf.

JRC (2017), *The 2016 EU Industrial R&D Investment Scoreboard*, database, No. JRC103716, Joint Research Centre, Brussels, http://iri.jrc.ec.europa.eu/scoreboard16.html

Marcel, M. (2016), "Economía y Territorio: Existe una Relación entre Desarrollo Territorial, Crecimiento e Inclusión?", in *El Arranque de la Descentralización: Desatando las Amarras del Centralismo Chileno*, Edited by Universidad de la Frontera, Temuco, Chile, December.

OECD (2017a), *Production Transformation Policy Reviews: Actions to Succeed in a Changing World*, OECD. Publishing, Paris, http://dx.doi.org/10.1787/9789264276628-en.

OECD (2017b), *The Next Production Revolution: Implications for Governments and Business*, OECD Publishing, Paris. http://dx.doi.org/10.1787/9789264271036-en.

OECD (2017c), "Making trade work for all", *OECD Trade Policy Papers*, No. 202, OECD Publishing, Paris. http://dx.doi.org/10.1787/6e27effd-en.

OECD (2017d), Key Outcomes of the Peer Learning Group (PLG) Meeting of the PTPR of Chile, hosted by the OECD in Paris, May, 2017

OECD (2016a), "Chile", in *OECD Regional Outlook 2016: Productive Regions for Inclusive Societies*, OECD Publishing, Paris, http://dx.doi.org/10.1787/9789264260245-en.

OECD (2016b), Start-up Latin America 2016: Building an Innovative Future, OECD Publishing, Paris, http://dx.doi.org/10.1787/9789264265660-en.

OECD (2014), *Perspectives on Global Development 2014: Boosting Productivity to Meet the Middle-Income Challenge*, OECD Publishing, Paris, http://dx.doi.org/10.1787/persp_glob_dev-2014-en.

OECD (2013a), *Perspectives on Global Development 2013: Industrial Policies in a Changing World*, OECD Publishing, Paris, http://dx.doi.org/10.1787/persp_glob_dev-2013-en.

OECD (2013b), *Start-up Latin America: Promoting Innovation in the Region*, OECD Publishing, Paris, http://dx.doi.org/10.1787/9789264202306-en.

OECD (2012), *Industrial Policy and Territorial Development: Lessons from Korea*, OECD Publishing, Paris, http://dx.doi.org/10.1787/9789264173897-en.

OECD (2011), *Regions and Innovation Policy*, OECD Publishing, OECD, Paris, http://dx.doi.org/10.1787/9789264097803-en.

OECD (2009), *OECD Territorial Reviews: Chile 2009*, OECD Publishing, Paris, http://dx.doi.org/10.1787/9789264060791-en.

UNCTAD (2017), *Trade and Development Report 2017/Beyond Austerity - Towards a Global New Deal*, ISBN: 9789211129137.

UNCTAD (2016), *Trade and Development Report 2016 - Structural transformation for inclusive and sustained growth*, United Nations Publication, New York and Geneva.

Xu, C. (2011), "The fundamental institutions of China's reforms and development", *Journal of Economic Literature*, American Economic Association, 49(4): 1076-1151.

Zilic, F. (2014), "Biobío Región Maderera. Una propuesta de valor agregado para la madera", Polomadera, Universidad de Concepción.

Chapter 3

Transforming industries: Perspectives on solar energy, mining and agro-food in Chile

The shifting global geopolitical and technological landscape coupled with changes in consumers' preferences is opening up a window of opportunity for Chile. The country could transform its economy, enlarge its knowledge base and increase productivity by leveraging on its natural assets in new, more innovative ways. However, the world is moving fast and opportunities will not be permanently available. To tap into them, a strategic approach and a shared vision between government, business and society is needed. Chile has started to do so through strategic initiatives that identify future opportunities and clarify gaps to be addressed. This chapter presents the Chilean experience in solar energy, mining and agro-food; in each case it presents a snapshot of key trends and future scenarios, developed through multi-stakeholder consultations, it describes the current policy approach and it identifies reforms to move forward.

Unleashing the potential of solar energy in Chile

This section presents a snapshot of the rise of solar energy in the country and summarises the results of public-private consultations on the opportunities presented by solar for Chile. It describes the current policy approach and it identifies reforms to move forward.

Solar energy is gaining ground in Chile

Solar energy is becoming globally competitive thanks to falling prices. Investment in the development of renewable energies globally is surpassing investment in fossil fuel technologies (OECD, 2018; IEA, 2016). Of these, investment in solar has increased the most since 2010. Global investment in the installation of solar technologies accounted for half of all investments in renewables in 2016 (Figure 3.1). High investment by the People's Republic of China in solar photovoltaic (PV), and the consequent reduction in module prices, have contributed to the substantial reduction in the cost of generating energy from the sun (Mathews, 2017). Solar energy has experienced the biggest price decline of all renewables, with the levelised cost of electricity (LCOE) for PV falling by 67% between 2010 and 2016 (Figure 3.2). Prices, of course, vary by location: China and India have the cheapest energy from solar PV (with a weighted average LCOE of utility-scale solar PV at USD 0.09 per kWh in 2016, down 68% from 2010). In OECD countries the average cost is USD 0.14 per kilowatt-hour (kWh), which has fallen by 61% since 2010. In the rest of the world the average cost is USD 0.17 per kWh. In 2016, the cheapest prices for PV were awarded through public bids in Abu Dhabi (USD 0.024 per kWh), Mexico (USD 0.026 per kWh) and Chile (USD 0.029 per kWh). The global record of USD 0.017 per kWh was registered in the second quarter of 2017 in Dubai (IEA, 2017b).

Figure 3.1. **Solar is capturing the lion's share of global investment in renewables**

Global investment by renewable energy technology, 2004-15

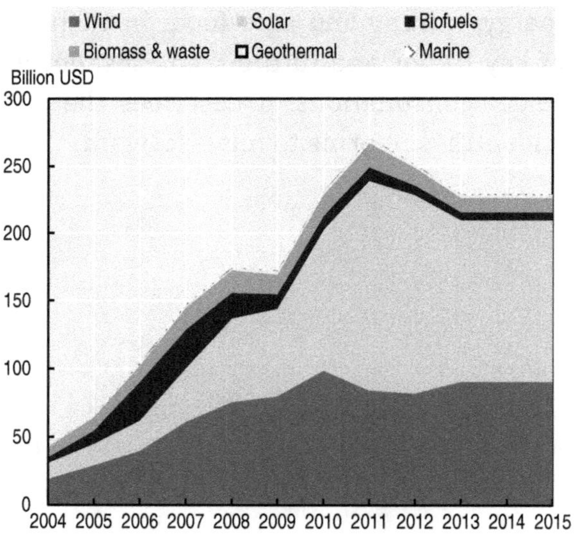

Source: Authors' analysis based on IEA (2016), "Statistics", and Global Trends in Renewable Energy Investment 2016. https://www.iea.org/statistics/

Chile is currently Latin America's main solar energy producer. Since 2008, non-conventional renewable energies (NCREs) have been gaining ground in Chile.[1] Biomass was the first to appear on a large scale, accounting for 175 megawatts (MW) in 2009, rising to 343 MW in 2013. Wind and solar then started to gain ground. By 2017, solar represented 43% of the NCRE capacity installed in Chile, at more than 1800 MW (Figure 3.3). Today, Chile leads solar energy production in Latin America, accounting for almost half of the total installed capacity in the region (Figure 3.4). This expansion has been coupled with record world prices. Indeed, in 2017, Chile and the United Arab Emirates earned the world record for the lowest prices, signing contracts for solar PV projects at below 0.03 USD/KWh for 2018 (IEA, 2017b).

Figure 3.2. **Solar PV has seen costs fall the most, 2010-16**

Average, minimum and maximum price, constant USD (2016)/kWh, by renewable energy source

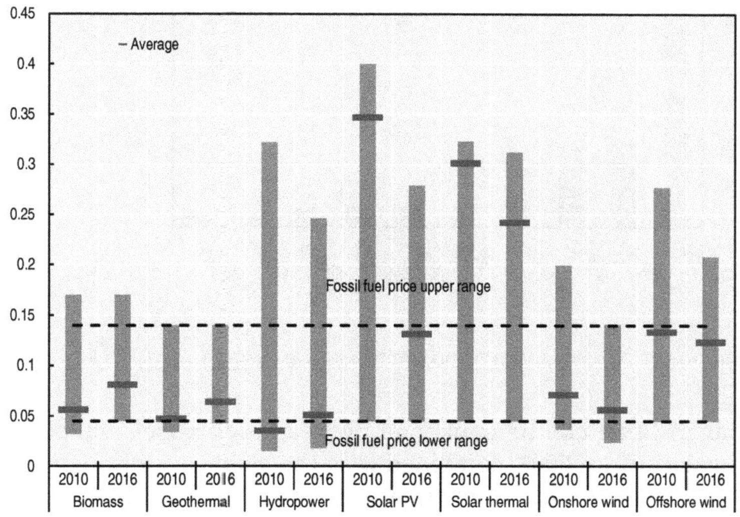

Note: Dashed line shows fossil fuel upper and lower price ranges.

Source: Authors' analysis based on IRENA (2017), IRENA Dashboard, http://resourceirena.irena.org/gateway/dashboard/

Figure 3.3. **Solar leads in installed electricity capacity in Chile, 2000-17**

Non-Conventional Renewable Energies (NCRE) installed capacity by energy type

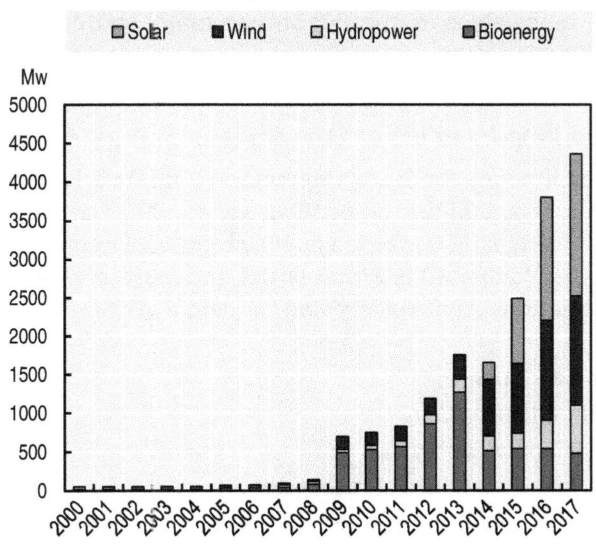

Source: Authors' analysis based on IRENA (2017), IRENA Dashboard, http://resourceirena.irena.org/gateway/dashboard; and official information from the Ministry of Energy of Chile, 2017.

Figure 3.4. **Chile is Latin America's biggest solar energy producer**

Installed capacity in solar energy, 2016

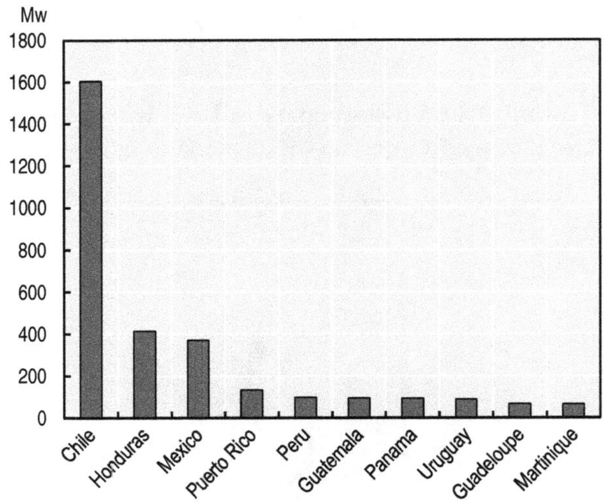

Source: Authors' analysis based on IRENA (2017), IRENA Dashboard, http://resourceirena.irena.org/gateway/dashboard/

The rise of solar in Chile can be explained by its energy policy, which has offered incentives for renewables since 2008, combined with the global evolution of the industry. Chile was a relative latecomer in introducing targets for renewable energy in its domestic energy policy (Table 3.1). Law 20.257 of 2008 implemented a target for electricity generators and/or suppliers to source at least 5% of their electricity needs from NCREs through a Renewable Portfolio Standard (RPS). Having reached the 5% target in 2013, Chile revised it upwards, requesting companies to source at least 20% by 2025 (Law 20.698). The target has been reached again in 2017, eight years in advance. The year 2015 marked a landmark in the energy policy approach as the country approved an energy policy with a road map towards 2050. This agenda was developed, for the first time in the country, through a multi-stakeholder consultation process that defined a shared national long-term vision for energy. In this policy, renewables matter not only as major sources of energy, but also as development drivers (Box 3.1).

Box 3.1. **A shared long-term vision: the Chilean Energy Agenda 2050**

The vision of the national policy for 2050, approved in 2015, is a landmark in Chile's energy policy-making process. Building on previous efforts, it is the first to set shared, agreed long-term goals. The agenda was based on the proposal of a committee chaired by the Minister of Energy, and composed of 27 ministries and representatives of key public institutions, trade associations, civil society and academia. The agenda rests on four pillars:

1. Supply quality and security
2. Energy as a driver of development
3. Environmentally-friendly energy
4. Energy education for efficient use of resources.

The agenda sets ambitious goals, including generating at least 60% of energy from renewables by 2035 and 70% by 2050, and reducing greenhouse gas emissions (GHG) by 30% by 2030.

Source: Ministry of Energy (2017a), "Chile, Energy 2050: Chile Energy Policy", http://pelp.minenergia.cl/

Table 3.1. **Chile came relatively late to the renewable energy agenda**

Energy policies for renewables, selected countries, 1978-2016

Year	RPS (quota policies)	Feed-in tariff
1978		United States
1983	United States	
1988		Portugal
1990		Germany
1991		Switzerland
1992		Italy
1993		Denmark; India
1994		Luxembourg; Spain; Greece
1997		Sri Lanka
1998		Sweden
1999	Italy	
1999		Norway; Slovenia
2001	Australia; Flanders (Belgium)	
2001		Armenia; France; Latvia
2002	United Kingdom; Wallonia (Belgium)	
2002		Algeria; Austria; Brazil; Czech Republic; Indonesia; Lithuania
2003	Japan; Portugal; Sweden	
2003		Cyprus; Estonia; Hungary; Slovak Republic; Republic of Korea
2004	Poland	
2004		Canada; Israel; Nicaragua
2005		China; Ecuador; Ireland; Turkey
2006		Argentina; Pakistan; Thailand
2007	China	
2007		Albania; Australia; Bulgaria; Croatia; Dominican Republic; Finland
2008	Chile; India; Philippines; Romania	
2008		Iran; Kenya; Liechtenstein; Philippines; San Marino
2009		Japan; Serbia; South Africa; Ukraine
2010	Republic of Korea	
2010		Belarus; Bosnia and Herzegovina; Malaysia; United Kingdom
2011	Albania;	
2011		Ghana; Montenegro; Netherlands; Syria; Viet Nam
2012	Norway	
2012		Jordan; Nigeria; State of Palestine; Rwanda; Uganda
2013		Kazakhstan; Pakistan
2014		Egypt; Vanuatu
2016		Czech Republic

Source: based on Sawin, J., K. Seyboth and F. Sverrisson (2016), REN21 Renewables Global Status Report 2016, www.ren21.net/wp-conten

All scenarios estimate that solar will be the leading energy source in Chile by 2045. The Ministry of Energy is scanning for possible futures. It has developed five future scenarios based on global trends and domestic conditions, and the parametrisation of multiple factors, including future demand, rate of technological change, environmental externalities and cost of investment (Ministry of Energy, 2017). In all five scenarios, solar dominates the domestic energy matrix of the future, ranging from 30% to 47% of the installed capacity by 2045 (Figure 3.5). PV is identified in all scenarios as the main solar energy type. Only two scenarios identify concentrated solar power (CSP) as another important form of solar energy generation. This is due to the high projected increase in energy demand (3.2% annual average) derived from the expansion of electro-mobility, the electrification of heating in apartments, and a high penetration of air cooling in the residential sector, coupled with the expected increase in the price of fossil fuels (for example, assuming a price for diesel oil of around USD 1 200/m3 in 2045).

Figure 3.5. **Five scenarios for energy in Chile by 2045**

Share of installed capacity by energy source

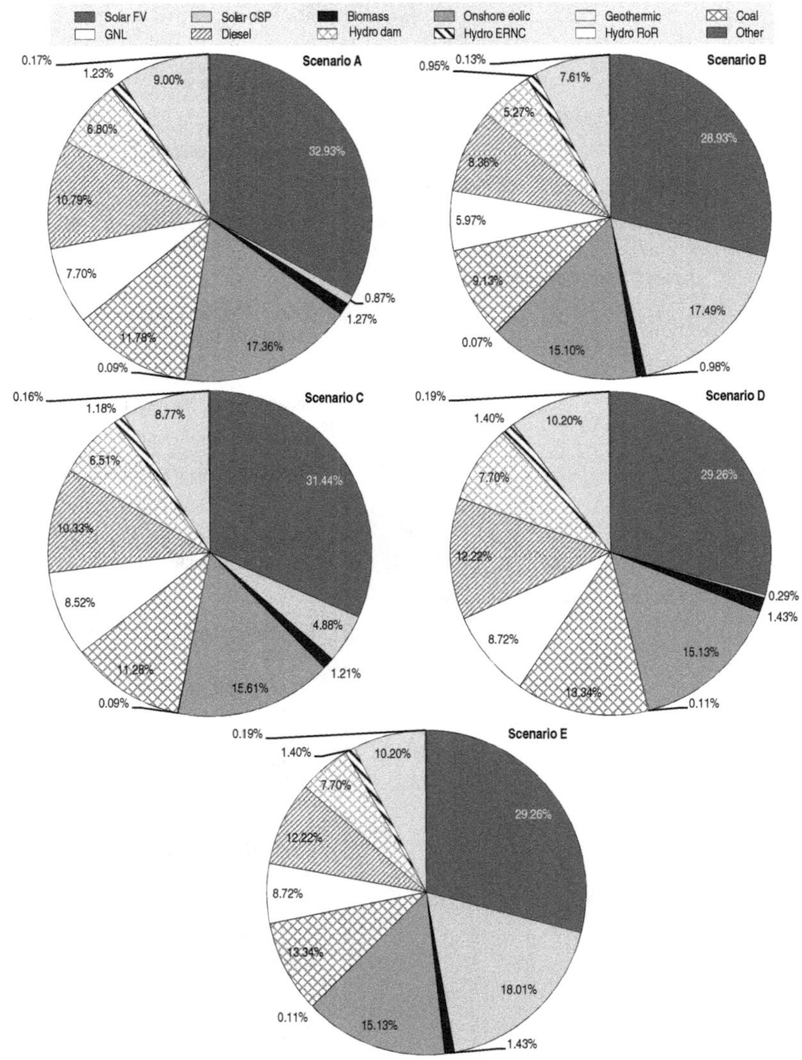

Note: CSP (concentrated solar power); LNG (liquefied natural gas), NCRE (non-conventional renewable energy). The scenarios are based on the parametrisation of six factors: social licences, energy demand, technological change in batteries storage, environmental externalities, cost of investment in renewables, and cost of fossil fuels. The combination of each factor along three different parameters led to the definition of five scenarios for 2045. For further information visit http://pelp.minenergia.cl/

Source: Authors' analysis based on Ministry of Energy (2017b), Long-Term Strategic Planning Database.

Solar could be the next driver of development

Chile's natural endowments, together with falling renewable energy prices and ongoing technological changes, open up a window of opportunities. Solar energy can help not only to green the energy matrix, but also to transform the economy and its growth model. The Atacama Desert in the north of Chile has a surface of 105 000 km2, receives 4 000 hours of sun a year, has the highest solar incidence in the world at 3 500 kWh/m2 DNI (direct normal irradiance), and UV-B radiation 65% above the European average. These unique geographical and geological conditions give Chile the opportunity to benefit from very cheap solar electricity, as well as thermal energy (Figure 3.6). In addition to the positive impact on mining and manufacturing, cheap electricity could also alleviate Chile's dependence on fossil fuel imports, which represent 70% of the country's total primary energy supply (in 2016). These are dominated by petroleum products (41%), followed by coal (19%) and natural gas (10%).

PV and concentrated solar power (CSP) are the two main technologies in the solar industry, and entail different value chains. The core component of PV is its cells, which are made out of a semiconducting material that transforms sunlight directly into electricity, whereas CSP generates electricity by using sunlight to heat a fluid that is then used to produce electricity. CSP needs greater economies of scale than PVs; the latter can be installed in smaller projects. Chile imports most PV modules from China, which accounted for 96% of the total imported PVs in 2016. Unlike PV technology, CSP has the advantage of being able to store energy. A CSP plant is currently under construction in the Atacama Desert; upon completion the plant is expected to have 110 MW of installed capacity and 17.5 hours of thermal storage. World-leading companies are planning to set up more CSP plants in the north of Chile. In addition, there are prospects for hydroelectric seawater pumped storage; combined with these new solar photovoltaic plants, Chile could be guaranteed a reliable, sustainable and permanent source of electricity.

Figure 3.6. **The solar value chain: natural endowments and potential impacts of PV and CSP in Chile**

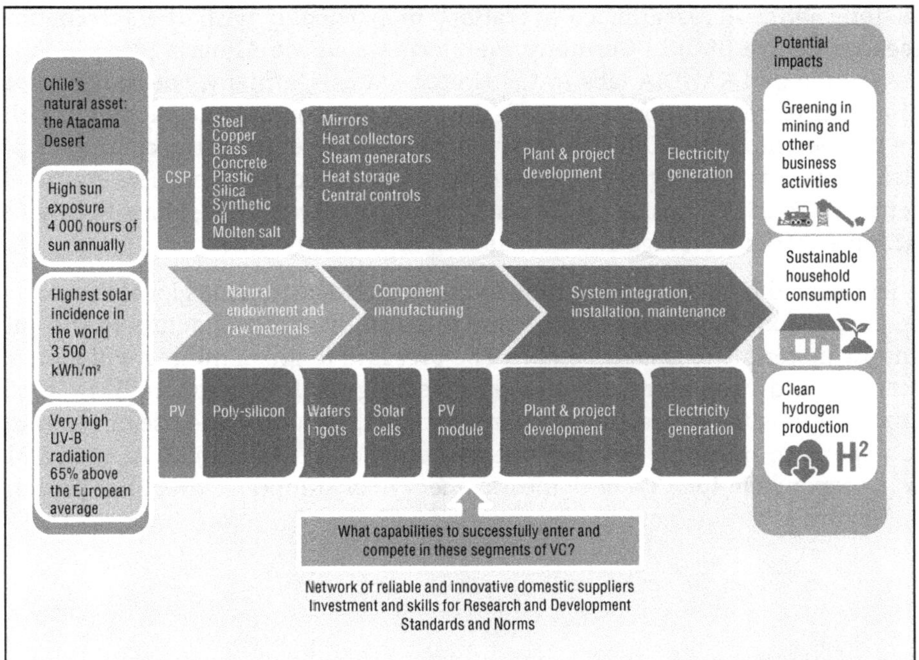

Source: Authors' analysis based on the outcomes of the Round Table on the Future of Solar Energy in Chile organised in the framework of the PTPR of Chile, hosted by CORFO in Santiago, Chile in June 2017.

Solar energy could also open up new opportunities for learning and innovation. Solar energy is the result of high value-added activities (Figure 3.6). Unlike fossil-fuel based energies, solar is not extracted through drilling or mining. It involves a manufacturing value chain and can be produced and used locally (Mathews, 2017). In PV, the space for local manufacturing suppliers is quite limited, as the industry has already developed based on PVs imported as ready-made packaged solutions into the country. Nevertheless the development of specific applications for high temperature and highly irradiated zones could be an opportunity for Chile to expand its knowledge base and take its first steps along the value chain. CSP offers more scope for business opportunities as the design, deployment and maintenance of CSP technologies require scientific and technical capabilities that are specific to the context in which the plants operate. In addition, in the case of Chile, existing technologies and business models need to be adapted to the specific local solar irradiation patterns in order to increase their profitability and effectiveness.

Innovating and identifying solutions for solar energy will require shared efforts from all actors in the ecosystem, including energy providers, academia and government. Chile already hosts world-leading energy providers, including Engie, Enel, SanEdison, SENER, Acciona and Abengoa. These players are important investors in Chile. Investments in electricity and energy projects accounted for 46% of total greenfield investments and 15% of all jobs created in Chile between 2013 and 2016. Over the same period, greenfield investments in solar accounted for USD 8.1 billion (Chapter 1). Establishing partnerships with these players could open up important innovation opportunities. For example solar thermal technology has been used worldwide for sanitary heating, but industrial applications that require higher temperatures (i.e. smelting) are emerging thanks to developments in CSP technologies. This is an important field of innovation as it applies to areas such as use, transfer and storage of heat for industrial processes and buildings.

Chile is exploring opportunities to strengthen its learning and knowledge base through global partnerships. Since 2011, Chile has been hosting the Solar Energy Research Centre (SERC) – a network of researchers and institutions focusing on solar energy. SERC is actively engaged in international research co-operation, in particular with the International Energy Research Centre (ISC) in Germany; Plataforma Solar de Almeria (PSA) in Spain; and NREL, Argonne and SANDIA labs in the United States. Germany, which has a long-standing tradition of cooperation with Chile in multiple economic development fields, has set up a partnership with CORFO to establish a research centre in the country as part of the Chilean government support for strengthening applied research. The Fraunhofer research centre (FCR-CSET), hosted by the Catholic University of Chile, plans to carry out applied R&D on electricity storage and heat as well as water treatment.

Solar energy could help to green mining in Chile. There is growing global demand for sustainable production. Greening the economy implies involving all actors in the value chain, from raw materials to final assembly. The pressure to green mining will increase. In fact, leading world companies are already investing in this direction. This implies searching for solutions to reduce environmental impact, including the use of renewable energies to cope with mining's growing energy demand. In Chile, in 2000, the mining industry was responsible for 13% of domestic energy consumption; that share reached 20% in 2015 (Figure 3.7).

Figure 3.7. **Final energy consumption by economic activity, Chile 2000-15**

Ton of oil equivalent (toe)

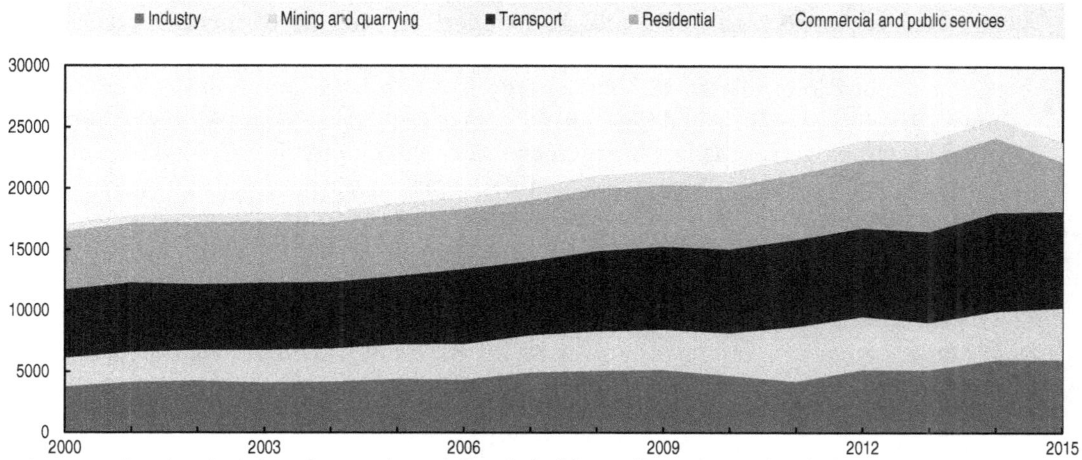

Source: Authors' analysis based on IEA (2017a), "Statistics", https://www.iea.org/statistics.

To realise the potential benefits of participating to the solar value chain, Chile faces several barriers (Table 3.2):

1. **Building capabilities in a rapidly changing technological environment takes time** and requires benefiting from global research and production networks. It has taken China more than two decades to become the main producer in solar PV modules (Quitzow, 2015). Production and trade linkages between Chinese manufacturers and German equipment makers and buyers, and R&D partnerships with global research centres, have played important roles in deepening China's technological capabilities in the industry (Quitzow, 2015). Chile could build on its reputation as a reliable partner and scale up its efforts to co-operate within the region and globally in this field.
2. **Chile is a latecomer with respect to leading countries and global competition to lead in the value chain is high**. Asian countries account for 90% of global PV module production, and China alone represents 65% of word PV module production (Sawin et al. 2016). China, Germany, the United States and Japan are the world leaders in this value chain They all have major leading firms, and have accumulated a high critical mass of technological and innovation capabilities, as well as skills and infrastructure. In PV, 14 out of the top 20 patents owners are from Japan and new entrants come mainly from China and Korea. In CSP, 6 of the top 20 patents owners are from Germany and 9 are from China (Helm et al. 2014). Strategic partnerships with investors could open opportunities for developing capabilities in specific segments of the value chain, as in Morocco and India.
3. **The current status of the power grid connection and low spot prices could limit future investments and hamper future development**. Chile's solar industry has expanded quickly but power grid infrastructure has not developed at the same pace. The lack of adequate transmission capacity in the northern section of the SIC (Central Interconnected System) to the additional three southern sections limits the capacity to transmit electricity, resulting in overcapacity in the northern section. To alleviate the solar overcapacity on the SIC, transmission lines and electrical sub stations for its interconnection with the Great Northern Interconnected System (SING) are underway and are supposed to be operative as of 2018. In addition, spot prices in some points of the north reached zero during a few hours of the day due to lack of demand (mostly caused by the reduction in copper prices and the overall

slowdown in GDP growth) and transmission constraints, increasing the operational risks for power plants owners and energy developers.

4. **The lack of specialised skills and knowledge, as well as of technological and innovation infrastructure, could limit the potential to move up the value chain.** Patent applications related to solar energy in Chile have increased considerably since 2012. By 2016, Chile had filed 238 patents in CSP, 70 in PV, and 40 in PV-thermal hybrid technologies. This is a big increase since 2012, when it had filed 59 patents in CSP, 16 in PV and 7 in PV-thermal hybrid. Despite this progress, Chile lags behind other countries in terms of domestic scientific and technical capabilities in this industry. The country's patent filings in solar energy in 2016 made up only 0.01% of total world patent applications in the field (IRENA, 2017).
5. **The social acceptability of solar energy should not be taken for granted.** Currently in Chile, renewable energies, and solar in particular, benefit from high social acceptance. This is due in part to a generalised perception that these energy sources are "good" for the environment and for the people (users and workers in the value chain), and in part to the major social dissatisfaction with big energy projects, such as polluting thermal plants, and the environmental impacts of large hydro-plants. However, the social licence which these energies currently benefit from will not be sustained in the long run if new agreements, negotiations and benefit sharing with local communities are not developed. New forms of dialogue and partnership with local communities will be needed.

Table 3.2. **Multi-stakeholder assessment of the future of solar energy in Chile**

Strengths	Weaknesses
• Strong solar irradiation Abundance of salts for storage for CSP • World biggest lithium reserve • Established presence of world leading energy companies • Long-term & shared vision for the energy policy • Open and stable economy • Existing public-private dialogue through the Solar Energy Strategic Committee	• Late mover in PV manufacturing value chain • Limited grid connection • Scant domestic S&T capabilities • Small domestic market • Low investment R&D • Reduced skills base
Opportunities	**Threats**
• Global rise in electro-mobility • Greening mining • Exporting specialised solutions for desert applications • Self-sustained energy production • Self-production for/in sparsely populated areas • Potential to develop locally adapted solutions for system installation (downstream)	• Desert context may not be ideal for PV (dust) • Technological uncertainty (form of manufacturing & storage technologies) • Social acceptance • Energy spot prices • Slow progress in regional integration • Lack of sustained commitment from leading companies

Source: Authors' analysis based on the outcomes of the Round Table on the Future of Solar Energy in Chile organised in the framework of the PTPR of Chile, hosted by CORFO in Santiago, Chile in June 2017.

The green shift needs a shared long-term vision and strategic actions

Recognising the potential opportunities for Chile offered by solar energy, in 2015 CORFO, in co-operation with the Ministry of Energy, set up public-private consultations to define a road-map for future actions. These consultations led to the identification of three gaps that require public investment if Chile is to maximise the benefits from solar energy:

- weak research and technological capacity, including the lack of a technology centre
- a limited supply chain base
- lack of adequate infrastructure, standards and norms.

In response, in 2016 CORFO set up a strategic solar programme with a time horizon to 2025. In line with international practices, this plans to foster value chain development through several channels (Table 3.3). The programme is managed by a committee chaired by the Minister of Energy and envisages the participation of both public and private sector. The Committee oversees 50 initiatives to address the three gaps, to support private sector development and to favour private investment. In particular, the programme aims to: 1) enable the creation of 100 new firms in the solar value chain; 2) reduce CO2 emissions by 4.5 tons every year; and 3) achieve a LCOE of USD 25 Mw for PV in desert zones. The estimated budget for the programme is USD 800 million up until 2025, of which approximately 15% is expected to be financed by the public sector and the rest by private stakeholders. For the period 2015-2018, USD 22 million have been financed by the government (CORFO, through the FIE and FIC), and USD 1.8 million by the private sector.

In particular, the solar programme encompasses actions in the following areas:

- **Technology and skills development.** Chile is helping to set up R&D consortia, and attracting foreign direct investment by creating conditions for investors to enter and co-finance innovation. The main action in this field includes the creation of the International Institute of Solar and Mining (IISM) to foster applied research in solar energy, mining and production of clean hydrogen and other energy-storage components. The estimated cost of the project is USD 94 million up to 2025 for building the infrastructure and the initial operational costs. Approximately, the private investment for the next ten years will amount to USD 80 million. The remaining USD 14 million will be conveyed through CORFO's fund for Technology Centres for Innovation. The International Institute of Solar and Mining (IISM) plans initially to employ 35 researchers who seek to develop applied research industrial applications. The country is also planning to finance a ten-year R&D programme to adapt PV technologies to high radiation conditions through a consortium involving local and international universities, research centres and firms.
- **Supply chain development.** Chile is planning to facilitate supply chain development in two main ways: 1) though an open platform, launched in 2017 and managed by Fundación Chile, to match demand and supply for developing solutions for operating in desert conditions; and 2) by setting up standards and regulations, including by standardising measurement, testing, and certification processes associated with the design, development, construction, operation and maintenance of solar power generation systems, as well as by setting standards linked to component design and manufacturing processes for specialised desert solar technologies. This appears crucial given the climate conditions that might affect the durability and performance of photovoltaic systems in the Atacama Desert.
- **Infrastructure development.** This involves 1) building a Solar Technology District, a large-scale generation plant that is expected to facilitate the development of specialised solutions for solar power generation and storage, as well as the participation of domestic suppliers by allowing all the actors in the supply chain to be located near one another; and 2) investing in developing the corridor Cuenca del Salado Solar, a pilot project that would allow widespread adoption of solar energy in the cities of Chañaral and Diego de Almagro.

Table 3.3. **Chile's strategic solar programme, 2017-25**

Areas	Actions	Estimated budget
Technology and skills development	International Institute of Solar and Mining (IISM)	USD 94m between 2017-27
Supply chain development	Open innovation platform	USD 6.6m between 2016-19
	Contribution to develop international standards and regulation	USD 2m between 2016-19
Infrastructure and territorial planning	Solar Technology District (DTS)	USD 0.8m between 2016-17 (pre-phase investment)
	Corridor Cuenca del Salado Solar	USD 0.5m between 2016- 17

Source: Authors' analysis based on official information from the Solar Strategic Committee of Chile.

The actions in Chile's solar energy programme are at an early stage (Table 3.4). In some aspects they are aligned with international practices, including:

- **Creating a long-term vision**. A road-map to 2035 drawn up with the active participation of all stakeholders is a positive step. Other countries are also creating long-term visions for increasing their capabilities in renewable energies. Since 2007, the European Strategic Energy Technology Plan (SET-Plan) has been promoting research and innovation to accelerate the EU's transformation to a low-carbon economy. The SET-Plan is the technology pillar of the European Energy and Climate Policy. It identifies specific actions for research and innovation, based on an assessment of the energy system's needs, on their importance for the energy system transformation, and on their potential to create growth and jobs in the EU. In 2015 the SET-Plan identified ten priority actions with a time horizon to 2030. The plan addresses the whole innovation chain, from research to market uptake, and tackles both financing gaps and regulatory framework needs.
- **Building consensus among diverse stakeholders**. Chile has been successful in bringing all stakeholders on board, including academia, civil society and the private sector, and it has implemented actions in line with international good practices. The formulation and implementation of the EU SET-Plan also relies on consensus building. Its priorities were set by a participatory process involving governments, firms and research, under 154 umbrella organisations representing 16 700 entities. The Technology and Innovation Platforms also provided relevant inputs. The European Technology and Innovation Platform Photovoltaics (ETIP PV) is a platform to gather together all relevant stakeholders in the PV sector, including firms, research centres, and industry associations. They engage in consultations with member and associated countries of the EU and EU Commission institutions, with a view to providing consensus-based advice on increasing the competitiveness of the European PV sector.
- **Information sharing**. The creation of the open platform in Chile to match clients and suppliers is another positive step in line with international practices. The SET-Plan Information System (SETIS) is a platform for sharing information on low-carbon technologies; assessing the impact of various technology policies, conducting cost and benefit analyses of various technological options, and estimating implementation costs. The Energy Research Knowledge Centre under SETIS collects and organises information on energy research programmes and projects, as well as their results and analyses. In Germany, the government's co-financed Fraunhofer Institutes co-operate with universities on industrial research and testing. The institutes favour information sharing between universities and businesses by allowing talent mobility between the institute and the firms and allowing students to gain practical experience in commercially-oriented research.
- **Territorial management for sustainable deployment**. The creation of the technology district will generate technology for commercial products and processes, enable

companies and research centres (both national and international) to test equipment and industrial processes on pilot manufacturing lines, and foster a continual flow of trained engineers and technicians to the private sector. It is important that the district embraces activities that go beyond industrial development, to incorporate infrastructure and territorial development. For instance, solar district heating in Europe supports supplier and local communities.[2] The large-scale solar thermal technology supplies renewable, zero-emission heat from large solar collector fields via district heating networks to residential and industrial areas, and at the same type they represent a laboratory for industrial application and research. Long-term experience is available from demonstration projects in Sweden, Denmark, Germany and Austria.

In going forward, there are additional aspects that would be important to address:

- **Scale up resources and foster private sector participation**. The budget allocation for 2017 represents only 2.8% of the total resources required to achieve the goals of the solar programme; private sector participation accounts for 8% of the total budget in 2017. The SET-Plan receives support from the European Union framework programme for research and innovation (Horizon 2020) for low carbon technologies and national governments, but the private sector also has an active role. In 2014, funding from Horizon 2020 reached EUR 1.1 billion and public investment from national research and development (R&D) programmes account¬ed for nearly EUR 4.2 billion. In 2014, total investments in the research priorities of the plan by European countries reached 27 EUR billion and the private sector contribution represented almost 85% of the total investment.
- **Strengthen opportunities for learning and innovation**. World leading research centers in solar, such as the German Aerospace Center (DLR) in Germany, benefit from a wide science base and networks with multiple fields of research that enhance not only the impact of research in solar, but also enable cross-fertilisation and self-discovery in multiple technological and industrial fields. In going forward it would be desirable to identify mechanisms to enlarge the mission of the solar institute in Chile, and to also explore interoperability with other renewable energies. Pursuing synergies with other renewable energies, such as wind, hydro and biomass, offers untapped potential. In Europe, for example, the SET-Plan has moved away from vertical and technology-specific approaches to a more horizontally integrated approach aiming to find complementarities across renewables and linking them with other enabling technologies, such as ICT, advanced manufacturing, advanced materials, industrial biotechnology, nanotechnology, photonics and nano-electronics.
- **Strengthen international and regional co-operation in research and supply-chain development**. Pooling resources for research at the regional level, exploiting synergies in Latin America, and creating opportunities for SME development by building on complementarities with neighboring countries would be important priorities in going forward. Strengthening regional ties in these dimensions could help to scale up investments and reach the critical mass needed to compete effectively at the global level. For example, European countries emphasise co-operation and resource pooling at a regional level. The European Research Area Network (ERA-NET) was launched in 2011 to support public-public partnerships and joint research between EU countries in solar energy. By the end of 2016, nine ERA-NET co-fund networks had been established in the priority areas identified by SET, with financing of EUR 217 million for 2012-15. International co-operation is also relevant. An interesting step in this direction is the South-South co-operation programme that Chile signed in 2017 with Morocco to foster learning and co-operation to strengthen capabilities in the solar value chain (Box 3.2).

Table 3.4. Progress overview of Chile's solar programme, 2017

Governance dimensions		
Anticipation capacity	√	Having a road-map with a long-term horizon (to 2025) takes Chile a step forward in line with international good practices. Aligning financing with the time-line of the road map will be an additional step forward.
Adaptation capacity	≈	In the fast changing technological environment the time for design and validating road-maps could be shortened from the current 13 months, while adaptability could be increased by introducing periodical revision of road-maps.
Learning and upgrading potential	√	The creation of the Solar Research Institute and the open platform to connect local providers fills two main gaps in enabling learning and upgrading in the value chain and are positive steps in line with international practices.
	×	The specific focus on current challenges (e.g. solar energy for mining and solar energy solutions for high radiation areas) could limit knowledge spillovers and self-discovery processes. There is room to identify synergies with other renewable energies (in the framework of Energy 2050) and with other industrial applications beyond mining.
	√	**Within government**. The programme benefits from multi-agency co-ordination and buy-in (e.g. Ministry of Energy, Ministry of Economy, InvestChile, etc.).
	×	**Private sector**. Businesses participated in the road-map process, but co-operation with lead-investors would be needed in going forward.
Interconnectedness propensity	√	**Academia**. The programme benefits from commitment and co-operation mechanisms with academia and research centres.
	≈	**Civil society**. There is room to increase the participation of civil society in the process, especially to realise the potential of solar energy beyond industrial applications (e.g. self-production and energy to sparsely populated areas).
	×	**Regional**. Strengthening regional ties could help to scale up investments and reach the critical mass needed to compete effectively at the global level.
Embeddedness potential	≈	Mechanisms to avoid rent seeking and capture are needed to ensure that publicly-financed actions benefit all stakeholders and deliver public and club goods not available otherwise. In this respect open government and effective monitoring and evaluation are needed to track progress and performance and identify areas for improvement.

Note: √: positive progress; ≈: margin for improvement; x: reform needed.
The definition of the five governance dimensions can be found in OECD (2017c) and in Box 2.1 in Chapter 2 of this report.

Box 3.2. How Morocco is building on its natural assets to participate in the renewable energies value chain

Morocco has significant renewable energy potential: 25,000 MW of wind power, 20,000 MW of solar (3 000 hours of sunshine/year), and 200 sites usable for hydraulic micro-power plants, equivalent to about 3 800 MW.

Morocco's proactive commitment to the energy transition process has resulted in significant improvements over the last several years, as a result of the successful first phase of the National Energy Strategy (2009-2015). Evidence points to an increase in the share of solar and wind energy from 2% in 2009 to 13% in 2016, and a reduction in the energy dependence rate, from 98% in 2008 to 93.3% in 2016. The second phase of the strategy (2016-2030), already well underway, aims at achieving a sizeable goal: to increase the share of renewables in the energy mix to 52%, and to reduce energy dependence to 82% by 2030. The strategy also aims at achieving energy savings of 15% by 2030 and a massive introduction of natural gas (Figure 3.8).

To reach a share of 52% of total installed capacity coming from renewables, Morocco is to develop additional capacity in electricity generation from renewable sources of about 10 100 MW, of which 4 560 MW from solar, 4 200 MW from wind, and 1 330 MW from hydro-power plants, between 2016 and 2030.

The development of renewable energies is expected to reduce CO^2 emissions by 20 825 kilotonne (kT) by 2030.

Box 3.2. How Morocco is building on its natural assets to participate in the renewable energies value chain *(Cont.)*

Figure 3.8. Projected evolution in the structure of Morocco's installed capacity, 2010-30

Share of installed capacity by energy source

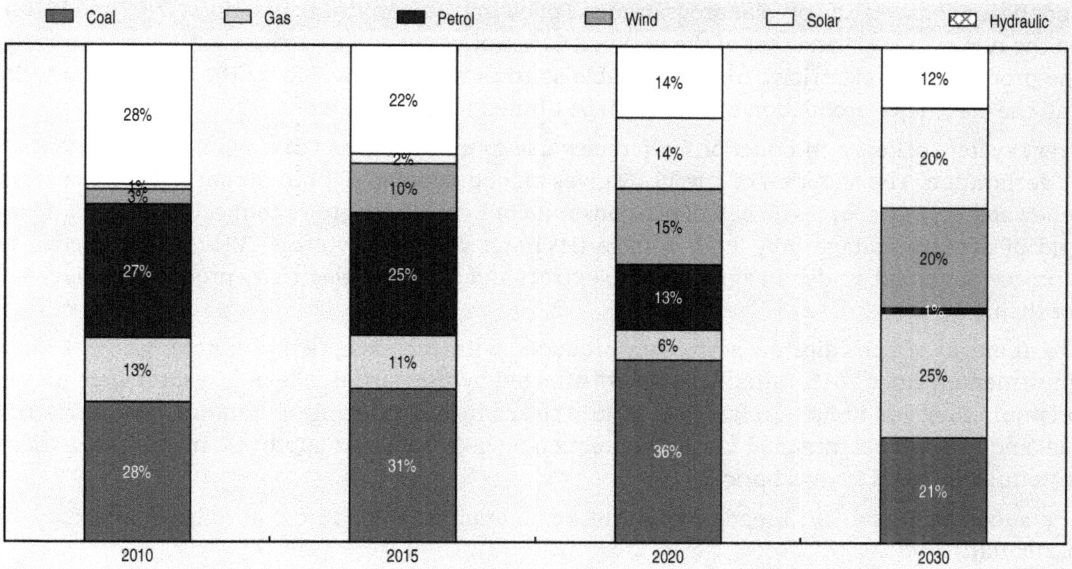

Morocco's strategic programme for renewable energies

Solar programme of 2 000 MW: with an overall cost estimated at USD 9 billion, this programme will be launched in 2020 with a view to producing 4 500 gigawatt hours (GWh) of electricity per year through different sites in the Kingdom. To this end, the successful operationalisation in February 2016 of the first solar plant (Noor 1) with a capacity of 160 MW, enabled the production of 400 GWh in 2016. At end of May 2017, its production grew 14% from the previous year. This site's solar electric capacity will be complemented by the launches of Noor 2 (200 MW) and Noor 3 (150 MW) by the end of 2017. On other sites, processes of pre-qualification for the project Noor Midelt (800 MW) and for corresponding financing have already started. The call for bids on the Noor PV I has also been awarded. With an overall capacity of 170 MW, this programme will foster the development of three photovoltaic plants on three separate sites (80 MW in Laayoune, 70MW in Ourazazate, and 20MW in Boujdour).

Wind programme of 2 000 MW: This programme includes the installation of 2 000 MW in wind power by 2020 and an annual production of 6 600 GWh of electricity, at an estimated cost of USD 3.31 billion. Following the completion of the Tarfaya plant (300 MW), the current total installed capacity is close to 780 MW. Scheduled in 2018 are the operationalisation of the wind park of Taza (150 MW), as well as the launch of the integrated wind power project with a capacity of 850 MW: Tanger II (100 MW), Jbel Lahdid (200 MW), Midelt (150 MW), Tiskrad (300 MW) and Boujdour (100 MW).

Hydroelectric programme of 2 000 MW: the capacity installed to date is of 1 770 MW, of which 460 MW is in the form of pumped hydroelectric energy station (PHES). The hydropower programme will be complemented, by 2020, by the construction of the hydroelectric complex of El Menzel (125 MW) and of the pumped hydroelectric energy station (PHES) of Abdelmoumen (350 MW). Furthermore, several micro-hydropower plants, totalling about 100 MW, are being developed by the private sector as part of the renewable energy law 13-09, and about 300 MW are currently being assessed.

Box 3.2. **How Morocco is building on its natural assets to participate in the renewable energies value chain** *(Cont.)*

Lessons learned

In 2010, the Moroccan Agency for Solar Energy (MASEN) was initially in charge of the development and the implementation of solar programmes. Following the adoption of two laws (57-09 and 38-16), on the role of MASEN and that of the national Office of Water and Electricity (ONEE) respectively, the production of electricity from renewable sources will be provided by the company MASEN and the electricity production of ONEE will be limited to fossil sources.

Every system of energy production from renewable sources is subject to a regime of authorisation or declaration. The adoption of law 13-09 gives an operator the right to produce electricity from renewable energy sources on behalf of a consumer or a consumer group connected to the national grid of average voltage (AV), high voltage (HV) and very high voltage (VHV). This applies to Morocco or abroad, under an agreement to extract and consume electricity produced exclusively for their own use.

The removal of subsidies on petroleum products, with the exception of butane gas, has been implemented since 2013. Initially, products affected by the partial indexing system were diesel, premium fuel, and industrial fuel no2. In 2014 the complete indexing of premium fuel, industrial fuel and special fuel intended for the production of electricity was approved. In 2015, fuel prices were fully indexed to world prices.

The adoption of law 58/15 made important amendments to law 13-09 on renewable energy, in particular:

- The opening of the market for electricity from renewable energy sources of low voltage was embedded in the regulatory framework: for producers of electricity from renewable energy sources, law 58-15 opens up the possibility of connecting to urban and rural low-voltage power grids, in order to promote the development of small and medium-sized industrial facilities, including photovoltaics.
- The increase of the threshold of installed capacity for hydroelectric power generation projects. The exclusion of projects whose electric power was more than 12 MW in the scope of law 13-09 was "a barrier to the exploitation of the maximum threshold given by the physical and hydrological characteristics of production sites". Law 58-15 has thus increased the threshold of installed capacity for projects of electric energy production from hydraulic source from 12MW to 30 MW.
- The point of view of the Hydraulic Basin Agency will now be taken into account in the process of provisional authorisation for the construction of systems for the production of electricity from renewable energy sources
- The possibility to sell surplus production that is not used by the operator to ONEE or the manager of the distribution network. For the latter, the operator cannot sell more than 20% of its annual energy production surplus.

The creation of the National Agency for Regulation of Electricity (NARE) following the adoption of law 48-15: for greater transparency, this law brings answers to better manage the transitional phase marked by the conflict of interest currently underway due to the current status of ONEE as a producer, carrier, and distributor of electricity.

Adoption of the law on self-power generation, allowing power generation greater than 300 MW: this law intends to give producers of over 300MW of electricity the possibility to access the national grid to bring the energy produced from the production site to the various places of consumption.

Adoption of order 2-15-772 on access to grids of average voltage: this reform aims at defining a regulatory framework that is attractive to potential investors in renewable energy systems connected to average voltage grids.

Source: Ministry of Economy and Finance of Morocco, as member of the Peer Learning Group (PLG) of the PTPR of Chile.

In Chile, mining needs to shift up a gear

This section focuses on mining. It discusses the current opportunities and challenges of this industry in a comparative perspective and it identifies key issues at stake for the future. It summarises what actions are needed from businesses and government to make mining a driver of sustainable and inclusive development.

Mining needs to increase productivity

Mining is the backbone of the Chilean economy. Chile is the biggest producer of copper in the world: with 5.5 million metric tons produced in 2016, Chile accounts for 30% of the world's copper production and reserves (Figure 3.9). Chile is also the world's leading producer of iodine (63.2% of world production), of rhenium (50%), and of lithium (39%); the third global producer of molybdenum (13.5% of world production), and the sixth producer of silver (4.6%). The Escondida mine, in the north of the Atacama Desert, produces 1 million tons of copper a year and is the world's largest open-pit copper mine as well as the largest contributor to Chile's copper output. Mining employs around 220 000 workers and has an important weight in Chile's GDP and exports. Over the last decade it accounted for 13% on average of national GDP and for 55% of domestic exports, 50% of which came from copper alone.

Figure 3.9. **Chile has the largest copper reserves in the world**

Share of global copper reserves, million metric tons, 2016

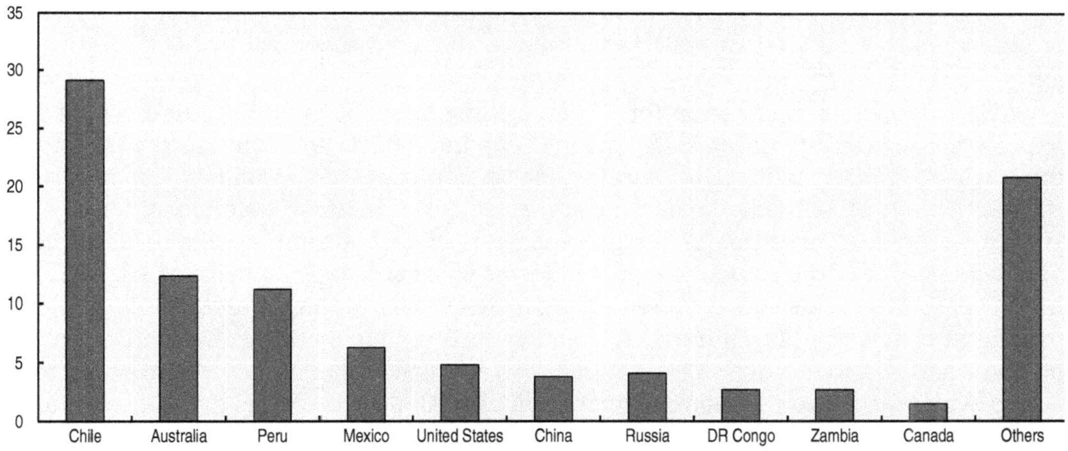

Source: Authors' analysis based on US Geological Survey and COCHILCO (2017), database, https://www.cochilco.cl/

In the last decade, Chile has increased its specialisation in extraction at the expense of smelting and refining. As of 2016, Chile accounted for 8.5% and 11% of world's smelting and refined production. The downward trend in smelting and refining has been due to the emergence of China, which increased its smelting and refining capacity fivefold between 2000 and 2016 (Figure 3.10). The Chinese appetite for copper ores has boosted Chilean mining exports; however it has also contributed to increasing specialisation in the less sophisticated segments of the value chain (see Chapter 2).

Figure 3.10. **Copper production stages, Chile and China, 2003-16**

Kilo metric ton (kMT) of copper content, by production stage

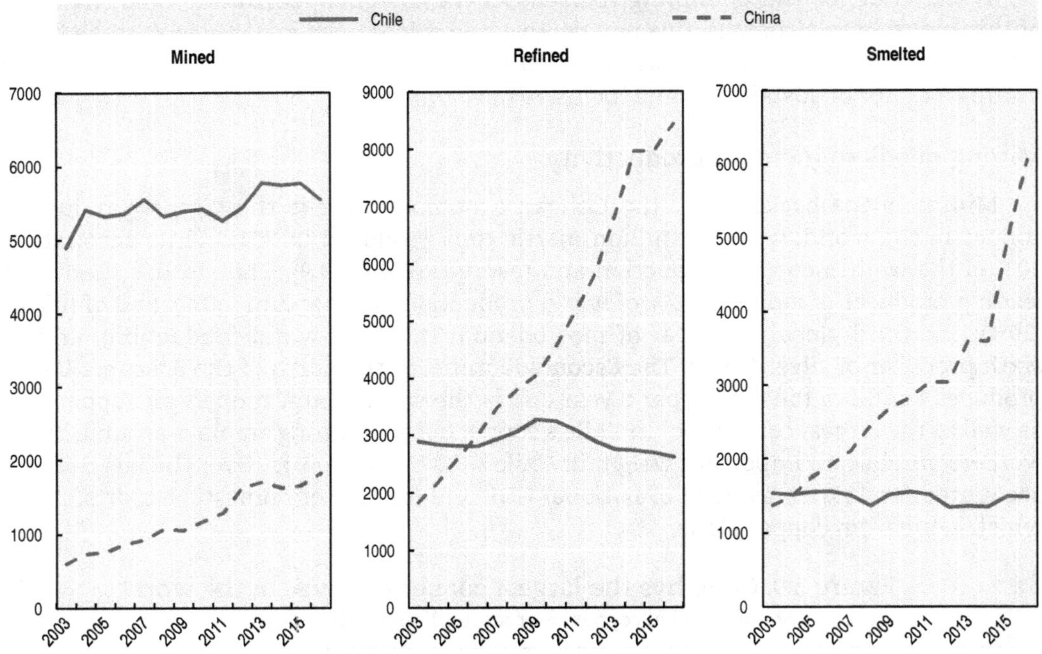

Source: Authors' analysis based on World Metal Statistics, www.world-bureau.com; and Cochilco database https://www.cochilco.cl/, 2017.

Asia is the main destination for Chile's mining exports. In 2016, Chile's copper ore exports mainly went to China (38%), Japan (22%), India (13%) and South Korea (8%), for a total value of USD 11 billion. In the same year, Asian countries combined also absorbed USD 9.8 billion of refined copper from Chile, with China alone accounting for 47% of the total. The decomposition of the gross exports of Chilean mining allows for a more detailed analysis of the source of inputs in terms of sectors and countries of origin. Chile has lower foreign value added content in gross exports (20%) than Sweden (25%). Chilean mining exports embed fewer inputs from other sectors than Sweden. The contribution of business services to mining is 21% in Chile, whereas in Sweden it is 30%. A similar pattern is also evident in the role of manufacturing, which in Chile contributes to 7% of total value added in mining exports, compared to 10% in Sweden (Figures 3.11 and 3.12).

Figure 3.11. **Decomposition of Chilean gross exports by origin and destination, mining, 2014**

Value added of gross exports by origin and destination (%)

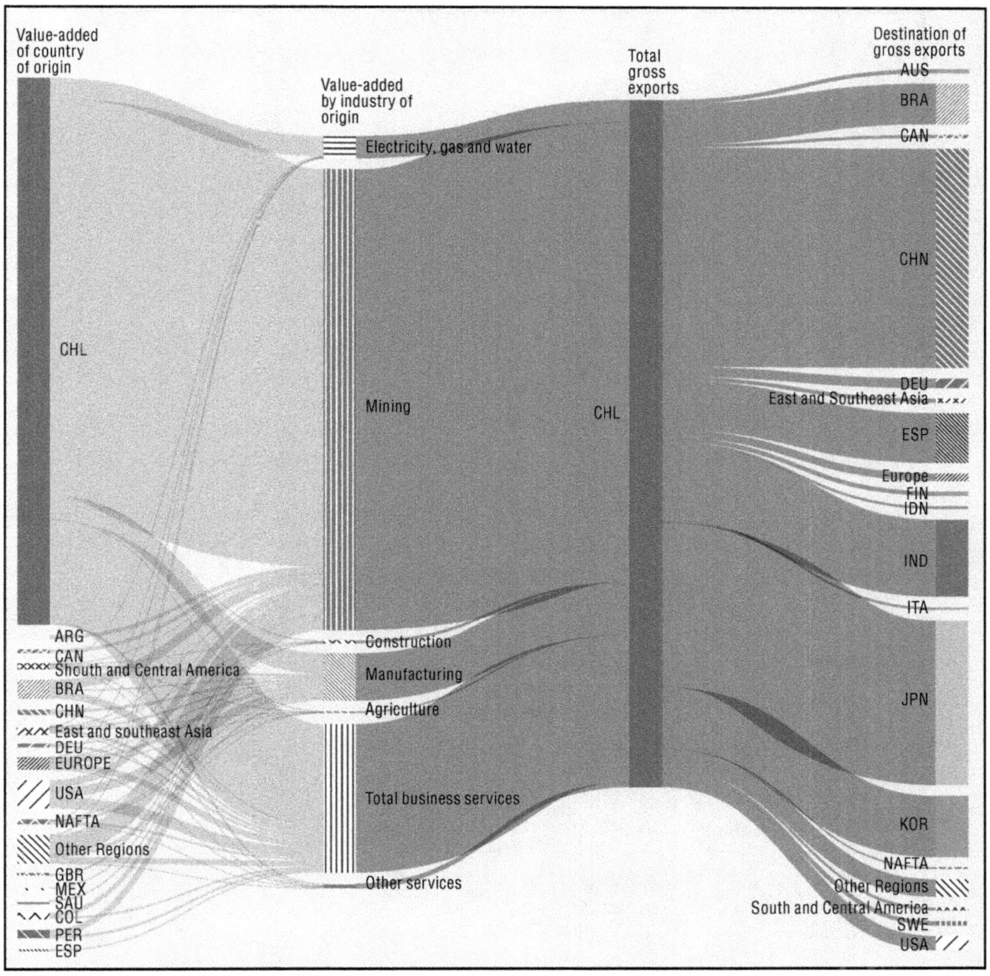

Note: Regional aggregates exclude member countries reported in the graph.

Source: OECD (2017b), TiVA Nowcast Database, http://stats.oecd.org/Index.aspx?DataSetCode=TIVA_NOWCAST; see also www.oecd.org/std/its/tiva-nowcast-methodology.pdf

Figure 3.12. **Decomposition of Swedish gross exports by origin and destination, mining, 2014**

Value added of gross exports by origin and destination (%)

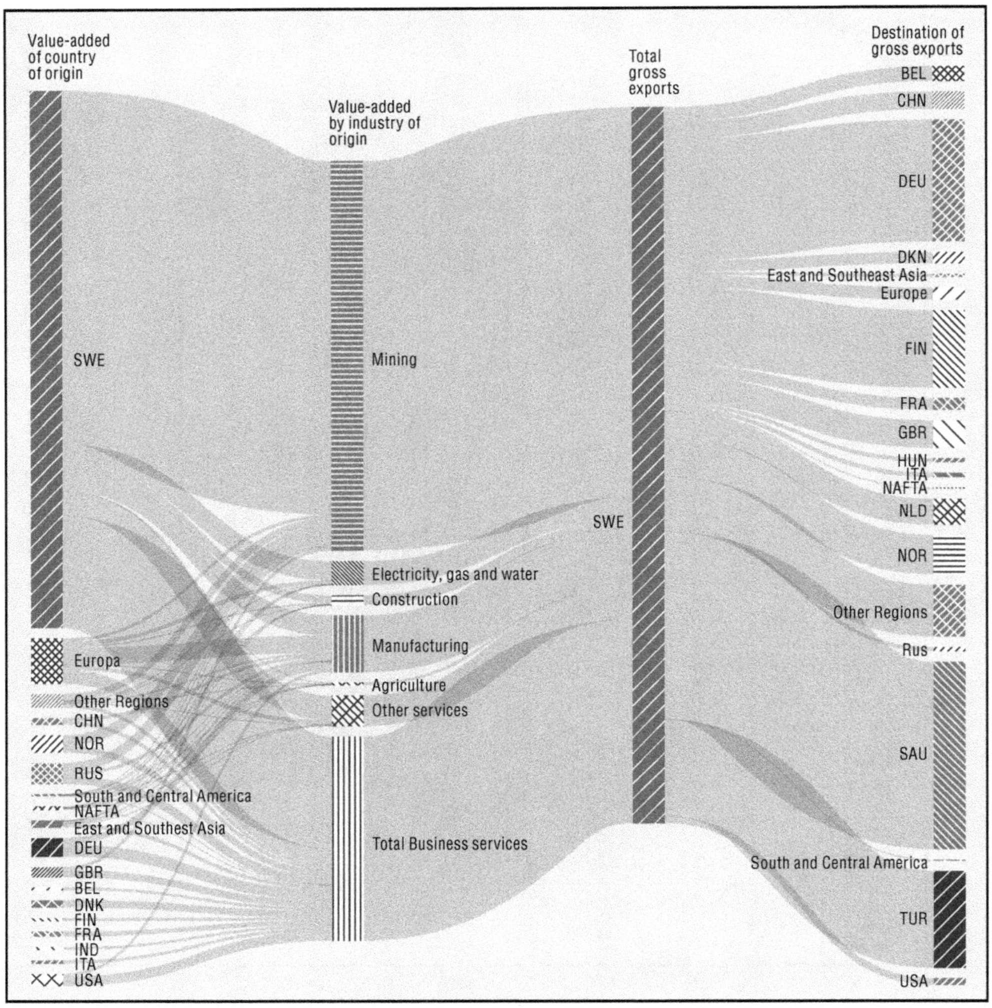

Note: Regional aggregates exclude member countries reported in the graph.

Source: OECD (2017b), TiVA Nowcast Database, http://stats.oecd.org/Index.aspx?DataSetCode=TIVA_NOWCAST; see also http://www.oecd.org/std/its/tiva-nowcast-methodology.pdf

Chile's high dependency on natural resources makes the country vulnerable to external shocks. The contraction of the Chinese economy in 2015, along with sluggish world economic growth and the expected appreciation of the dollar, have affected copper prices, which dropped to USD 2.10 per pound (lb) in 2016, almost USD 2.00/lb lower than the peak of 2012. The decline in copper prices has had a direct effect on employment. Employment rates in mining dropped by 5.5% on average between 2012 and 2016, and the impact has been particularly severe in mining regions. The unemployment rate during the first quarter of 2017 reached 6.8% nationally, but was 8.3% in Antofagasta, and 8.9% in Atacama. Although the second half of 2017 saw copper prices stabilise around USD 3/lb, the recent contraction reveals how structural problems are affecting the industry. Rising costs, declining productivity, and increasing concerns about social and environmental sustainability are all hampering the country's historical position as a global leader. Some of these structural problems are discussed next.

Since the 2000s, the productivity of mining in Chile has been declining. This is not a uniquely Chilean problem: between 2000 and 2015, many commodity-rich countries faced productivity declines in industries associated with natural resources. For example, the value added per hour worked in Norway's mining and services sectors fell by a yearly average of 4% between 2000 and 2015. In Australia, it fell on average by 5% per year between 2000 and 2011, while in Canada, the average decline was 1% per year between 2007 and 2013. Available estimates by the National Productivity Commission of Chile reveal that between 2000 and 2014, Chile's copper production increased by 19%, while the use of inputs for production increased by much more: energy requirements grew 79%, labour 157%, and capital investment 178% (CNP, 2017). This combination of a modest increase in output with high growth in the use of inputs led to an overall decline in total factor productivity. Additionally, there was a sharp reduction in labour productivity. Depending on the methodology used, and accounting for several factors including ore grade deterioration, labour productivity fell by 15% to 50%. When comparing the Chilean mines with an international benchmark, the results are even more worrying. In 2015, moving 1 000 tons of material in the world's best-practice mining sites in Australia, Canada, Sweden and the United States required on average 30 hours, less than half the time required for the average Chilean site of 67 hours. Moreover, mines in Chile employ 1.8 technical support people per plant while the international benchmark average is 1.3 (CNP, 2017).

The decline in mining productivity can be explained by several factors. On the one hand, Chile's main mining sites are experiencing ore grade deterioration, leading to lower productivity. In 1991, the average ore grade in Chile was 1.4%. Current estimates show that ore grades now range between 0.7% and 1%, and are expected to be 0.6% by 2020 (CNP, 2017). When a copper resource is developed, mining begins by extracting ore close to the surface. Once this is removed, ore is extracted from increasing depths. Deeper pits lengthen the process before milling can start, and decreasing ore grades mean that greater amounts of material must be moved and processed to achieve the same quantity of final product, which results in greater energy consumption and water use (Figures 3.13 and 3.14). The increasing water demand is an additional challenge for mining in Chile, as most sites are located in the northern regions, next to the Atacama Desert, one of the driest places in the world. The region of Antofagasta alone requires 5 000 litres of water per second, and demand for water in Chile's mining industry is expected to increase to 500 million cubic litres by 2020. To meet this increase in water demand, water will need to be desalinated and pumped to the mountains, a process that is costly and highly intensive in energy consumption.

Figure 3.13. **Chilean ore grades are falling while energy consumption is rising, 2001-15**

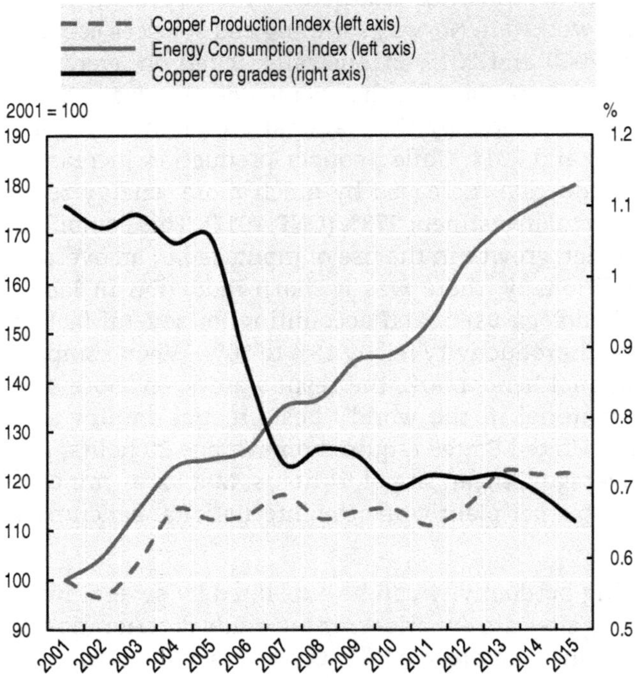

Note: The Copper Production Index measures thousands of tons exctracted and the Energy Consumption Index measures terajoules necessary for extraction.

Source: Authors' analysis based on US Geological Survey and COCHILCO (2017), database, https://www.cochilco.cl.

Figure 3.14. **Total water consumption by region, Chile 2015**

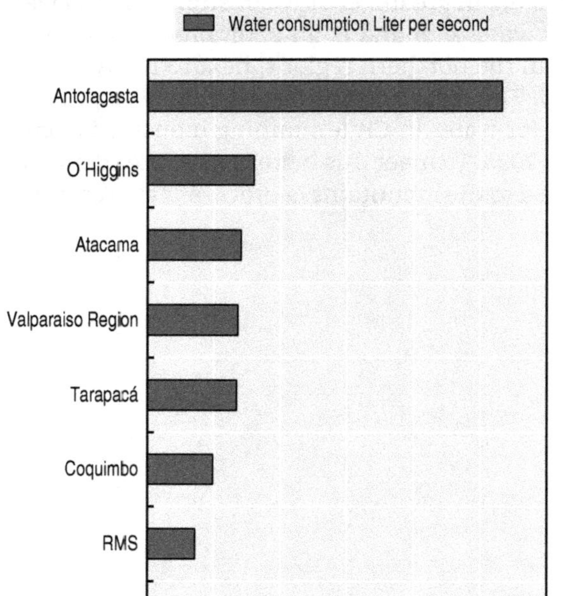

Source: Authors' analysis based on COCHILCO (2017), database, https://www.cochilco.cl.

Chile's mining business is mostly focused on extraction and invests little in innovation. Increasing specialisation in extractive activities, along with the industry's focus on maximising volume during the super cycle of commodity prices of the 2000s, overshadowed the importance of research and innovation. When the cycle ended, inefficiencies were revealed in operations and organisational structures. A sustained effort in innovation is essential to compete at the international level. Total business expenditure in R&D over total gross value added in the mining industry is 0.15% in Chile, versus 2% in Australia, 1.5% in the United States and 1% in Sweden (Figure 3.15, Panel a).

Qualified human capital is necessary to fully exploit new technological advantages. Chile's specialisation in low value-added segments of the mining value chain means its labour force is largely composed of low-skilled workers, often with short-term contracts. In Australia, 21.4 out of every 1 000 mining employees are dedicated to R&D activities; in Sweden and Norway the numbers are 13.3 and 11.4 respectively. In Chile that number is only 1.2 (Figure 3.15, Panel b). Chile is aware of the need to increase its skills base for the future of mining, and some initiatives have been put in place to do so. In the region of Antofagasta, a public-private partnership involving the University of Antofagasta, the Centre for Industrial Training (CEIM) and the Catholic University of the North has set up the Andes Pacific Technology Access (APTA) programme. Its aim is to increase knowledge transfer between universities and firms through on-campus and off-campus training. Companies are also co-operating with universities and technical schools to build skills. For example, the Chilean state-owned copper company CODELCO is co-operating with the technical school Don Bosco-Calama to train workers in extraction and industrial mechanics.

Figure 3.15. **Chile lags behind world leading mining countries in innovation**

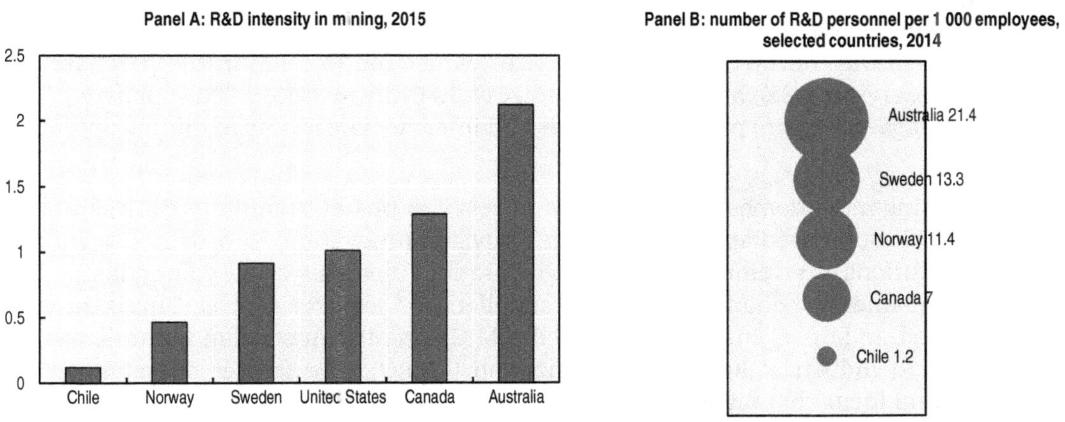

Note: Panel a: R&D intensity in mining is the ratio of total business enterprises' expenditure on R&D over total gross value added in the mining sector (ISIC rev 3.1); Panel b figures refer to private sector employment, 2015: Chile, 2014: Norway, 2013, Australia and Canada, 2010: Sweden.

Source: Authors' analysis based on OECD STAND stats.oecd.org; ILO Statistics, www.ilo.org/ilostat; and Australian Department of Employment, https://www.employment.gov.au (databases), 2017.

Mining is also facing a skills gap at the technical level. Estimates from the public-private Council for Competitiveness in Mining in Chile forecast a gap in 16 000 technical profiles by 2024. The gap will be critical in technical areas such as mechanical and electrical maintenance, as well as operators of both fixed and mobile equipment. On the other hand, there is an oversupply of university professionals in the extraction, exploration and development (production geology) areas (Figure 3.16). Available estimates reveal that the profiles with less demand, for example mining professionals and geologists, continue to show an increase in university enrolments (CCM, 2016). Addressing this skills mismatch will be an important driver of productivity growth in the future.

Figure 3.16. **Skills gap in mining, 2015-24**

Thousands of employees

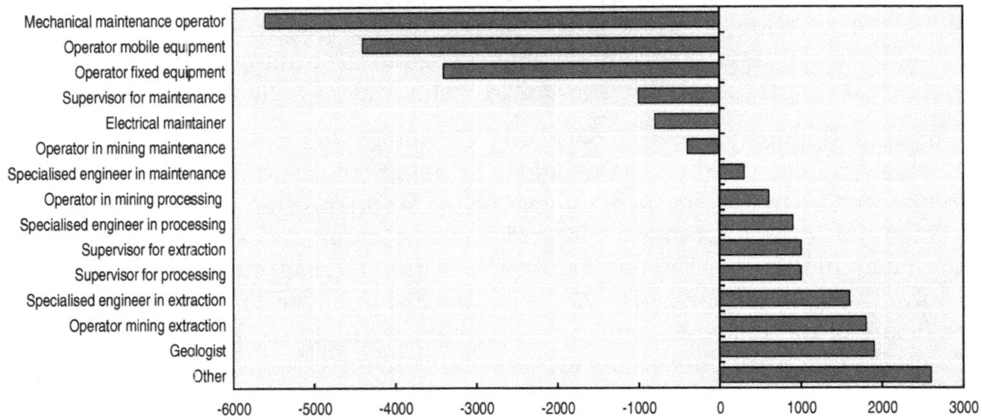

Source: Estimates from *Consejo de Competencia Minería* (CCM), 2017.

Chile could take more advantage of the opportunities offered by services linked to mining. The mining of the future will be more focused on the efficiency and sustainability of extraction and smelting activities. Integrating service-related activities in upstream and downstream segments can boost the total value added of the sector. Services represent 35% of the value added of mining exports in Sweden and New Zeeland, while in Chile the same figure is around 20%. In addition, while emerging economies like Peru and South Africa have increased the value added of services in mining exports, in Chile value added declined from 30% in 2000 to 23% in 2014 (Figure 3.17). This reduction can partly be ascribed to the contraction of copper prices, which led to a fall in the purchases of operational services (-8%) between 2012 and 2014. In Chile in 2015, 4 500 suppliers (1 500 in the Antofagasta region) provided services and intermediate inputs to mining operators (CNP, 2017).

Generating more domestic value added in services linked to mining requires a shift towards a solution-based approach to technology and innovation. New technologies and business solutions often emerge through collaborations along the whole value chain, when mining companies work hand in hand with suppliers and research centres. This is the case for the Canadian Mining Innovation Council (CMIC), and the Australian Commonwealth Scientific and Industrial Research Organization (CSIRO). The former operates with a cross-sectoral focus that favours knowledge transfer and accumulation, and which aims to strengthen ties among the operators along entire value chains. These channels have served very well as a platform for collaborative innovation amongst the competitors to solve shared challenges, especially around socio-economic and sustainability issues.

Figure 3.17. Services value added content of mining and quarrying gross exports, Chile and selected countries, 2014

Domestic and foreign services value added as share of gross exports

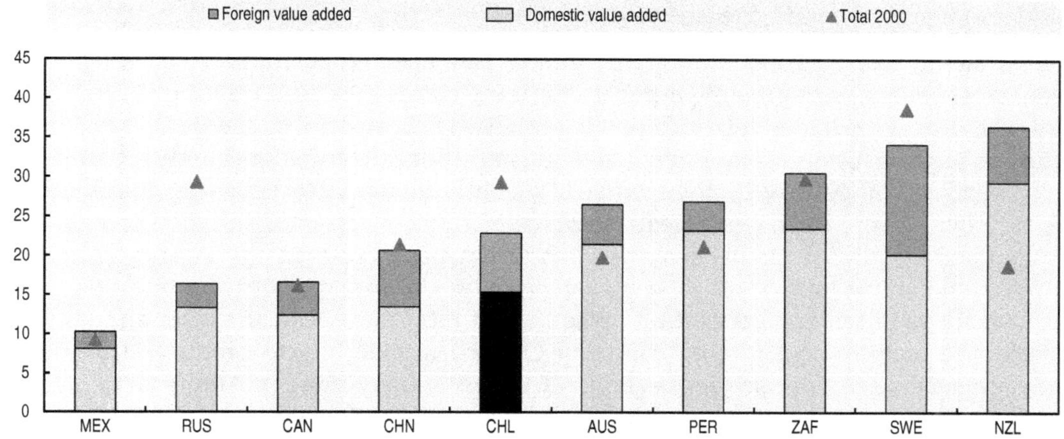

Source: Authors' analysis based on OECD Trade in Value Added (TIVA), 2017. stats.oecd.org/

New technologies and demands are reshaping the global mining industry

Automation and artificial intelligence are driving productivity growth in mining, and are enhancing safety in the work place. Autonomous mine haulage trucks are estimated to have the potential to increase output by 15-20%, to lower fuel consumption by 10% to 15%, and to reduce maintenance costs by 8% (OECD, 2017a). Automation is also becoming increasingly relevant as mining is shifting from open-pits to underground mining. Automation increases the productivity and changes the skills profile of employees. In 2014, Sweden's leading companies, including Boliden and ABB, inaugurated the world's most automated mine in Garpenberg. The project required private investment of USD 480 million and achieved up to 25% energy savings by using smart ventilation. Mining extraction doubled as automation enabled a 24-hour extraction process.

Digital technologies are improving strategic planning and decision making through the use of real-time data, analytics and predictive tools. In 2016, the largest gold mine in the world, Canada-based Barrick Gold, teamed up with Cisco to set up an analytics hub. The new tools will not only allow Barrick Gold to improve planning and financial management, but also to enhance transparency and business-community relationships by sharing real-time data with civil society. The hub will also enable the design and implementation of innovations to improve safety, productivity and environmental performance. The company estimates that by automating its equipment, using predictive algorithms to gain greater metallurgic precision, and using digital technologies to streamline its permitting activities, it can reduce production costs from USD 800 to less than USD 700 per ounce of gold (Deloitte, 2017). Sweden's mining business is also active in identifying opportunities to transform mining through new mobile communication technologies. The Pilot for Industrial Mobile Communication in Mining (PIMM), started in 2016, brings together a group of Swedish companies in mining and ICT in a consortium to identify shared solutions for new business models for increasing productivity, maintenance and safety.

The mining industry is also responding to the growing global demand for sustainability and is searching for green solutions. Greater co-operation between governments and businesses is needed in this area, as most projects involve business-specific solutions and the provision of public goods. In Sweden, the steelmaker SSAB has partnered with mining company LKAB and utility provider Vattenfall to develop breakthrough technology to decarbonise its operations over the next 20-25 years. Through this partnership, the companies aim to use hydrogen fuel instead of fossil fuels in the steelmaking process, achieving waste product of pure water and no carbon dioxide emissions. This project is at an early phase and is currently looking for public support to bridge the financing gap and shift from prototype to scale (see also Chapter 2).

Growing energy consumption in mining can open opportunities for integrating renewable energies. A growing number of mining companies are investing in renewable energy, often in partnership with public authorities. In Australia, the DeGrussa copper mine is implementing a solar project that aims to reduce the mine's dependence on diesel by investing in a 10.6 MW PV plant with 6 MW of lithium ion battery storage. The objective is to provide more consistent, clean, and cost-effective electricity. The total cost of USD 30 million is 50% co-financed by the Australian Renewable Energy Agency (ARENA). Commissioned in June 2016, solar power provides the majority of the mine's daytime electricity requirements, offsetting up to 20% of total diesel consumption annually. In Chile, the state-owned mining company Codelco is planning to produce sustainable copper cathode. A pilot project began in 2013 in the Gaby mine in Antofagasta. In this case the Pampa Elvira solar thermal plant, which produces 54 megawatt hours per year of electricity (MWh/y), covers 85% of the heat needed to refine copper and has reduced the mine's CO2 emissions by 15 000 tons a year since 2014.

Renewed partnerships could boost mining and transform it into an innovative and sustainable industry

Public and private stakeholders in Chile's mining ecosystem are aware that global trends offer opportunities to shift gear and transform it into an innovative and sustainable industry (Figure 3.18 and Table 3.5). Chile's natural endowments in copper and lithium make mining an obvious driver of future growth, development and diversification. Ongoing transformations in the global mining industry (e.g. the shifts towards green and automated mining), coupled with the challenges that Chile is facing (e.g. the need to sustain productivity in an industry that is shifting from open-pit to underground with growing energy requirements), call for a renewed approach to public-private partnership in this field.

Figure 3.18. **Trends in Chile's copper value chain, 2017**

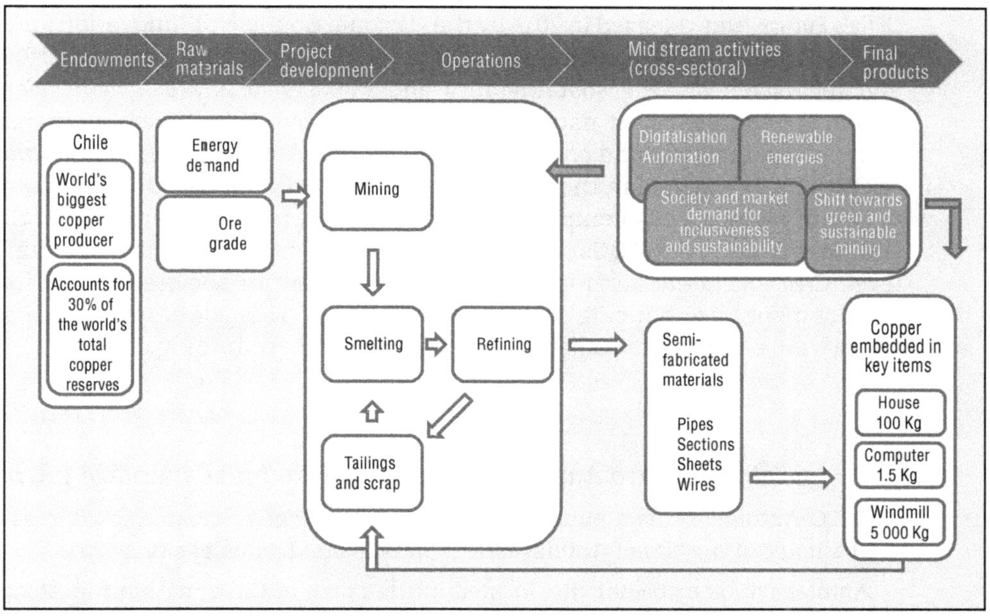

Source: Authors' elaboration based on the outcomes of the Round Table on the Future of Mining in Chile, organised in the framework of the PTPR process, hosted by CORFO in Santiago, Chile in April 2017..

Chile already has an established public-private dialogue with lead firms in the mining industry. The programme "World Class Suppliers", co-financed in 2009 by Fundación Chile and BHP Billiton, and since joined by CODELCO, has helped to strengthen trust between the government and the private sector. It has matched the needs of lead firms to save costs and increase efficiency in their operations, with opportunities to strengthen the domestic supply chain by fostering partnerships with local suppliers. In the first three years of the programme, over 100 innovation projects were submitted for consideration, 20 of which led to contracts with BHP Billiton.

Table 3.5. **Multi-stakeholder assessment of smart and green mining in Chile, 2017**

Strengths	Weaknesses
• World biggest reserves of copper and lithium • Largest copper producing company in the world (CODELCO) • Stable macroeconomic situation	• Decrease in productivity • Decline in copper ore concentration • Shift from open pit to underground mining • Increasing demand for energy • Water scarcity in mining regions • Market concentration • Low-skilled labour force • Poor science and technological innovation
Opportunities	**Threats**
• Rise in electro-mobility • Green mining value chain • Synergies with other sectors (i.e solar industry)	• Exogenous price variation of copper • Reduction in global and Chinese demand • Environmental and social impacts

Source: Authors' elaboration based on the outcomes of the Round Table on the Future of Mining in Chile, organised in the framework of the PTPR process, hosted by CORFO in Santiago, Chile in April 2017.

The trust built over time between government and businesses in mining has enabled Chile to take a step forward in defining a shared vision for the future: *Mining: A Platform for Chile's Future*, was released in 2014 by the National Council for Innovation and Development (CNID, 2014). This identifies three pillars for going forward: productivity, sustainability and inclusiveness. The sustainability and inclusiveness areas have been turned into two major initiatives. At national level the initiative *Valor Minero* promotes actions that foster social dialogue and ensure the positive social and environmental impact of mining operations. In particular, the project for Territorial Dialogue (IDT) has set up roundtables to identify how mining companies could contribute to the achievement of the Sustainable Development Goals (SDGs) in the communities in which they operate. At the local level, *Creo Antofagsta* aims to provide opportunities for socio-economic integration and development by enhancing social capital (Box 3.3). This is a result of the commitment of the private sector and local authorities in the northern mining city.

Box 3.3. ***Creo Antofagasta*: a long vision for sustainable growth**

CREO Antofagasta is a public-private strategic initiative created to address the growth challenge of the city of Antofagasta. It aims to build a model city by 2035.

Antofagasta is a coastal city, located in the north of Chile, within the Atacama Desert, where mining is the mayor economic activity (65% regional GDP). In terms of incomes and job satisfaction, Antofagasta has one of the highest performances within Chilean cities; however, to achieve a more sustainable development and better quality of life, the city needs to deliver higher quality and access to public services, urban amenities, affordable housing and community participation. To address these challenges, Creo Antofagasta has developed a masterplan for Antofagasta, with a strong focus on public spaces, socio-spatial integration, environmental sustainability, community participation, enhancing social capital and public-private collaboration. This is the first plan of its kind in Chile, as it has managed to bring together public sector, private companies and the community into one city vision and a portfolio of over 300 initiatives that should bring USD 1.3 billion of concerted investment by 2035.

This plan also includes a short-term portfolio to develop 38 initiatives and more than USD 160 million of investment by 2021, some of which is already underway. These initiatives include:

- the development of a 22 km waterfront as the city's main urban park
- an integrated urban mobility strategy, focusing in transit and no-motorized modes like walking and cycling for re-connecting the disadvantaged neighbourhoods to urban services and public spaces in a more sustainable way
- the reuse of wastewater to irrigate and make feasible the aim to increase green areas and plant trees through the city
- a waste management programme to boost recycling and compost generation to improve soil quality in parks

Box 3.3. *Creo Antofagasta*: a long vision for sustainable growth (*Cont.*)

Creo Antofagasta is organised through an executive board led by the Regional Government and the Municipal Government of Antofagasta including, among its members, NGOs, regional universities and private companies' representatives.

Lessons for the future:

- build a shared vision with a rooted and realistic plan
- complement and support, not replace, local government
- focus on long-term strategic projects and delivering early wins with public sector leadership
- build trust by strengthening local capacity, developing an inclusive governance and boosting an active - not passive - collaborative culture
- secure public and private funding through formal investment agreements and accelerating feasibility and design processes.

Source: Information provided by Creo Antofagasta, www.creoantofagasta.cl.

Chile is implementing two major initiatives at the national and regional level to address the productivity challenges. *Alta Ley* is a public-private partnership, co-ordinated by CORFO in partnership with the Ministry of Mining, to identify long-term priorities to transform Chile's mining industry. It builds on the successful experience of the World Class Supplier Programme mentioned above. Through public-private dialogue, *Alta Ley* has developed a shared vision and road-map for 2035 that aims to mobilise investments and partnerships to increase productivity, competitiveness and innovation in the national mining industry and among its suppliers (Table 3.6).

Table 3.6. Shared public-private goals for mining, 2015-35

Objectives	Baseline 2015	by 2035
Increasing production	5.5 metric tons of copper	7.5 metric tons of copper
Increasing global leadership	40% of production in the 1st quartile of cost	80% of production in the 1st quartile of cost
Developing world class suppliers	65 firms	250 firms
Increasing annual exports of goods and services	USD 537 million	USD 4 000 million

Source: Authors' analysis based on information from CORFO, 2017.

The public-private partnership has identified four shared needs that require public and private action (Table 3.7):

1. developing technology-based solutions to ensure tailing's safety and sustainability
2. increasing the efficiency of smelting and refining processes
3. facilitating the shift towards smart mining and the adoption of autonomous solutions
4. enabling bottom- up innovations, facilitating the participation of domestic suppliers to the value chain and fostering the export orientation of these providers.

Consultations between the public and the private sector revealed gaps in four areas – skills, financing for innovation, standards, and supply chain development. Specific actions have been planned to address these gaps. The estimated budget for implementing these actions is around USD 100 million by 2035. As of 2017, the government had committed USD 35 million and the private sector had invested USD 10 million.

Table 3.7. **Priorities, gaps and actions for the future of mining in Chile, 2015-35**

NEEDS	Developing technological solutions to ensure the safety and sustainability of tailings			Increasing the efficiency of copper smelting and refining processes	Shifting to smart mining & autonomous solutions	Increasing the participation of domestic firms as suppliers of specialised goods and services	
GAPS	Human capital	R&D and innovation			Standards & regulation	Supply chain	
ACTIONS	Create a Technical Training Centre	Support smart tailing through online monitoring	Enable treatment and recovery of valued metals	Create a technological programme for copper smelting and refining processes	Develop standards for mining interoperability	Support internationalisation	Set up a Mining Innovation Platform
Expected public budget up to 2026	USD 7.43 million	USD 8.17 million	USD 3.19 million	USD 0.86 million	USD 8.17 million	USD 4.51 million	USD 8.04 million

Source: Authors' analysis based on official information from CORFO, 2017 on the mining strategic programmes.

The actions at the national level through *Alta Ley* are complemented by initiatives at the local level. The Mining Cluster of Antofagasta replicates the structure of national actions, but focuses on the regional ecosystem. This cluster program aims to increase mining competiveness in the region by fostering the development of a high-value added supply chain to exploit opportunities in the provision of technological services and by supplying specialised human capital. The program, which came about through public-private consultation, identifies several projects around a road map to 2025 for a total joint public and private expected budget of USD 5 million.

Alta Ley and the Mining Cluster of Antofagasta build on past experiences and previously-established trust between the public and private sector. Setting up effective spaces for consultation with the private sector strengthens the competitiveness programmes by ensuring the commitment of the business community. While it is too early to assess their impact, as they are in the early stages of implementation, some good practices in line with international experience (e.g. from Sweden, see Box 3.4) can be identified, along with some possible areas for improvement (Table 3.8):

- **Establishing trust between government and the private sector to achieve a shared vision for the future.** Chile, in line with international practices, has invested in trust building. Mining is, in fact, one of the areas in which Chile actually has a common practice of private-public consultation. *Alta Ley* has marked a step forward by making government and businesses looking into the future to identify opportunities and challenges to identify a road-map for action.

- **Getting the right stakeholders at the table**. Setting up effective public-private consultations is an important step in defining better policies. The effectiveness of these consultations depends, however, on the representativeness and inclusiveness of the participants. Over the last decade, Chile has strengthened the public-private dialogue with lead mining firms. In going forward it would be important to strengthen the participation of civil society, entrepreneurs along the entire value chain and local governments and communities.
- **Aligning the long term vision with long term financing**. Mobilising resources for innovative, high risk projects requires multi-annual budgeting. Enabling the multi-annual commitment of resources also favours partnerships with the private sector. The recently created Strategic Innovation Fund (FIE) is a step towards enabling financing strategic projects. Moreover it is important to reinforce the complementarity among the different programs, avoid duplicate interventions, resources and administrative procedures as well as overlapping in governances.
- **Fine tuning the policy mix with the objectives**. The dialogue with the private sector contributes to reveal competitiveness gaps in multiple areas. It is important to identify which instruments are more effective in addressing these gaps. In line with international practices, Chile is now shifting from a logic of simply providing financing to offering services to businesses. The creation of an innovation platform where lead firms in mining can interact with potential suppliers is a good step in this direction. Chile also has a gap in terms of technological capabilities and the creation of a modern technology institute that could address the challenges of mining together with the energy challenges seems a promising step in closing the gap in terms of technological and scientific capabilities.
- **Enabling learning and innovation in mining and beyond**. Facilitating innovation in mining could also open opportunities for innovation and learning in the overall economy. On the one hand, Chile could leverage on the transition of mining towards industry 4.0 to reveal the gaps that Chile will need to address to enable that its stakeholders participate and effectively compete in industry 4.0 types of business environments. These gaps include ensuring a high speed, resilient and redundant internet connection and enabling training for having the right skills for the digital world. On the other hand, the shift towards digital mining will expose the national innovation system (universities, researchers, firms) to these new technologies and will favour learning and potential spillovers to the whole system.

Box 3.4. **Smart and green mining: lessons learned from Sweden**

In Sweden, an innovation and solution-oriented private sector is leading the shift towards smart and green mining.

The high trust and social capital of the system, and the effective connection between businesses, universities and government, make the Swedish industrial system highly responsive to embracing change. This is coupled with the long-term financing that innovative and risky projects require. In Sweden, the fund "VINNOVA – Regional Growth through Dynamic Innovation Systems" finances large-scale initiatives and guarantees a public contribution of up to 50% of the total project cost for 10 years, for up to EUR 1 million annually. An evaluation of 12 of the first projects financed - up to 12 year financing - found clear impacts in strengthening the quadruple helix model and in the innovations focus of the regions.

Box 3.4. Smart and green mining: lessons learned from Sweden (Cont.)

The government and the private sector have built trust and capacity to work together to achieve a common vision over time. For example the Strategic Innovation Programme for the Swedish Mining and Metal Producing Industry (STRIM) follows a quadruple helix approach and is embedded within the strategic innovation programmes backed by high political commitment. The programme includes participation by national government, firms, universities, NGOs and municipalities. The programme has identified an agenda to 2030 that includes both industrial and social challenges. The programme finances full-scale innovation and pilot projects along the entire value chain: exploration, resource characterisation, mining, metallurgy, recycling, reclamation and environmental performance. In 2017, 51 projects were under implementation.

The government is highly responsive to business needs, and the private sector operates with high social and environmental standards, thus focusing not only on business growth, but also on how this growth is achieved (in terms of social and environmental impact) and how the benefits are shared across the community and society.

Sweden values highly a participatory approach in policy making and national policies benefit from structured mechanisms to consult with civil society, and with regions, local authorities, and communities.

Source: Contribution by International Council of Swedish Industry (NIR) to the Round Table on the Future of Mining in Chile, organised in the framework of the PTPR of Chile and hosted by CORFO in Santiago, Chile in April 2017.

Table 3.8. Progress overview of the mining strategic programme, Chile, 2017

Governance dimensions		
Anticipation capacity	√	The two long-term road-maps (to 2025 for the cluster programme and 2035 for national programme Alta Ley) bring Chile a step closer to international best practices. Aligning the two road maps with financing limited to 2018 will be an additional step forward that will secure impact.
Adaptation capacity	≈	The road-maps could be revised in light of changing international and domestic market dynamics. In a fast-changing technological environment the time for design and validating road-maps could be shortened from the current 13 months, while adaptability could be increased by introducing periodical revision of road-maps and of mid-terms targets.
Learning and upgrading potential	√	The focus of the programme and road-map on four specific gaps (human capital, R&D and innovation, standards & regulation, and the supply chain) is a step towards a logic that embraces all dimensions of the production system and that allows for the expansion of the knowledge base.
	√	Facilitating innovation in mining could also open opportunities for innovation and learning in the overall economy. Chile could build on the transition of mining towards industry 4.0 to reveal the gaps it will need to address if its industries and services are to work in an industry 4.0 environment.
	√	**Within government**. The programme benefits from multi-agency coordination and buy-n (e.g. Ministry of Mining, Ministry of Economy, Fundación Chile etc.).
	×	**Multi-level governance**. The presence of various programmes and actions at national and regional level over several dimensions may lead to a certain degree of overlap that could result in duplication of efforts and investment. It is important to reinforce the complementarity of the various programmes, avoid duplicate interventions, resources and administrative procedures, as well as overlap in governance structures.
Interconnectedness propensity	√	**Private sector**. Businesses participated in the road-map process and are represented within the governance structure of the programme.
	≈	**Civil society**. There is room to increase the participation of civil society in the process. Local community tends to have a negative opinion of mining operations in Chile.
	√	**Academia**. The programme benefits from commitment and co-operation mechanisms with academia and research centres.
Embeddedness potential	≈	Mechanisms to avoid rent seeking and capture need to be in place to ensure that publicly-financed actions benefit all stakeholders and deliver public and club goods not available otherwise. In this respect open government and effective monitoring and evaluation are needed to track progress and performance and identify areas for improvement.

Note: √: positive progress; ≈: margin for improvement; x: reform needed.
The definition of the five governance dimensions can be found in OECD (2017c) and in Box 2.1 in Chapter 2 of this report.

The future of agro-food: towards high-quality and functional food

This section focuses on agro-food in Chile. It presents a snapshot of the characteristics of the industry in Chile highlighting its strengths and weaknesses. It provides an overview of global trends with a view to discussing the future opportunities and challenges for Chile. It concludes by reviewing the current policy approach in a comparative perspective, and identifies avenues for going forward.

Chile has been successful in positioning its exports globally

Agro-food is an important economic activity for Chile, comprising agriculture, fishery and food processing industries. Together these account for 8% of Chile's GDP, contributeto more than 20% of domestic exports, and employ 17% of the national work force. The food and beverages industry accounts for almost 40% of total national manufacturing value added. Agro-food related activities are mostly concentrated in the Central Valley, even though the production frontier has been progressively shifting south due to climate change, making new areas cultivable. Almost 30% of Chilean firms (approximately 320 000) operate in activities linked to the agro-food value chain. They are specialised in agriculture (which alone accounts for 10% of total domestic firms), food processing (2.5% of total domestic firms) and retail. The market is dominated by a few, large companies, while 70% of the firms are micro-enterprises. Large firms (i.e. firms with an annual turnover above USD 4 million) represent 1.3% of firms in agriculture and 2.7% in food processing. Medium sized companies (i.e. firms with an annual turnover between 1 and 4 USD million) represent 2.9% of firms in agriculture and 3.6% in food processing, while small companies account for 23% of the total firms in agriculture and 25% in food processing (SII, 2016). On the export side, large firms outpaced others. Although SMEs represent 50% of exporting firms large firms account for 90% of total export for a value of 7.3 USD billions (Table 3.9).

Table 3.9. **Large companies account for the bulk of Chile's agro-food exports, 2016**

Size class	No. of firms	Share of firms	Export value USD millions	Share of exports
Large	617	35.4%	7 299	89.2%
SMEs	830	47.6%	625	7.6%
Micro	148	8.5%	22	0.3%
Unclassified	148	8.5%	233	2.8%
Total	1 743	100%	8 179	100%

Note: Tabe includes firms in agriculture and food processing.
Source: Official information from DIRECON-Pro-Chile and SII, 2017.

Chile mostly exports primary products for consumption, and its exports are less diversified than other countries. For example, primary products account for 41% of Chile's domestic agro-food exports, compared to 15% and 11% in Italy and France respectively (Figure 3.19). In 2016, 49 products accounted for 90% of Chilean exports of agro-food. In comparison, 112 products explain 90% of Italy's exports, 121 in France and 165 in the Netherlands. Chile is specialised in the export of fresh fruits and has emerged as a leading exporter in the wine industry. Grapes, pome and stone fruits account for 50% of total domestic agricultural production and 50% of agricultural exports. In 2016 Chile was the 8th world largest wine producer and the 5th world exporter, accounting for 8% of total international trade, by volume. Chile exports 70% of its production of wine to 150 countries, reaching on average 1.5 billion consumers per year (AAWE, 2017).

Figure 3.19. **Trade in agro-food by type, cumulative share 2013-16, selected countries**

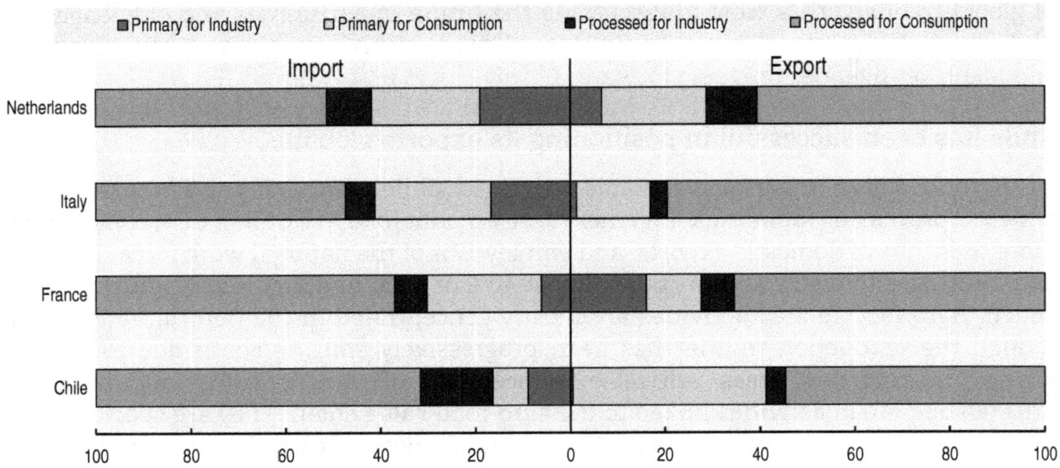

Note: Trade in agro-food by type is obtained by combining the Harmonized System (HS) classification with the Classification by Broad Economic Categories (BEC).
Source: Authors' analysis based on UN Comtrade (2017), Comtrade database, https://comtrade.un.org.

The export market has been highly dynamic in the last decade. Agro-food and beverages exports, which together account for half of Chile`s non-mining exports, have been more dynamic than overall domestic exports. They have been growing on average 10% annually between 2005 and 2015, while total domestic gross exports grew on average 2.5% annually over the same period.

An effective and open trade policy managed by DIRECON, combined with targeted efforts to strengthen Chile's reputation and image abroad, have contributed to the expansion of this industry. In 2015, 94% of agriculture, food and beverage processing exports were destined to the 64 markets covered by the 25 preferential trade agreements that Chile has in place. The primary market for the Chilean agro-food industry is the United States, accounting for 32% of Chilean agricultural exports and 24% of its food and beverage exports in 2015 (Figure 3.20). Japan is the second destination market, accounting for 15% of all Chilean food and beverage processing exports. Other important destination markets are the Netherlands (8% of total domestic exports), the United Kingdom (5%) and Brazil (4%). In the food and beverage processed industry, besides the United States and Japan, other important destination markets include China (6.5% of domestic exports), the Russian Federation (5%), Mexico (4.5%) and Korea (3.5%) (Figure 3.21). Chile's top 10 destination markets absorb 75% of total domestic agro exports and 70% of domestic exports of food and beverages.

Figure 3.20. **Decomposition of Chilean gross exports by origin and destination, agriculture, 2014**

Value added of exports by origin and destination (%)

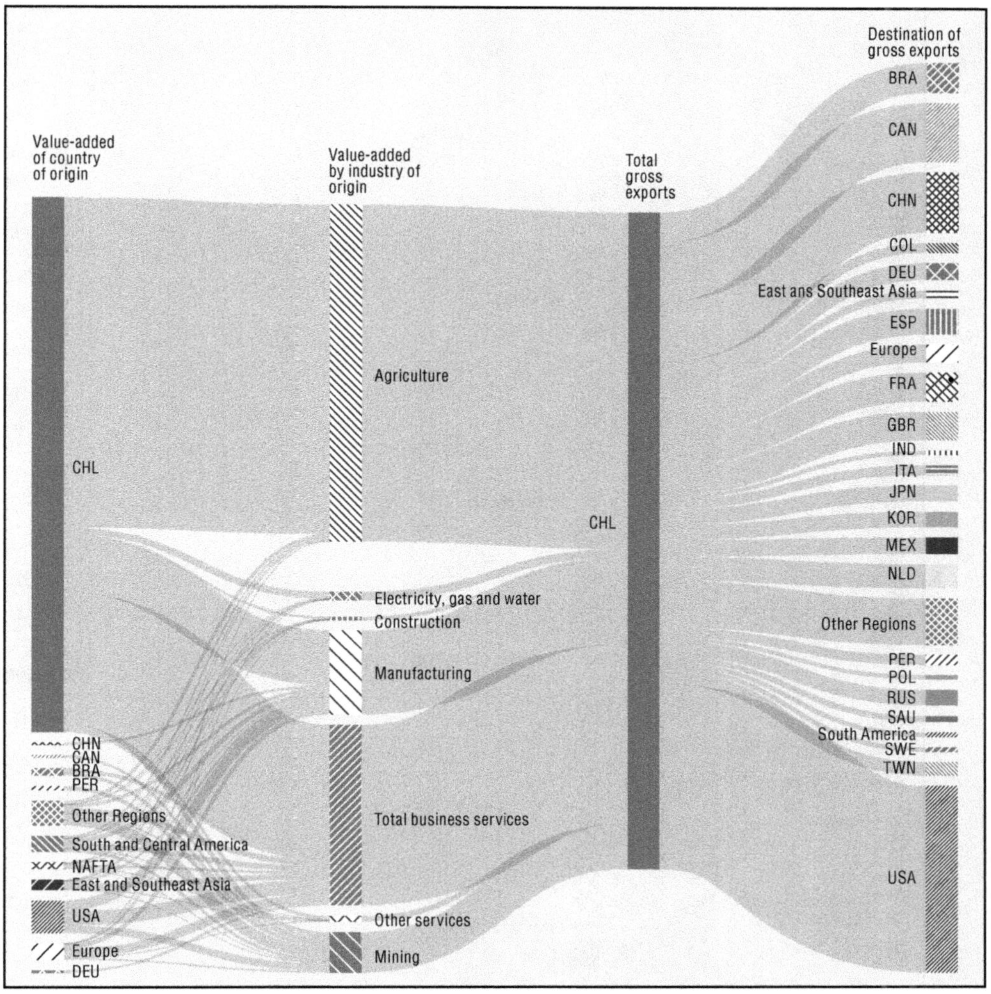

Note: Regional aggregates exclude member countries reported in the graph.

Source: OECD (2017b), TiVA Nowcast Database, http://stats.oecd.org/Index.aspx?DataSetCode=TIVA_NOWCAST; see also www.oecd.org/std/its/tiva-nowcast-methodology.pdf

Chile has the potential to increase land productivity and the value of its agro-food exports (Figure 3.22). Despite having 15 million hectares of cultivable land, Chile only exports agricultural products worth USD 6 000 million annually, while the Netherlands, with a cultivable surface of only 1.84 million hectares, exports agricultural products worth USD 28 000 million.

Figure 3.21. Decomposition of Chilean gross exports by origin and destination, food manufacturing, 2014

Value added of exports by origin and destination (%)

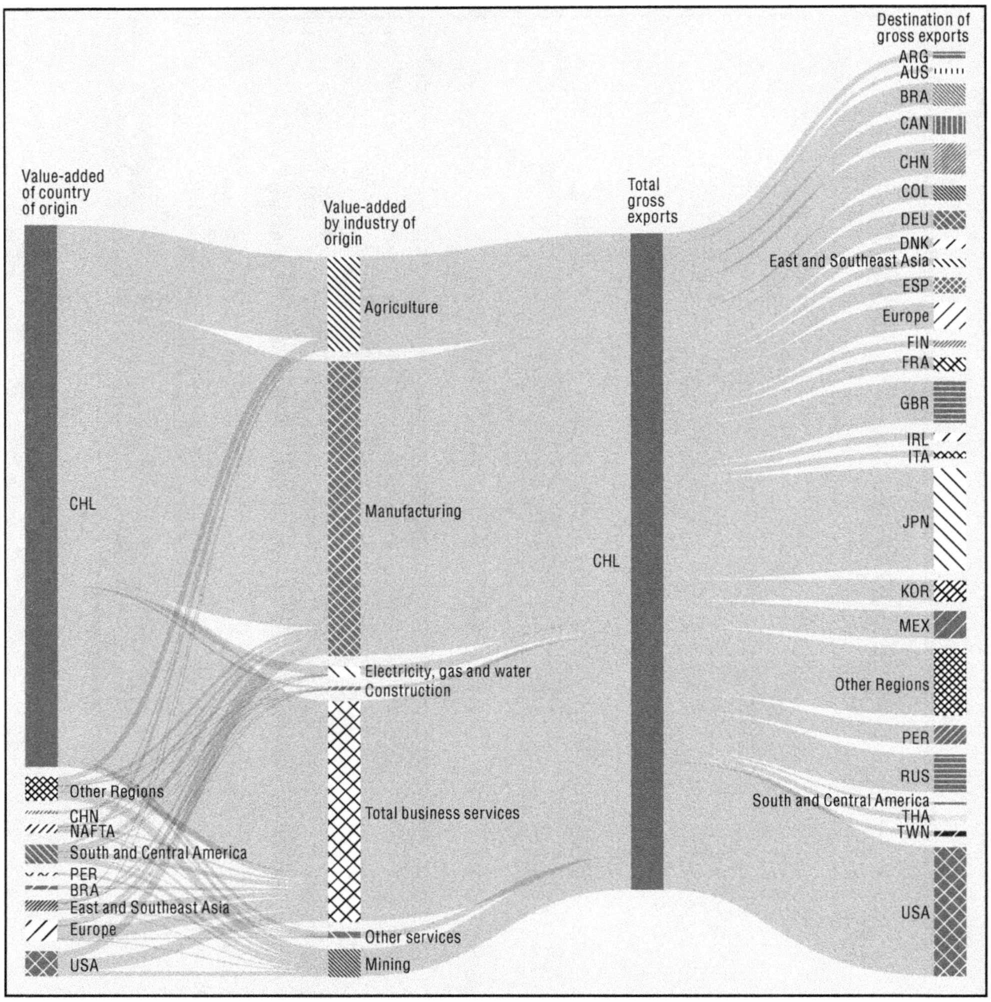

Note: Regional aggregates exclude member countries reported in the graph.

Source: OECD (2017b), TiVA Nowcast Database, http://stats.oecd.org/Index.aspx?DataSetCode=TIVA_NOWCAST; see also www.oecd.org/std/its/tiva-nowcast-methodology.pdf

Increasing the impact of applied research and development in the agro-food value chain could help to increase the value added of domestic production. In Chile, the R&D intensity in agriculture, measured as a share of R&D expenditures on agriculture-related matters in agricultural value added, is higher than the national average (1.6% versus 0.4%). In Latin America, Chile is second only to Brazil for its R&D intensity in agriculture-related areas, where it is 2%. However, the gap with other emerging and advanced countries remains high. In South Africa, investment in agro-related R&D amounts to 2% of agricultural value added; in Australia the indicator reaches 5% and in Netherlands 10% (Figure 3.23).

Figure 3.22. **Agricultural exports and land area, 2015**

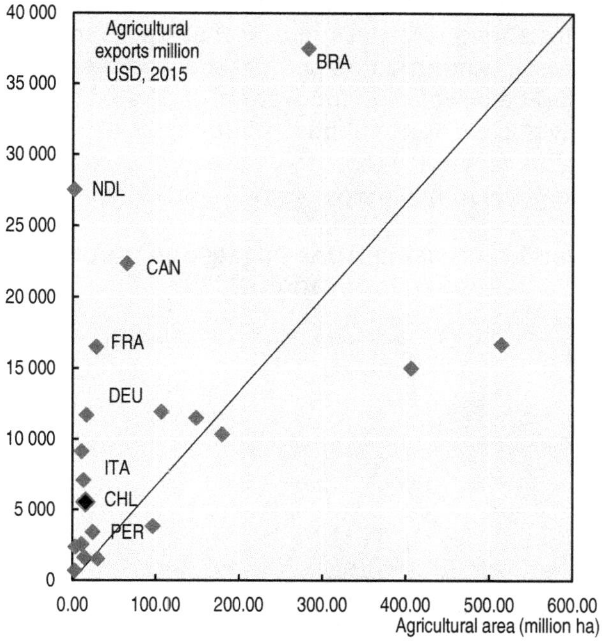

Source: Authors' analysis based on OECD National Accounts https://data.oecd.org/ and FAO Statistics database www.fao.org/faostat/, 2017.

Figure 3.23. **R&D expenditure in agricultural science as a share of value added in agriculture, 2014**

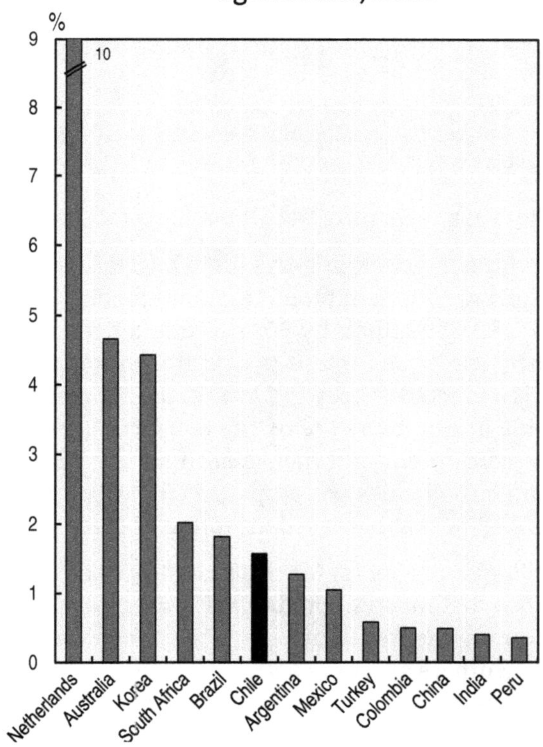

Note: R&D figures refer to 2014 or last available year: 2011 for South Africa; 2013 for the Netherlands, Australia, Korea, Brazil, and Peru

Source: Authors' analysis based on OECD National Accounts https://data.oecd.org and ASTI-IFPR https://www.asti.cgiar.org, 2017.

The private sector commitment to innovation in Chile's food processing industry is below that of international leaders. In Chile fewer firms introduce innovations, and among the innovators, Chilean firms tend to be less radical than firms in other countries and they tend to focus on process, rather than on product innovations. In Chile, 40% of food processing companies report being active in innovation, compared to 70% in Belgium and around 60% in France, Italy and the Netherlands. Additionally, 27% of Chile's innovators report having introduced a process innovation, 19% have introduced product innovations, and 17% have introduced organisational innovations (Figure 3.24).

Figure 3.24. **Share of food processing firms engaged in innovation activities by type of innovation, 2014**

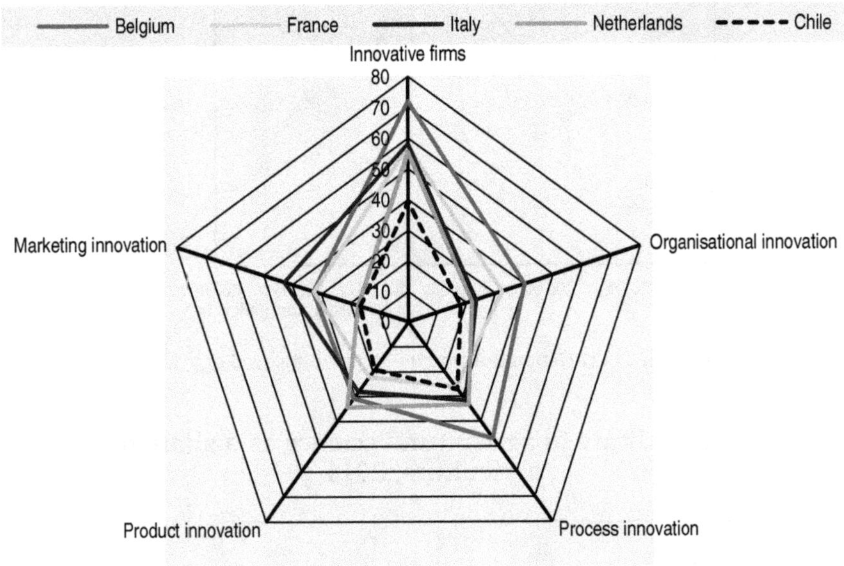

Note: For comparing different innovation surveys we adopted the scheme proposed by Crespi et al (2016).
Source: Authors' analysis based on Eurostat (2014), "Community Innovation Survey", http://ec.europa.eu/eurostat/web/microdata/community-innovation-survey; and Chilean Innovation Survey 2013-14, 2017.

New trends in global markets are reshaping the global agro-food value chain

New consumer preferences are changing the global agriculture, food and beverage markets (Figure 3.25). The global functional food[3] market reached USD 140 billion in 2015 and is expected to exceed USD 250 billion by 2024. While a decade ago the demand for sustainable, safe and healthy food was limited to a niche market, the trend has recently become more diffused and is expected to keep growing in the future (Grand View Research, 2016). Consumers worldwide are more aware of the consequences of long and complex food value chains for the environment and their health. In the US, total food sales were up 1.9% in 2015 while organic food sales were up 16.9%. The market for functional and healthy food is growing, linked to the increased attention of middle classes to wellbeing.

Demand is shifting to "local" products (0-Km products), and "authentic" and unique products, often coming from distant markets but with a recognised impact on health. This is the case for the booming market in quinoa, a product almost unknown a decade ago in Western markets. Consumers are more aware of the impact of food on their quality of life, on the environment and on the people involved throughout the value chain, and demand for local and foreign products is growing. However, these trends come with higher requirements in terms of transparency and information on the characteristics of each product, the environment it comes from, the processing methods, and the overall sustainability of its production and distribution. Many lead firms in the food and beverage industry are taking steps in this direction. Some of these firms are strengthening the accountability procedures of their sourcing practices and their relationship with industrial suppliers and farmers, and are shifting from a logic of traditional responsible business conduct (RBC) to a logic of partnerships for competitiveness and development.

These changes are influencing the whole agro, food and beverage value chain standards, traceability and innovation, which are increasingly important! The standards linked to ISO 22000 define international norms for food safety. In addition to that, there are currently multiple bottom-up initiatives for setting sustainability norms for production, processing, and use of ingredients. The proliferation of these various standards makes it increasingly difficult for small and medium-sized companies to access the market. Clarification of international standards will be needed to ensure consumers' interest and fair market access for producers (OECD, 2013).

Innovations linked to new ingredients, smart packaging, new forms of production and distribution, and new energy sources are helping to redefine the value chain and the competitiveness opportunities for lead firms and suppliers. Major innovations are taking place in packaging, as focus is increasingly drawn to sustainable solutions, such as biodegradable packaging. As Chile mostly exports fresh fruit, smart packing is needed to preserve the products' freshness during transport, and to ensure a high-quality experience for the final consumer. Renewable energies also open up new opportunities to green the agro-food value chain, which accounts for 30% of global energy consumption (Sims et al., 2015).

Figure 3.25. **The future of global agro-food: new markets, innovation and standards**

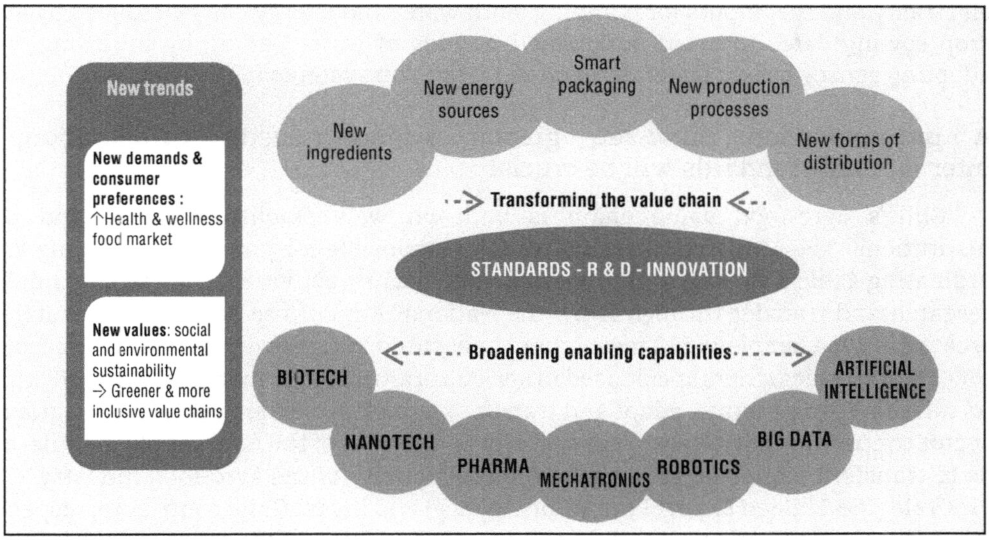

Source: Authors' elaboration based on the outcomes of the Round Table on the Future of Agro-food in Chile, organised in the framework of the PTPR of Chile, hosted by CORFO in Santiago, Chile in April 2017.

The agro-food value chain is increasingly sophisticated and a growing number of scientific and technological areas will drive competitiveness in the future. Bio and nano technologies will be increasingly relevant for the value chain, but also competences linked to pharmaceuticals and new forms of packaging and manufacturing. For example, natural bioactives, including phytosterols, are used as ingredients in creating functional foods. However, because of their lack of solubility, stability and bioavailability, many of these ingredients cannot be directly consumed by people. Nanotechnology research is helping to improve the solubility and stability of these bioactive ingredients to transform them as inputs for functional food products. Research in chemical and pharmaceuticals is also increasingly relevant for the agro-food value chain, as food and chemicals are combined to develop nutritional products to prevent and treat diseases. The region of Emilia Romagna

(Italy), is investing USD 20 million in 74 applied research projects with a time horizon of 2014-2020 to connect the regional agro-food value chain to new technologies. The projects involve six regional universities, four regional research centres and the business community, including the Consortium of Parmigiano Reggiano.

Robotics, big data and cloud computing are also major enablers of future competitiveness. The global market for agricultural robotics is expected to grow from its current USD 1 billion to USD 28 billion by 2025 (Business Wire, 2016). Applied to smart farming, the Internet of Things and Big Data will shape precision agriculture through smart sensing and monitoring, smart analysis and planning, leading to increased yields and productivity and reduced environmental impact. Data science also benefits the sector through enhanced traceability and greater food safety. Big data coupled with neurosciences, behavioural sciences, and linguistics will also be increasingly relevant as they will contribute to develop new marketing techniques and will increasingly be used to define "nudging schemes" for inducing healthier consumer choices.

In Chile, world-leading neuro-scientists have contributed to the work of the Future Commission in the Senate, leading to the approval of a law that sets nutritional standards for food products that are allowed to be distributed in Chilean schools. Digital technologies can also help to green the whole value chain by helping farmers reduce their energy consumption. Precision irrigation systems based on GPS information can provide reliable and flexible water application and facilitate wastewater reuse. Crops often take up less than 50% of the applied irrigation water, so there is potential to improve efficiency by reducing water run-off and evaporative and infiltration losses. This can result in fewer electricity and fuel inputs for pumping. Both water and energy can be reduced by altering crop sowing dates to avoid anticipated periods of water deficit, by mulching, and by adopting sensor-based, water demand-led irrigation systems (Sims et al., 2015).

A pro-innovation mind-set, greater science-industry co-operation, and international standards will be crucial

Chile's agro-food value chain is built on well-established public and private institutions. The Ministry of Agriculture is responsible for promoting, steering and co-ordinating Chile's agricultural, livestock and forestry activities. It fosters technological research and transfer through INIA (the National Agriculture Research Institute). INIA, created in 1964, employs 320 researchers (measured in full-time equivalents), accounting for 45% of all researchers specialised in agricultural-related activities in Chile (IFPRI, 2016). Its mission is to generate, adapt and transfer technologies to ensure that the agricultural sector contributes positively to the security and quality of the food supply in Chile, as well as to transfer technology to increase the productivity of the agro-food industry. CORFO, ProChile (the Chilean Export Promotion Agency) and Invest Chile contribute, respectively, to strengthen domestic capacity, favour exports and attract foreign investment. The three operate with a combination of horizontal programmes and targeted actions for the agro-food value chain. CORFO focuses on enabling innovation and production development, especially in small firms. It also supported the creation of a universities consortium in 2016, which resulted in the creation of the Technological Centre for Food Innovation (CeTa). The centre aims, in co-operation with the private sector, to close the country's infrastructure and technological gap in order to facilitate the upgrading of the Chilean agro-food firms into functional and sophisticated food value chains. The Ministry of Foreign Affairs, through DIRECON-Prochile, promotes exports and access to foreign markets and facilitates trade through awareness raising, image promotion and partnerships, whereas Invest Chile is aiming to attract investments conducive to achieving the world frontier in the global functional and healthy food industry.

The setting up of the Chilean Agency for Quality and Food Safety (ACHIPIA) in 2005 to regulate phytosanitary and food safety in the country is another positive step. The agency defines and ensures compliance with standards and measures related to food safety and quality. The Agricultural and Livestock Service (SAG) is responsible for enforcing Chile's import regulations concerning alcoholic beverages, organic foods, animal and plant quarantine; the grading and labelling of beef and some processed food products, both for human and animal consumption, including pet-food, feed and feed supplements. In this respect, alignment with international standards is necessary to facilitate trade.

Lead firms count on strong business associations and have an export-oriented attitude. The Association of Fruit Exporters (ASOEX) and the Chilean Fresh Fruit Trade Association (FEDEFRUTA) are active in export promotion, targeting especially the United States, Europe, and Latin America. The Federation of Food Processing Industries of Chile (CHILEALIMENTOS ex-FEPACH) advises exporters on foreign trade issues, conducts statistical and tariff reviews of new markets, advises members on the proper use of export incentives, and advises exporters on certificate of origin issues. Chile is also home to some pioneer firms in functional food. For example, Granote was founded in 1981 with a mission to increase the value added of the wheat and grain value chain by focusing on technological solutions for nutrition, biotechnology and health.

For a country like Chile, in which the agro-food value chain accounts for 16% of employment and 12% of all firms, and contributes to 25% of domestic exports, it is essential to scan for and monitor global trends, and to identify niches where the country, with its limited production base, can compete effectively (Chile accounts only for 1.6% of global agricultural production). The business community and government share the vision that Chile has potential to benefit from emerging trends in the industry. Stakeholders also recognise that overcoming several barriers to scaling up in the global agro-food value chain will require co-operation among various actors. These barriers are related to: 1) enabling conditions for business development, such as reducing red tape, creating incentives for public-private R&D, and improving physical and Internet connectivity; and 2) specific issues linked to the agro-food value chain, such as co-ordination among the various actors and reaching a critical mass of investment in research and development to keep up with global trends (Table 3.10).

Table 3.10. **Multi-stakeholder assessment of the functional agro-food value chain, Chile, 2017**

Strengths	Weaknesses
• Availability of high-quality inputs (e.g. fruit) for functional food • Counter-seasonal supply to the north hemisphere • Effective image and reputation • High openness of the economy and effective trade policy • Ongoing international business to business co-operation with foreign companies	• Low productivity of micro enterprises • Low propensity to innovation in food processing • Limited co-ordination within and between government • Geographical distance from main destination markets that increases logistics costs & shelf-life challenges • Limited technology transfer capacity between universities, research centres and firms • Limited investment and installed capacities in ingredient development and smart packaging
Opportunities	**Threats**
• New, more sophisticated consumer tastes • Growing demand for functional food • New technologies to address logistic challenges • Leveraging on existing institutions for applied R&D in agriculture • Big domestic companies with a Latin American (and global) aspiration • Strengthened regional integration	• Small-scale production • Lack of appropriate standards and traceability systems • Climate change • Increasing water scarcity

Source: Authors' elaboration based on the outcomes of the Round Table on the Future of Agro-food in Chile, organised in the framework of the PTPR of Chile, hosted by CORFO in Santiago, Chile in April 2017.

In response to global trends, Chile has set up a process to identify a shared vision for the future and to clarify priorities for public investment. CORFO, with its mandate to foster business development in the country, has capitalised on past experiences and since 2014 has led a process of dialogue between businesses, academia and government agencies. In line with what is happening in other countries and regions, CORFO set up a consultative public-private process to define a vision and a road-map for 2025 in co-operation with the Ministry of Agriculture and the Ministry of Health, INIA, other government agencies, and in consultation with the private sector. The process involved 71 firms, 17 business associations and 17 public and private universities and research centres. The public-private dialogue led to the shared objective of positioning Chile among the top 10 world leading countries in the production and commercialisation of sustainable and functional food products. CORFO is co-ordinating the process, and it has helped to set up a road-map for 2025 with specific goals linked to increasing export diversification and sophistication and augmenting the value of exports (Table 3.11). This current national programme, *Transforma Alimentos*, builds on its precursor programme, PIAS (*Programa de Innovacion en Alimentos Saludables*). Set-up in 2012 the programme encouraged and promoted the development of a sustainable food value chain in Chile.

Table 3.11. **Vision and objectives for agro-food in Chile, 2013-25**

GOAL: To be among the leading global processors and exporters of healthy foods			
Targets	Indicator	Baseline 2013	by 2025
Diversifying exports	Number of agro-food products that cover 90% of exports	64	74
A more sophisticated export basket	Average Product Complexity index	0.61	0.50
Increasing export value	Free on board (FOB) export value	USD 18 billions	USD 32.2 billion

Note: The Product Complexity Index measures the knowledge intensity of a product by considering the knowledge intensity of its exporters. For more information see Hidalgo & Haussmann 2009: http://www.pnas.org/content/106/26/10570.short

Source: Authors' analysis based on official information from CORFO, 2017.

The road-mapping exercise identified six main gaps: 1) infrastructure; 2) human capital; 3) innovation; 4) co-ordination; 5) market access; and 6) standards for enabling the development of new food categories and high-value ingredients for specific consumer groups, as well as for ensuring high-quality inputs (e.g. fresh fruit), and the development of new packaging techniques to ensure effective shelf-life, quality and safety of Chilean products (Table 3.12). The government is mobilising public resources of around USD 30 million, and the private sector is contributing USD 10 million for the period 2015-18. The planned overall investment by 2025 is USD 100 million, of which 63% is expected to come from the public sector. The national actions are complemented by four regional plans: fruit in Valparaiso, horticulture in O'Higgins, semi-processed agroindustry in Maule, and high value-added processed food in Los Rios. The regional programmes foster co-ordination among the different actors, including farmers, producers, universities and local and national research centres. These regional programmes are managed by CORFO and co-financed by FIC (Innovation and Competitiveness Found) and FIE (Strategic investment Fund).

Table 3.12. **The Chilean agro-food strategic programme: gaps and actions by 2025**

GAPS & ACTIONS	Developing and promoting new food categories for specific consumer groups	Developing high-value ingredients from natural sources	Increasing productivity and quality of fruit exports taking into account climate change	Developing packaging to ensure effective shelf-life, quality and safety of Chilean products	Ensuring high quality inputs (e.g. new tubers for natural colorants, etc.) for specific demand from dynamic markets
INFRASTRUCTURE	Lack of adequate infrastructure for applied research and technology transfers => Creation of an Innovation & Technology Centre				
	USD 27.84 million				
HUMAN CAPITAL	Lack of adequate technical skills => Provision of extension services (USD 3.83million)				Lack of adequate technical skills => Provision of extension services (USD2.30million)
R&D & INNOVATION	Little investment in research for industry-related problem solving and innovation => R&D grants with request of matching funds from firms and services				
	USD 5.25 million	USD 18.10 million	USD 14.46 million	USD 6.78 million	USD 2.55 million
NETWORK and CO-ORDINATION	Scant co-ordination across and within regions => Grants for joint financing and for technology transfers				
	USD 0.51 million	USD 7.94 million	USD 1.10 million		USD 1.56 million
MARKET ACCEwwS	Financing for business scaling up		Financing and services for access to market		Financing for suppliers development
	USD 7.81 million		USD 0.35 million		USD 0.18 million
INFORMATION, STANDARDS, REGULATIONS	Lack of adequate standards & norms => Modernisation of the National System for Assessment, Quality and Food Safety => Modernisation of the traceability system				
	USD 0.69 million	USD 0.08 million	USD 0.29 million		USD 4.50 million

Source: Authors' analysis based on CORFO information, 2017.

The programme is in the early stages of implementation so it is too difficult for any type of impact assessment, but comparing the Chilean approach with international benchmarks can help identify key issues in going forward (Table 3.13):

- **Foster self-discovery and long-term thinking.** Chile's visioning approach is in line with global trends. All countries and regions with an exports-oriented agro-food industry are currently scanning for ongoing and potential future opportunities in the global market in response to changing demand and technology. Most countries are involved in exercises to identify long-term goals through public-private consultations. One example is the region of Emilia Romagna in Italy (Box 3.5).
- **Identify gaps that need public action.** The gaps and areas for public intervention identified by Chile also reflect international trends. These include: 1) public support, in the form of financing and/or services for infrastructure development, and in particular strengthening the research base; 2) skills development, with a particular focus on competences linked to technological convergence and digitalisation, and scientific areas relevant for the future of the industry; 3) market access facilitation; 4) co-ordination among different actors in the ecosystem; and 5) investment in standards and regulations.
- **Mobilise public and private resources for amounts that reflect global challenges.** The competitiveness challenges posed by the ongoing technological and demand revolutions require high mobilisation of resources. The Emilia Romagna region, with less than 5 million inhabitants, is mobilising USD 800 million between 2015 and 2020 for investments to improve the competitiveness of its agro-food system. Chile, according to current plans, is aiming to mobilise one-eighth of this amount (USD 100 million from 2014 to 2025). Considering Chile's future priorities to reduce

public debt, actions involving regional and global partnerships could help the country overcome its funding limitations.

- **Monitor implementation and assess impact.** New technologies offer new opportunities to guarantee easier and real-time access to information linked to the implementation of public action. Setting up a clear, easy-to-access mechanism for tracking implementation increases accountability and enables actions to be adjusted when expected results are not achieved. The region of Emilia Romagna has an open platform that monitors the implementation of actions linked to the agro-food system. It shows indicators of output (number of projects financed, firms participating, research centres, etc.) and impact (investment in R&D by firms, patents, among others).[4]

Table 3.13. **Progress overview of Chile's agro-food programme, 2017**

	Governance dimensions	
Anticipation capacity	√	The road-map to 2025 represents a step forward in line with international best practices. Alignment of the road map with financing limited to 2018 will be an additional step forward to secure impact.
Adaptation capacity	√	The programme is in line with global increasing demand for functional and healthy food products. The programme is also the result of long- standing tradition and relies on past experiences.
Learning and upgrading potential	x	Beside the national programme, other regional and national programmes are currently under implementation. These concern other complementary activities in the agro-food value chain, such as livestock, fishing and fruticulture. It is important to avoid excessive splitting of programmes, which could result in overlapping actions and information asymmetries.
	≈	The programme encompasses several lines of work. Nevertheless it should incorporate specific actions to better promote learning through technology complementarities with such as big data, smart farming and the Internet of Things, as well as the potential offered by renewable energies.
Interconnectedness propensity	√	**Within government**. The programme benefits from multi-agency co-ordination and buy in (e.g, Ministry of Economy, Ministry of Agriculture).
	≈	**Private sector**. Though businesses participated in the road-map process there is lack of buy in from a broad section of value chains, particularly those in upstream activities.
	√	**Academia and research centres**. The programme benefits from commitment and co-operation mechanisms with academia and international research centres, such as Fraunhofer Chile Research.
	x	**Regional co-operation**. Chile is a small economy that could build on its openness to foster greater integration at regional level to achieve critical scale in order to be competitive in the international market.
Embeddedness potential	≈	Mechanisms to avoid rent seeking and capture need to be in place to ensure that publicly-financed actions benefit all stakeholders and deliver public and club goods not available otherwise. In this respect open government and effective monitoring and evaluation are needed to track progress and performance and identify areas for improvement.

Note: √: positive progress; ≈: margin for improvement; x: reform needed.
The definition of the five governance dimensions can be found in OECD (2017) and in Box 2.1 in Chapter 2 of this report.

Box 3.5. Scanning possible futures in agro-food: the experience of Emilia Romagna, Italy

Emilia-Romagna is a world-leading region for agro-food. The industry benefits from complementarities between excellence in production, unique products and regional strengths in the whole value chain, including high quality capabilities in specialised machinery, education, training and research.

The agro-food system employs more than 16% of the regional workforce, employing around 313 000 people spread across agriculture (25%), food industries (20%), retail (20%), mechanical engineering (11%), chemical and complementary industries (2%), and other related services (22%). More than 770 co-operative firms are active in the region and generate 60% of the turnover of agro-food.

In 2013 the government of the Emilia Romagna region carried out a technology foresight process to define a strategy to sustain the competitiveness of the agro-food industry in line with the Horizon 2020 European Structural Funds. The process was co-ordinated by the regional government and the regional Agency for Research (ASTER). The process also involved the private sector and universities. As a result the region has identified 4 main challenges that have been associated with 11 areas of intervention (Figure 3.26).

Figure 3.26. Scanning future challenges to set priorities for agro-food in Emilia Romagna

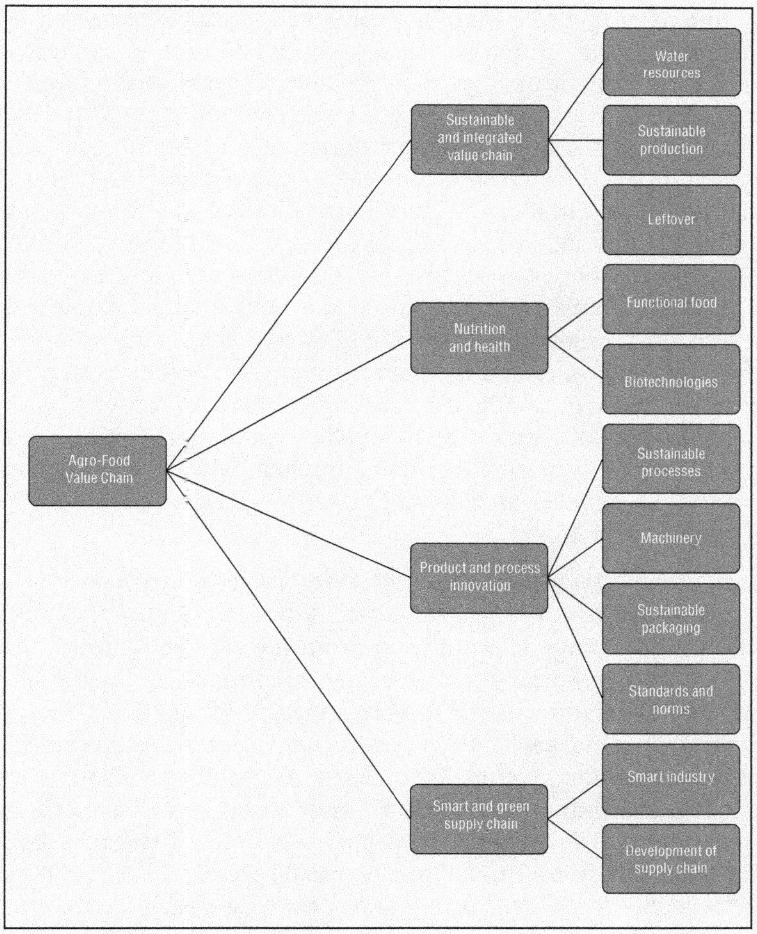

Source: Regional Government of Emilia Romagna, 2017.

Conclusions

The changing global technological and economic landscape is opening up new opportunities for Chile. The definition of long-term agendas based on trust and dialogue between the government and the private sector is the cornerstone of future progress. This chapter has reviewed Chile's current public-private dialogue and roadmaps for the future in solar energy, mining and agro-food.

Solar energy could open up new opportunities for learning and innovation. Chile has a unique natural advantage in this industry. Unlike fossil-fuel based energies, solar is not extracted through drilling and mining, but is the result of high value-added activities. It involves a manufacturing value chain and can be produced and used locally. Innovating and identifying solutions for solar energy requires shared efforts from all actors in the ecosystem, including energy providers, academia and government. Chile is investing in closing the knowledge and regulatory gaps to unleash the potential of solar energy. Identifying potential synergies with other renewable energies and economic activities and strengthening regional ties to scale up investments and reach the critical mass needed to effectively compete at the global level will be important. In going forward, the social acceptability of solar energy should not be taken for granted. The social licence from which these energies currently from will only be sustained in the long run if new agreements, negotiations and benefit sharing with the local communities are developed. New forms of dialogue and partnership with local communities will therefore be needed.

Mining has been, and will remain, a key economic activity in Chile. Global trends are transforming mining into a more inclusive and sustainable sector. Green mining is already a business priority, in part because of high and growing energy costs, and also because of growing demand for "greener" products, pushing the need to green entire value chains. Chile could build on its effective partnerships with lead firms in the value chain to participate in this transformation at an early stage. This will require a pro-development attitude from the business community, and targeted policies to foster learning and innovation. Chilean mining will benefit from a shift in logic away from using technology as a "ready-made technical solution", to a discovery process that requires partnerships and trust between technology providers and mining operators. Working together to identify innovative solutions is the next step for trust-building between government and businesses in mining. *Alta Ley* is a promising step in this direction. The results will depend on effective monitoring of the implementation process, and on the capacity of government to adjust accordingly. It will also depend on the capacity to generate synergies with other industrial development opportunities, most notably solar energy. In going forward, a more integrated approach between social and environmental sustainability will be needed, as well as greater integration among different activities, such as *Alta Ley* and *Valor Minero*.

Chile's long-standing tradition in the agro-food value chain is reflected in its definition of actions and targets towards a more sustainable and productive system. In going forward, Chile needs stronger commitment from the private sector to innovate; greater co-operation between research and the business community; and effective policies to facilitate business development and enable strategic innovation through partnerships between academia, businesses and the government. Moreover a more holistic approach that avoids duplicated efforts would be important. Chile also needs to be actively involved in international discussions on standards and norms, as these will be increasingly relevant in the agro-food value chain and especially in the functional food segment. The institutional capabilities in this area that are already present in the country will be key for creating the transparent and stable regulatory framework needed to enable production development and trade.

Notes

1. Excluding hydroelectric larger than 20 megawatts (Mw).
2. For more information see http://solar-district-heating.eu/SDH/forheatsuppliers.aspx.
3. Functional foods are those types of food that provide additional health elements generated around a particular functional ingredient, for example foods containing probiotics or prebiotics.
4. The information is available here: http://www.regione.emilia-romagna.it/s3-monitoraggio/risultato.html.

References

AAWE (2017), *American Association of Wine Economists database*, www.wine-economics.org/data.

Alston, J. (2010), "The Benefits from Agricultural Research and Development, Innovation, and Productivity Growth", *OECD Food, Agriculture and Fisheries Papers*, No. 31, OECD Publishing, Paris. http://dx.doi.org/10.1787/5km91nfsnkwg-en

Ang, G., D. Röttgers and P. Burli (2017), "The empirics of enabling investment and innovation in renewable energy", *OECD Environment Working Papers*, No. 123, OECD Publishing, Paris. http://dx.doi.org/10.1787/67d221b8-en

Austmine (2013). Australia's New Driver for Growth. Mining Equipment, Technology and Services.

Business Wire (2016). Agricultural Robots Market Analysis & Trends - Product, Technology - Forecast to 2025

Carbaugh, R. J., & St Brown, M. (2012). Industrial policy and renewable energy: Trade conflicts. *Journal of International and Global Economic Studies.*

CCM (2016), "Fuerza Laboral de la Gran Minería Chilena 2015-2024: diagnóstico y recomendaciones", Consejo de competenza Minera.

CNID (2014), *Mining: A Platform for Chile's Future. Report to the President of the Republic of Chile Michelle Bachelet*, National Council for Innovation and Development, Santiago, www.cnid.cl/wp-content/uploads/2015/06/Mining_a_platform_for_chilean_future.pdf.

CNP (2017), "Productividad en la gran minería del Cobre", Comisión Nacional de Productividad, Santiago.

Codelco (2017), "Annual report, 2017", Codelco.

COCHILCO (2017), "database", Ministry of Mining, Government of Chile, https://www.cochilco.cl.

Crespi, G., Tacsir, E. and F. Vargas (2016), "Innovation dynamics and productivity: Evidence for Latin America", In: *Firm Innovation and Productivity in Latin America and the Caribbean* (pp. 37-71). Palgrave Macmillan US.

Deloitte (2017), "Tracking the Trends 2017. The top 10 trends mining companies will face in the coming year", https://www2.deloitte.com/global/en/pages/energy-and-resources/articles/tracking-the-trends.html.

Eurostat (2014), "Community Innovation Survey", Eurostat, Brussels, http://ec.europa.eu/eurostat/web/microdata/community-innovation-survey

Grand View Research (2016), *Functional Foods Market Analysis by Product and Segment Forecasts, 2014 to 2024*, Grand View Research, San Francisco.

Helm, S., Tannock, Q. and I. Iliev (2014), *Renewable Energy Technology: Evolution and policy implications—Evidence from patent literature. Global Challenges Report*, World Intellectual Property Organization, Geneva.

Hidalgo, C.A. and R. Haussmann (2009), "The building blocks of economic complexity", PNAS 106(26): 10570–10575, http://www.pnas.org/content/106/26/10570.short.

IEA (2017a), "Statistics", International Energy Agency, Paris, https://www.iea.org/statistics.

IEA (2017b), *Global EV Outlook 2017: Two million and counting*, International Energy Agency, Paris, http://dx.doi.org/10.1787/9789264278882-en.

IEA (2016), *World Energy Outlook 2016*, International Energy Agency, Paris, http://dx.doi.org/10.1787/weo-2016-en.

IEA (2009), *Chile Energy Policy Review 2009*, International Energy Agency, Paris, http://dx.doi.org/10.1787/9789264073159-en.

IFPRI (2016), "Chile: Agricultural R&D indicators factsheet", International Food Policy Research Institute, Washington, DC, http://ebrary.ifpri.org/cdm/ref/collection/p15738coll2/id/130291.

IRENA (2017) *IRENA Dashboard*, International Renewable Energy Agency, Masdar, http://resourceirena.irena.org/gateway/dashboard/.

IRENA (2015),"Renewable energy in the water, energy & food nexus", The International Renewable Energy Agency (IRENA), Masdar.

FAO (2013). WFP, The State of Food Insecurity in the World 2013. The multiple dimensions of food security.

Johnson, O. (2013). Exploring the effectiveness of local content requirements in promoting solar PV manufacturing in India.

Jorge Cabrera,& Hans Grosse. (2015). State of the World's Forests 2016 Section 4.2 Country Case Studies: Chile final report (Original Version). DOI: 10.13140/RG.2.1.2517.7843

Korinek, J. (2013), "Mineral Resource Trade in Chile: Contribution to Development and Policy Implications", *OECD Trade Policy Papers*, No. 145, OECD Publishing, Paris. http://dx.doi.org/10.1787/5k4bw6twpf24-en

Kuntze, J. C., & Moerenhout, T. (2012). Local Content Requirements and the Renewable Energy Industry-A Good Match?.

Marin, A., Navas Alemán, L., & Perez, C. (2015). Natural resource industries as a platform for the development of knowledge intensiveindustries. economisheensocialegeografie, 106(2), 154-168.

Mathews, J. A. (2017), *Global Green Shift: When Ceres Meets Gaia*, Anthem Press.

Molina, O., Olivari, J., &Pietrobelli, C. (2016). Global Value Chains in the Peruvian Mining Sector. Inter-American Development Bank.

Ministry of Energy (2017a), "Chile, Energy 2050: Chile Energy Policy", Ministry of Energy, Santiago, http://pelp.minenergia.cl/.

Ministry of Energy (2017b), *Long-Term Strategic Planning Database*, Ministry of Energy, Santiago.

Quitzow, R. (2015), "Assessing policy strategies for the promotion of environmental technologies: A review of India's National Solar Mission", *Research Policy*, 44(1), 233-243.

Sawin, J., K. Seyboth and F. Sverrisson (2016), *REN21 Renewables Global Status Report 2016*, REN21 Secretariat, Paris, www.ren21.net/wp-content/uploads/2016/05/GSR_2016_Full_Report_lowres.pdf.

Sims, R., Flammini, A., Puri, M. and S. Bracco (2015), "Opportunities for agri-food chains to become energy-smart", FAO and USAID, Rome and Washington DC, www.fao.org/3/a-i5125e.pdf.

ODEPA (2015) Oficina de Estudios y Políticas Agrarias, Chilean Agriculture Overview 2015

OECD (2018), *OECD Economic Surveys: Chile 2018*, OECD Publishing, Paris.

OECD (2017a), *The Next Production Revolution: Implications for Governments and Business*, OECD Publishing, Paris, http://dx.doi.org/10.1787/9789264271036-en.

OECD (2017b), *TiVA Nowcast Database,* http://stats.oecd.org/Index.aspx?DataSetCode=TIVA_NOWCAST, OECD, Paris.

OECD (2017c), *Production Transformation Policy Reviews: Actions to Succeed in a Changing World*, OECD Publishing, Paris, http://dx.doi.org/10.1787/9789264276628-en.

OECD (2016a), *Agricultural Policy Monitoring and Evaluation 2016*, OECD Publishing, Paris. DOI: http://dx.doi.org/10.1787/agr_pol-2016-en

OECD (2015), *OECD Economic Surveys: Chile 2015*, OECD Publishing, Paris. http://dx.doi.org/10.1787/eco_surveys-chl-2015-en

OECD (2015b), *Overcoming Barriers to International Investment in Clean Energy*, OECD Publishing, Paris. http://dx.doi.org/10.1787/9789264227064-en

OECD (2013), *Agricultural Innovation Systems: A Framework for Analysing the Role of the Government*, OECD Publishing, Paris. http://dx.doi.org/10.1787/9789264200593-en

OECD (2011), *Maintaining Momentum: OECD Perspectives on Policy Challenges in Chile*, OECD, Publishing, Paris, http://dx.doi.org/10.1787/9789264095199-en.

OECD (2010), *Agricultural Policies in OECD Countries 2010: At a Glance*, OECD Publishing, Paris, http://dx.doi.org/10.1787/agr_oecd-2010-en.

Pegels, A., & Lütkenhorst, W. (2014). Is Germany's Energy Transition a case of successful Green Industrial Policy? Contrasting wind and solar PV, *Energy Policy*,

REN21(2017). Renewables 2017 Global Status Report, Paris REN21 Secretariat.

UN Comtrade (2017), *Comtrade Database*, United Nations, New York, https://comtrade.un.org.

Urzúa, O. (2013). The emergence and development of knowledge intensive mining service suppliers in the late 20th century (Doctoral dissertation, University of Sussex).

WTO, OECD and UNCTAD (2014), Reports on G20 Trade and Investment Measures: Mid-November 2013 to mid-May 2014, available at: http://www.oecd.org/daf/inv/investmentpolicy/11thG20report.pdf

Zhang, S., Andrews-Speed, P., Zhao, X., & He, Y. (2013). Interactions between renewable energy policy and renewable energy industrial policy: A critical analysis of China's policy approach to renewable energies. *Energy Policy*, 62, 342-353.

OECD PUBLISHING, 2, rue André-Pascal, 75775 PARIS CEDEX 16
(41 2018 01 1 P) ISBN 978-92-64-28833-1 – 2018

www.ingramcontent.com/pod-product-compliance
Lightning Source LLC
Chambersburg PA
CBHW061217240926
51846CB00006B/1259
* 9 7 8 9 2 6 4 2 8 8 3 3 1 *